Rekindling Democracy

Rekindling Democracy

A Professional's Guide to Working in Citizen Space

Cormac Russell

FOREWORD BY
John L. McKnight

AFTERWORD BY
Julia Unwin

CASCADE *Books* • Eugene, Oregon

REKINDLING DEMOCRACY
A Professional's Guide to Working in Citizen Space

Cascade Books
An Imprint of Wipf and Stock Publishers
199 W. 8th Ave., Suite 3
Eugene, OR 97401

www.wipfandstock.com

PAPERBACK ISBN: 978-1-7252-5363-6
HARDCOVER ISBN: 978-1-7252-5364-3
EBOOK ISBN: 978-1-7252-5365-0

Cataloguing-in-Publication data:

Names: Russell, Cormac, author. | McKnight, John L., 1931–, foreword. | Unwin, Julia, afterword.

Title: Rekindling democracy : a professional's guide to working in citizen space / Cormac Russell ; foreword by John L. McKnight ; afterword by Julia Unwin.

Description: Eugene, OR : Cascade Books, 2020 | Includes bibliographical references and index.

Identifiers: ISBN 978-1-7252-5363-6 (paperback) | ISBN 978-1-7252-5364-3 (hardcover) | ISBN 978-1-7252-5365-0 (ebook)

Subjects: LCSH: Community development. | Community development—Political aspects.

Classification: HN49.C6 R90 2020 (print) | HN49.C6 R90 (ebook)

Manufactured in the U.S.A.   05/29/20

In memory of my father, Michael Russell (1943–2018)

Contents

*Foreword by John McKnight, Cofounder, Asset-Based
    Community Development Institute* | xi

Preface | xiii

Introduction | 1

Part One: Rekindling Society

*Communities are all around us, close at hand, awaiting the
community building that will make the invisible assets within
them visible in all their abundance.*

1   "Discoverables," Not Deliverables: The World of Asset-Based
    Community Development | 13

2   Black Swans, White Swans, and Ugly Ducklings: Why Top-Down
    Approaches (Mostly) Don't Work | 24

Part Two: Rekindling Community in
a Consumer Society

*We can all reverse the Bernays curse and make the long jour-
ney from consumer to producer, but it requires a collective will,
which is fundamentally countercultural. It is thus that deep
democracy is cocreated and enduring social justice realized.*

3   The Bernays Curse: Countering the Seven Tactics of
    Hidden Persuaders | 33

4   Paradise Lost: Cargo Cults and Austerity | 43

5   Too Small to Fail: Lessons from E. F. Schumacher, Stan Hallett, and Marian Tompson | 54

6   In Critique of Development: Choosing Sufficiency over Greed | 63

7   Economic Imperatives: Departing the Marketplace and Rekindling Local Economies | 72

Part Three: Rekindling Well-Being in a Sickness-Making Society

Imagine a world where every institution, whether within the sphere of commerce, government, or civil society, had an active policy to reduce dependence on their service, by increasing interdependence in community life. If such a world were ever to exist it would be radically different from the one we know today.

8   Pulling Back from the Edge: Growing Old in the West | 87

9   It Takes a Village: In Search of Medical Heretics | 99

10 Rekindling Well-Being from the Inside Out: Learning from Institutional Radicals | 113

Part Four: Deepening Community

Local democracy is not a product to be consumed but a way of living that must be cocreated by citizens.

11 Generating Change and Innovation: The Leadership Question | 123

12 Growing Collective Power: Power from the People, Power to the People | 129

13 Building Community and Pathways to Citizenship: Deschooling Society and Practicing the Art of Motorcycle Maintenance | 139

14 Restoring the Village: From Youth at Risk to Youth at Promise | 146

Part Five: Making It Real

To answer the question, "What can I do to make these principles visible?" the next four chapters offer practical tips for applying seven community-building principles in back-home, real-world contexts.

15 Seven Principles of Community Building: Working in the BY Space | 155

16 Working at the Speed of Trust: Serving while Walking Backward | 163

17 Practicing the Art of Connectorship: Starting with What's Strong | 168

18 Thinking Small: Animating Community at the Human Scale | 177

Part Six: Connecting Community and State

The effective state recognizes that civil society does not in fact expand commensurate with the number of citizens' needs addressed by the state, but to the extent that people's assets are connected and expressed in free space.

19 Widening Our Sphere of Influence: Enacting Democracy with a Whisper | 187

20 The Tools for Social Change: Growing an Association of Associations | 193

21 Enacting Democracy: Behind the Veils of Technocracy, Consumerism, and Globalization | 202

22 Rekindling Democracy: The Wide View | 210

Conclusion: Serving in Civic Space | 219

Afterword by Julia Unwin, DBE | 233
Acknowledgments | 235
About the Author | 239
About Nurture Development | 241
Notes and Sources | 243
Index | 255

Foreword

Cofounder, Asset-Based Community
Development Institute

IN SWEDEN THERE IS a housing development where the residents are encouraged to do something individually or collectively to improve their neighborhood. When they have completed the initiative, they are given a colorful yellow jacket with a logo containing a flame and the words "FIRE SOUL" underneath the flame. These visible Fire Souls are the kindling that brought this community to life.

This book is written by one of the world's greatest Fire Souls: Cormac Russell. He guides us along a dangerous path into a creative safe space where local neighbors can light the fires of community. It's a dangerous path because there are threats along the way to the possibility that any community might come alive. Often these threats remain hidden from view, invisible; in these pages, Cormac makes them visible.

He tells us that the first invisible threat results from living in a culture of consumerism. In this kind of culture, the members believe that they can buy everything they need for a good life. However, Cormac reminds us that the only thing they can't buy is community, and community is the essential producer of a good life.

He reveals the second threat as the world of professionalism. In that world, the message is "you will be better because I know better." Cormac reminds us that a community is made up of people who know best how to create the future that will kindle a good life.

The third threat Cormac makes visible is governments and institutions that claim they want to help. Their help most often creates a benign dependency rather than the freedom for citizens to act powerfully.

After leading us along this perilous path, Cormac shows us where to find the kindling that can light up our communities and empower our democracy. And as we light this fire, we can clearly see the way to become productive citizens who imagine the future and make it come true.

In *Rekindling Democracy*, we have the privilege to walk alongside Cormac, whose phenomenal experience leads us to a pathway where every neighbor can become a Fire Soul. What good fortune that you have found this book, for it will light and lighten your life!

Preface

Humpty Dumpty sat on the wall,
Humpty Dumpty had a great fall.
All the King's horses and all the King's men
Couldn't put Humpty together again.

JUST AS IN THE nursery rhyme "Humpty Dumpty," in which "all the King's horses and all the King's men couldn't put Humpty together again" after his great fall, institutional systems and the professionals who work within them can't put us back together again. Hospitals, schools, and law courts all have important functions, but they do not have a monopoly on the production of health, wisdom, and justice. Having spent the last sixty years enthralled with all that institutions can do for our well-being, perhaps now, in the wake of the international banking crisis, the opioid crisis, our burgeoning healthcare systems, and the recurring scandals of so many of our residential care facilities from cradle to grave, we can see what exists in civic space beyond the limits of institutions. With this rekindled clarity, we can enjoy greater personal and collective freedom and more functional services. Getting there will require a new and better story than the hyper-rational, commodity-based one that currently dominates modern industrialized thought.

Effectively reweaving our human story necessarily begins by asking different questions and taking unconventional paths toward the future. Instead of asking, "How can we get our agencies to add more value to, for, or with communities?" we must ask, "How can agencies create more space so that communities can produce the things they value?"

The answer, at least in part, is to start with what's strong, not what's wrong, then to liberate what's strong to address what's wrong, and to make what's strong even stronger. This is a far cry from the usual institutional way of doing things.

The impulse to shift the question from what institutions can do "to" or "for" us (from the top down) to what we as citizens would like to begin to create (from the bottom up) is grounded in the belief that social progress is about the expansion of freedom, not the growth of services.

What might have happened if Humpty Dumpty had fallen backward—over the other side of the wall? This book in large part is about what's on the other side: the noninstitutional, community side. On the community side—with some searching—we can hope to find the nest that hatches and the associational life that catches the humanness within us and between us all, and from there get better at being human together, since to be human is to be social. We can hope to once again see like a community. This book is also centrally about how professionals can work more effectively with citizens in civic space. A citizen is not someone sitting crouched over kindling, waiting for someone else to light their fire, so this is a guide for professionals interested in working with citizens so that they can rekindle democracy for themselves and each other, from the bottom up and the sidelines in.

Decentering, Not Demeaning

Throughout this book, I argue that citizens must be at the center of any authentic and powerful democratic response to our current socioeconomic challenges and that we ourselves must be the vitalizing starting point for a more sustaining future for all life. My secondary aim for this book is to decenter, not to demean, institutions and professionals, since this is the only way to restore citizenship and community to the center of democracy.

As I wrote this book, I regularly found myself looking back somewhat pensively on my early days as a helper working for the Irish Health Board in residential child care. I recognized that the top-down, rescuing impulses I critique and argue for decentering in the pages that follow were part of how I showed up—along with a know-it-all attitude and unquestioned certainties—in the lives of the people I served. Socrates was famed for questioning such certainties; his epigram "I know only that I do not know" is among the best-known philosophical dictums. I'm afraid it did not form part of my repertoire in those days.

It took me quite some time before I began to question my certainties, a process that involved setting aside the maps I had constructed or learned and instead getting my whole self into the territory. By "maps" I mean the heady assumptions I had made, or received from others, about someone or somewhere, or "those people." And by "getting into the territory" I mean sitting with and getting to know a community or visiting a place with real curiosity and humility, and by invitation. I have come to understand that one of the consequences of spending too much time in any large institution, even as a professional, is that you too can become institutionalized and disconnected from life on the ground just as much as the people who are traditionally thought of as clients.

The reason institutions can achieve impact at scale is that they depersonalize their objectives (the underlying rationale is an institution should never rely on any one person) and they elementalize (specializations and siloed departments dominate). This is also the trouble with institutions; institutions don't care, because they can't. People care. As professionals from this depersonalized, specialist, unsituated position we can come to know everything in general and very little in particular. The trouble with that is that citizen space is filled with people who know everything in particular and are not all that interested in our generalizations. And so often institutions and communities, professionals and citizens are ships passing in the night.

Repeatedly, across my professional life, when I have truly listened, I have heard people say they want interdependence within communities that celebrate them as gifted people with something to contribute to the well-being of those communities. In other words, they want a life, not a service. Like Humpty Dumpty they were not seeking more of the king's horses and men; they were yearning for the hatchers and the catchers in a life of their own choosing. In the early days of my career, I found myself on the wrong side of the Humpty Dumpty wall—without a ladder. My journey since then, with many co-conspirators for company, has been a mix of prospecting for ladders, traversing the narrow perimeter that divides the institutional worlds and community life, and increasingly seeking out the hatchers and the catchers in home places and communities around the world.

That's not always easy; there are many barriers to authentic connection. I know from painful experience, for example, that one of the best ways to stay removed from a person or a place is to label them. The more obvious methods of distancing, such as name-calling and stigmatizing, I've always found easy to guard against. It is less obvious and far more complicated to catch oneself in the act of the labeling that results from attempts at helping.

For many years one of my deeply held certainties was that "certain people" needed my help. I believed, for example, that people I labeled as "poor people" needed my help most. Especially "poor people" in the Global South—most especially if they were children and suffering from famine and persecution. Those certainties have been deeply undermined over the years, and, in many respects, this book is an autobiographical reprise of many years of inner dialogue and open debate with others to that end. To this day, I'm daily reminded of how easy it is to slip into labels that are well intended.

I have formerly labeled others in order that I might take responsibility for helping them; I now understand that I was misunderstanding the meaning of *response-ability*, and I began to redefine it as Ivan Illich would have us do, as receiving the ability to respond as a gift from the other.

Labels obscure gifts. Even when well intended, labels are loaded with all sorts of ideological judgments and presuppositions about the other, which act as barriers to genuine connection between people and places. The label "poor person/poor people" is a case in point. Too often it's a way of othering, creating a them-and-us narrative, and relegating the person to the status of an alien while suggesting that being "poor" is intrinsic to who they are as a human being. Better to use a term like "economically marginalized," since it describes how the world is currently organized and is affecting that person by isolating them from opportunities that others have at their fingertips. It also highlights an obvious pathway toward addressing such issues, which, as discussed in chapter 7, involves looking back at what advantaged the advantaged and doing that for everyone.

Yet repeatedly, in the early part of my career, I created situations where I, as the helper, had authority over the people I helped. Without realizing it, I labeled myself solely with reference to my assets (such as my credentials) and mostly ignored my deficits (such as the fact that most of the time I didn't know what I was doing). At the same time, I labeled those I was helping in the exact opposite way: I viewed them solely in terms of what they were missing (such as a home if they were "homeless"), while being blind to what they had (such as personal capacities and relationships).

My certainty that I was needed blinded me from seeing that I needed their needs. It obscured the realization that, in many respects, I had sought to fix other people's versions of my problems—problems I was often too unaware of or too scared to own. And it masked the reality that I was working within systems that viewed people as needy clients, not needed citizens. Not only was I a wounded healer, I was also a wounding healer.

As time has gone on I've made friends with uncertainty—these days my motto to every assertion that people make about a person or a place is "Maybe it is so; let's go see if it is." Interestingly, it is never just so. Certainties continue to be overstated when checked against people's stories and the endless surprises and mysteries of a given place. There is therefore only one thing of which I am sure, and that is the value of questioning certainties. The part I continue to find most challenging, though, is discovering what my certainties are, so thank goodness for honest fellow travelers who call them out. This is an account of what I have learned from these honest pilgrims.

Introduction

And I believe that we're in a unique moment in history. Maybe you're seeing the same thing. I'm feeling it as I'm traveling not just around D.C. but around the country. But people really want to get involved. They really want to. They're looking for a way to turn their frustration, excitement, anxiety into action.

—Michelle Obama

Allow me to tell you a story about a community of hatchers and catchers. One day several years ago, Carin stepped out of her travel trailer and walked a few minutes into the community she would soon fall in love with: the Voorstad-Oost neighborhood in the Dutch city of Deventer. Although still hurting from a difficult divorce, her natural curiosity about the people and place where she found herself meant it did not take long for her to hear the rumors that the old neighborhood school was being sold off. Within days of hearing this news, she found herself working with her new friend Lotte and a band of other residents getting organized to save their school. City developers had looked at this old building and seen an apartment block, but the Voorstad-Oost locals saw past the husk of its red bricks and grey mortar, and its financial potential, to envision their own community center.

And so began the adventure. It turned out that saving the building was the easy part. Having succeeded in gaining a permit from the municipality to turn the old school into a community center, they then had to figure out how to transform this forlorn structure, with its empty classrooms and echoing corridors, into a vibrant community center, and to do it without external funding.

Carin and Lotte, like the other members of the group, appreciate the power of openly asking for what they want. With a directness typical of the region, Carin and Lotte turned to each of their neighbors and asked, "What would you like to do to help create our community center? We have no money right now, so whatever you do will be a gift to your community." They discovered that people were just waiting to be asked. Over time, as money came in, they paid local craftspeople whenever and whatever they could, ensuring investment in the local economy. But in those early days it was down to what the people in the neighborhood were prepared to contribute.

Carin, Lotte, and their neighbors might not have used the term but they were operating within a "gift economy"—so much so that today most locals can walk by that former school building and say, "I helped to transform that into the beautiful community center you see there." The sense that "my neighbors and I made this" is of incredible consequence: the sustainability of such an endeavor can be measured by the number of local fingerprints found on the walls and the furniture of the place. The more fingerprints, the more collective ownership; the more shared ownership, the more investment in sustaining it and, more importantly, in creating the future expressions of the community's gathering place. Indeed, most people do not simply walk by the building; they walk in and contribute.

Besides having a powerful origin story, the Voorstad-Oost community center is distinct from many other centers I've seen around the world. First, it is completely managed and run by local people. Second, although it provides services such as childcare, they do not feel like "services." The ethos that pervades the center is one of family, not factory; of covenant, not contract. While there, you see the children mixing freely with the adults from the community; the playground is reminiscent of a village square, with young and old playing, talking, and laughing together. It is a far cry from the fortresslike environments of many modern childcare facilities, where the rooms are softened and child-centered but the steel railings around the perimeter send a clear message to the community: stay away, these youngsters are the private property of their parents, who have paid us to "care" for them. The message to children in those facilities is clarion also: the people who care for you are your family and the people they pay; your neighbors are strangers, and potentially dangerous.

Voorstad-Oost and similar stories stand in stark contrast to how most modern Westerners experience their childhoods. People who are more than fifty years old can perhaps still remember the care of the village, growing up under the watchful eyes of neighbors, but those under thirty-five will have mainly experienced the care of parents or extended family and the professionally run kindergarten and school. In Voorstad-Oost they still believe it takes a village to raise a child and they are doing something about it. Here people hatch and catch their neighbors and, in a beautifully reciprocal motion, are themselves opening up to life's possibilities and flourishing from inside out.

"Strange" but True

Another story is being played out in Grand Ledge, Michigan, where Brenda Hydon teaches eighteen students, ages five to twelve, in a one-room schoolhouse. There you see one teacher and a teacher's aide demonstrating the possibilities of a learning site built on a community rather than a corporate model. If not new, it is utterly unusual. And it's working.

The Strange School, as it is known—it gets its name from a local highway—has operated in its current building since 1879, but its history and longevity are not the story here. What's important is that the teacher teaches the older kids, the older kids teach the younger, and the youngest ones learn at their own pace by listening in. What's more, the art of community is learned by in-school experience; the kids learn to be the productive keepers of a public place and are distanced from the huge diversion from learning that is competitive sports.

Voorstad-Oost and Strange, Michigan, are just two images of what's in store should we get serious about rekindling democracy: we see a future where local citizens rely on one another to cope with the limits of the industrial model for everything, including the classroom and the community center.

In this book, you will read dozens of such stories, most of which have little to do with schools or clinics or other such institutions. Instead they are centered on what happens when people collectivize around a shared vision that they have created themselves. If it were possible to view these disaggregated, local, highly particular creative efforts in the aggregate, what you would see is democracy, in all its glory.

Democracy Redefined: Shifting from
Institution-Centered to Citizen-Centered

In a democracy, effective central and local governments and not-for-profit institutions function as an extension of civic life and serve to protect it. When institutions begin to replace civic life—doing things to or for citizens that they can do themselves or with each other—a shift from a democratic to a technocratic way of life takes hold. Technocratic governing relegates citizens to second place; it turns them into clients and consumers of government services and positions "experts" and "officials" as superior to the people they serve. Over time, five unintended consequences of this arrangement become evident:

1. People who need support due to economic isolation or fragility become defined as problems to be fixed, not as people to be valued and connected, people who possess the assets and resources that are critical to addressing their challenges.

2. A significant portion of the money intended to support those who are economically marginalized goes to paid service providers, not to the economically marginalized people themselves.

3. Active citizenship begins to retreat in the face of ever-growing professionalism and expertise. People not credentialed by a professional "guild" become increasingly more dependent on institutional services to do what previously was done by participating in community life.

4. Economically marginalized communities begin to internalize a map—a map drawn by outside experts—that defines them as helpless people populating hopeless places. Not surprisingly, the people who live in communities that have been defined by others as backwaters of pain and suffering come to believe that things will get better only when someone with the right resources and expertise comes in from outside to make them better.

5. Citizens begin to believe that a good life is not to be found in interdependent relationships at the center of community life, alongside near neighbors, but in services and programs at the edge of their communities, provided by salaried strangers. Many of those who are surrounded by a wide range of such services have been exiled from community life into "serviceland," the environment within which services and programs dominate. They are no longer known as a sister, brother, son, daughter, friend, or neighbor; they have been redefined as a service user, a patient, someone endlessly waiting to be fixed. The many services coalesce to form a new environment around the person that transposes their role from citizen to client.

In most parts of the world these consequences are combining to erode the social and political foundation of everyday life. This adds up to a creeping crisis that may be thought of as a rip in the social fabric of our collective lives, evident in ever-increasing disconnection—and loneliness.

In Canada, for example, one in four people is estimated to be lonely (Desjardins, 2018). A study by researchers at Brigham Young University found the ill effects of loneliness are as bad as smoking fifteen cigarettes a day (Holt-Lunstad, 2015). The study looked at more than three million participants and found increased social connection is linked to a 50 percent reduced risk of premature death. The United Kingdom is so concerned about the issue they appointed a minister for loneliness to tackle social isolation (Prime Minister's Office, 2018). Throughout Europe, North America, and Australia more than 20 percent of the people consulting their doctors are not bio-medically ill—they are lonely (Edwards et al., 2010).

What is the solution? Community.

Professor emeritus Myrra Vernooij-Dassen of Radboud University, The Netherlands, tells us in no uncertain terms that if we want to address loneliness the evidence is clear on what not to do: treat loneliness as yet another condition (Vernooij-Dassen and Jeon, 2016). People living with loneliness do not want to be associated with the stigmatizing term "loneliness." To address loneliness and other symptoms of the unraveling of our social fabric we must reconnect people into reciprocal relationships based on their capacities, not their deficits or labels.

Searching for Songlines

Chronic loneliness and a sense of being inadequate to the task of social and political change were once experienced by only a few; now it seems they are the inheritance of many. But this situation need not be inevitable. After all, things are not getting worse, they are getting clearer, and with clarity comes a whispering call to civic action and a move toward the restoration of commons. This book aims to amplify that call by seeking out what some may think of as an ordinance for civic renewal. I like to think of this book as a search for songlines, the pursuit of useful pointers in the same way indigenous Australians did in times past.

Songlines are cues from the landscape, and sometimes the skies, that enable us to remember important cultural insights, values, and practices; they open up pathways toward "re-membering," effecting cultural renewal in the collective sense. Indigenous Australians have the longest continuous cultural history of any group of people on earth. For them, as for many indigenous communities who use other cultural invocations, songlines are a powerful means of preserving and sharing their history and cultural heritage. They function as a cultural memory code, through nuanced stories, dance, song, and art, wisdom about the creation of the world. Through songlines more modern concerns and social laws are also remembered and shared. The information that is passed on and passed down is not all metaphysical or esoteric in nature either; in fact, most of it is practical. By rooting these cultural codes in the natural environment, across the generations, indigenous people have cultivated an immense memory of thousands of the flora and fauna across the continent. The knowledge and wisdom contained in their songlines could well rival Wikipedia, and in terms of functionality could be thought of as forerunner of the World Wide Web—no less sophisticated, but a great degree more sensible, which is to say rooted, embedded, experience-based, and life-giving.

Today, the most pressing challenge facing people and their governments in Australia and the rest of the Western world, and indeed in those countries that are rapidly becoming Westernized, is to reverse the developments of the last fifty years that have turned active citizens into satisfied or dissatisfied clients and passive consumers. Reversing the trend is about showing up more in our own and other people's lives as active citizens, as the primary producers of a more satisfying shared future. I consider this to be at the heart of the democratic challenge. While it is a perennial endeavor, the urgency of rekindling our communities and rebooting democracy could not be greater than it is today. We will never reclaim the community spirit of times past, yet we certainly can find and connect the current cultural ties that enable us to bind collectively in the world as it is, in order to re-create the world as we wish it to be.

Challenging the Institutional Assumption

Getting to that world is not about reforming our systems; it is about re-functioning our families and neighborhoods and our human service institutions, so that they can reorientate themselves toward their primary function: to support citizenship and community building. The current assumption that services and programs will be sufficient to address our biggest challenges is as ubiquitous as it is misguided. Placing the provision of services and programs in a more proportionate role alongside support for citizenship and community building is critical to the future of local democracy. The evidence clearly shows that it is not services and programs but our community assets that primarily determine our well-being—that is, the extent to which we are well and how quickly we recover when unwell. Of course, institutions have a role to play in supporting our well-being, but it is a supplementary one.

Epidemiology (the scientific study of what determines human well-being) is clear that the five determinants of well-being are

1. personal capacity;

2. associational life;

3. economic status;

4. environmental conditions; and

5. access to health and allied services.

The World Health Organization has significantly evolved their thinking on health from 1948, when health was simply understood as the absence of disease. Today we operate with new definitions of positive health defined by the presence of well-being. From the work of Machteld Huber (2011), Barbara Fredrickson (2013), and Jan Walburg (Walburg et al., 2006), we can conclude that health and well-being are determined overall by six more specific drivers:

1. A meaningful life/goal in your life/purpose.

2. Positive emotions—Fredrickson, for example, shows a "positive life" is equivalent to ten additional healthy years of life.

3. Meaningful relations with other people, being connected—associational life. This driver reduces the risk of premature death in the following year by 50 percent. Robert Waldinger's (2016) now-famous Harvard study on longevity offers compelling evidence around the importance of associational life.

4. Enjoying small things, living an attentive life, mindfulness of principles like sufficiency.

5. Doing something for someone else, sharing gifts/talents.

6. Living in a healthy way: attending to movement/exercise, food, alcohol, smoking, and other lifestyle decisions.

The evidence (which will be presented in later chapters) in other domains of our lives also shows that institutions are not the primary producers of our wisdom, prosperity, justice, or democracy. Communities are.

Over the last five decades, however, in the areas of health and well-being, education, local economics, environment, justice, and public safety, the role of community assets has been relegated to second place, treated as irrelevant to the primary concerns of social, political, and economic change. Institutions have replaced citizens as the primary inventors of the solutions to social and political problems. At the same time, institutional leaders have forgotten that their institutions were hatched from associational nests, and yet their institutional machinery often acts as the instigator of so many of the so-called problems they were established to resolve, and regularly, albeit unintentionally, causes such conditions to prevail or worsen. Accordingly, health—which is primarily a social and political matter—has come to be thought of as a medical one, and technocratic solutions have come to be considered more desirable and trustworthy in all instances than the tacit knowledge of citizens and communities. No longer is the home the place where we are born and die, where we learn and work. Institutions are widely considered to be benign, and the notion that institutions may sometimes be counterproductive is often viewed as a fringe position, propagated by troublemakers and crackpots.

Indeed, across a wide range of issues, from gang crime to dementia, the dominant assumption is that where a social problem exists, generating a solution is the primary responsibility of one institution or another (and more recently, a cluster of institutions working in concert in pursuit of collective impact). Yet the evidence clearly shows that this approach is not only counter to what science tells us, it is also counterproductive when it comes to rekindling democracy. Instead of precipitating collective citizenship and neighbor-to-neighbor interdependence, this process increases dependency on institutions and decreases interdependency in community life. Ultimately, it defines democracy as institution-centric instead of citizen-centered.

Rebooting Democracy

It is time to reboot democracy. This book cheers on and stands shoulder to shoulder with savvy civic and institutional leaders as it seeks to resource, support, and gently challenge them as they work to ensure an authentic and effective shift from institution-centric, top-down approaches to more citizen-centered, bottom-up approaches.

In the final analysis, institutions are not benign; their gravitational pull will draw them back time and again to doing things "to the people," "for the people"—and only on occasion "with the people." Time and again they will do things that belong in the domain of citizen-to-citizen work done *by* the people. Clearly there are things best done by families and communities; in such instances, government does well to create a dome of protection around them and ensure adequate space for them to blossom.

There are also things that are best done with citizens in the lead but with support from outside agencies or the marketplace. Here government does well to ensure those partnerships are well governed and benefit communities most. Communities at the same time must ensure that such social contracts are collaborative and democratic—and dissent when they are not.

And finally, there are things that governments and people with specialized expertise are best placed to do; in such instances government does well to support those specialists to do that work collaboratively, affectively as well as effectively, and transparently.

This book shows how we may catalyze the reboot that's needed for all of us to live more satisfying lives while walking lightly on the planet. It also sets out some of the primary steps for taking this approach from concept to enduring and authentic action. It is the second in a series dedicated to this aim. The first, *Asset-Based Community Development: Looking Back to Look Forward—in Conversation with John McKnight*, explored the intellectual influences of the cofounder of the Asset-Based Community Development (ABCD) Institute in framing the ABCD approach. Some of that background is summarized in this book, especially in chapter 1.

The consistent thread is the asset-based community development perspective. It is through this lens that I look out at this cross-pressured world of ours and consider how best to vitalize our communities and rekindle democracy. I say "rekindle" for two reasons. First, because the embers have not gone out: we have what we need to build community and reimagine democracy, if we connect what we have. Second, the word lends itself to playful interpretations—for example, it contains other words, such as *kin*, *kind*, *elder*, and so on—and it also reminds me of the German word *Kinder* (child), which immediately brings to mind the adage that it takes a village to raise one. Given that the asset-based community development approach provides the Archimedean point and Rosetta stone from which I explore a wide interdependent vista, from raising children to reimagining democracy, the next chapter explores what this approach actually means and offers an outline of what it might offer the world we all inhabit.

Part One: **Rekindling Society**

Communities are all around us, close at hand, awaiting the community building that will make the invisible assets within them visible in all their abundance.

Chapter 1

"Discoverables," Not Deliverables

The World of Asset-Based Community Development

*The world is full of magic things, patiently
waiting for our senses to grow sharper.*

—W. B. YEATS

ASSET-BASED COMMUNITY DEVELOPMENT (ABCD) is about people living in local places and taking responsibility for each other and their local resources. It is a description, not a model, of how local residents grow collective efficacy (Sampson et al., 1999) and what they use to do so (McKnight, 2009). The work of ABCD involves paying attention to what is already present in a local place, not what we think should be there, or what isn't there. What can be found in a local place are called its assets; they include

- the gifts, skills, knowledge, and passions of local residents;
- the power of local social networks/associations;
- the resources of public, private, and nonprofit institutions;
- the physical resources of the place;
- the economic resources of the place; and
- the stories of its residents' shared lives.

Setting aside our preconceived maps and genuinely coming alongside a given local community (assuming that there is an invitation to do so) demands an act of radical humility on the part of helping agencies. It's the opposite of diagnosing, fixing, or prescribing. It means our attention shifts from "deliverables" to "discoverables."

The logic of shifting the focus from deliverables to discoverables is grounded in four simple but inalienable truths:

1. People can't know what they need until they first know what they have.

2. An outside agency's map of the community will never be the same as the territory.

3. If you don't know the territory, you can't support the community and you run the risk of causing harm.

4. Communities do not work in silos or in tune with institutional targets or their predefined outcomes. Take health as a case in point: most of the activity that is health-producing is done by people who do not think or realize that what they are doing is health-producing.

The majority of sociopolitical challenges are three dimensional: they are personal, environmental/social, and institutional. The challenge that democratic societies face is in trying to address three-dimensional socioeconomic and political issues using a two-dimensional framework consisting of:

- institutional interventions (services, programs, policies, legislation); and

- individual behavior change.

In the pursuit of more sustainable and enduring change that is ecologically and socially sound we need to attend more to the third dimension: environmental/social. Environmental and social change is not the result of behavioral change, nor does it come about as a consequence of institutional reform. It happens as a consequence of effective grassroots community building at the neighborhood level (Monbiot, 2016).

Doing community building this way calls on all of us as citizens to start seeing our neighborhoods as the primary unit of change. Making the neighborhood the primary unit of change enables the discovery, connection, and mobilization of individuals, associations, and cultural, environmental, and economic assets. The magic is in the connections between all these domains, not in any particular technique, model, or siloed approach. This is why working within small places is so pivotal to more citizen-led action and ultimately to deeper democracy and environmental sustainability.

ABCD Principles and Practices

Identifying, connecting, and mobilizing a neighborhood's assets is a messy and complex endeavor, one that does not come with an instruction booklet. The ABCD approach does, however, come with a set of principles and practices that act like a compass in community-building work. Those principles and practices fall into five categories:

1. Citizen-led
2. Relationship-oriented
3. Asset-based
4. Place-based
5. Inclusion-focused

Citizen-led

There are certain things that only citizens, in association with one another, do best. ABCD is focused on this domain of change. From this perspective, sociopolitical, cultural, environmental, and economic change efforts are viewed through the lens of the following questions:

- What is it that residents in communities are best placed to do together?
- What is it that residents can best do with some outside help?
- What is it that communities need outside institutions to do for them?

Relationship-oriented

ABCD goes beyond individuals and their capacities to tap into relational power. Sadly, the power of relationships tends to be undervalued in industrialized societies. Notwithstanding, relational power, outside of hierarchical structures such as the workplace, presents a powerful and often untapped force for good. It enables consensual grouping behaviors to amplify and multiply the capacities of individuals, ensuring the societal whole is greater than the sum of its individual parts. Relational power, also referred to as associational life, is a key determinant of individual well-being, public safety, response to natural disasters, and vocational opportunities.

Asset-based

The starting point for ABCD is what's strong, not what's wrong. Some misunderstand this catchphrase as an attempt to minimize life's challenges or normalize injustices; nothing could be further from the truth. ABCD is the process by which relational power is mobilized to produce sustainable and satisfying change. With that in mind, it starts with what's strong and enables local people to get organized to address what's wrong and make what's strong even stronger. It also asks searching questions of those who seek to define certain neighborhoods by the sum of their deficits.

Place-based

Small local places are the stage on which a good, sustainable, and satisfying life unfolds. Seeing the neighborhood as the primary unit of change is a powerful strategy for addressing some of our most intractable sociopolitical challenges. It is, however, a strategy that is countercultural, in that it seems to contradict the vast majority of helping strategies, which see individuals or institutions as the most legitimate domains for change. While personal transformation and institutional interventions have their place, we have seen that by intentionally organizing relational power at the neighborhood level, local residents can connect local human, associational, environmental, economic, and cultural resources and, by aggregating them at a hyper-local level, come up with solutions that escape the reach of top-down institutions.

In more than thirty-five countries around the world I have witnessed the power of collective efficacy trump the capacities of innovative individuals and even the collective impact of institutional partnerships that purport to address "wicked issues," such as child poverty, obesity, and dementia. I have also come to recognize that true partnerships between citizens and institutional systems will emerge only when institutions begin organizing in the way people organize their lives—and by that I mean humbly localizing and offering their human and other resources to grow community, after first appreciating what is there already, instead of expecting people to organize their lives in the way institutions have traditionally organized their services and functions.

Neighborhoods and small towns are the scale at which local residents come to believe they can make an impact. This neighbor-to-neighbor impact is not about service provision; it is about neighborliness. A small local place also provides the context within which the multiplicity of helping agencies (each currently working within its own silo) can agree on common ground that automatically takes them beyond their administrative boundaries, to work across silos. "Neighborhood" is the potential context within which everything can come together, where relational civic power, when needed, can join with the power of civic professionals and their institutional resources. In sum, places can exist and thrive without people, but people cannot exist and thrive without places.

Inclusion-focused

Communities have imperceptible perimeters inside which are those deemed to belong and outside which are those considered to be strangers. ABCD principles and practices direct our attention toward working with local people to support them in creating a welcome for the "strangers" at the edge of the community's perimeters. A community that does not have a place for the people they have labeled outsiders has no place for anyone, since if they do not actively welcome everyone's gifts they disable themselves and others and build a bastion against authentic community. Every gift builds power, and civic power grows further when gifts, through sharing, are amplified and multiplied within associations.

In short, the principles and practices of ABCD are about investing in the group life of the neighborhood, recognizing that collective efficacy is measured not by the strengths or capacities of its leaders and programs but by the power and connectivity of its groups. Imagine how different things would be if well-intentioned helpers took care to first discover the informal ways communities sustain themselves. You can never know what a community needs until you first know what a community has.

It is important to note that ABCD is not a substitute for services, just as services or professional programs are not a proxy for genuine friendship and community-led inventiveness. Asset-based community-driven efforts recognize the following:

1. Everyone has certain capacities: a gift (they are born with), a skill (they have learned and practiced, and could potentially share/teach), a passion (they act on), and knowledge they can contribute to the well-being of their community.

2. Social movements grow stronger when these capacities are discovered and connected into productive reciprocal relationships with associations, the local environment, the economy, and culture.

3. Power grows from the bottom up, and from the sidelines in, when people identify what they care about enough to act on collectively.

The current community engagement strategies used by outside agencies, far from taking such place-based community-building approaches to heart, continue to be extremely siloed. All the while, they are attempting to engage communities before the work of building communities has actually begun. Consequently, such community engagement efforts are overly focused on named target groups, such as "youth at risk" or "frail older people" (themselves deeply unhelpful labels), instead of connecting diverse parts of the community across common fault lines and possibilities.

The Neighborhood as the Smallest Unit of Democracy

To my mind, the central task of democracy today is to look back to look forward, so that it can look with fresh eyes at the early vision of democracy that put citizens at the center and put governments, technocracy, and corporations in the servant's quarters. The vision has yet to be made visible. Still, when compared to our current versions of democracy, it is clear we have a long and difficult road ahead. Notwithstanding, once our vison is clear we can start from where we are right now and find the resources required within and between us, and then, together, make the path by walking it.

Of course, the path will be steep and sometimes treacherous. Any hope for more citizen-centered democracy exists against the backdrop of a dominant narrative in the twenty-first century that has all too often devalued, demeaned, and condescended to the talents and tacit knowledge of uncredentialed people—that is, people who primarily describe themselves as "just from around here" or "just a volunteer." Yet, our current map of democratic society has led us into a moral, political, and economic cul-de-sac. The primary error of this map is the "institutional assumption," which leads us to believe that the only way things are going to get better is if an outside expert or agency comes in to make our lives and communities better.

The sad but liberating fact is that social change hardly ever works that way. It is very, very rarely a unilaterally top-down affair. The rightful expectation of citizens is that institutions intervene in our lives in a proportionate and accountable way. When they do not, the role of citizens is to treat those institutions as we do automobiles that no longer function: trade them in for better-functioning alternatives. To fulfill this role of citizenship we need to focus on the functions of our institutions, not on their form, if we are to avoid ending up with dysfunctional jalopies. But a more primary focus is needed on our shared lives and the places where we live them.

David Brooks (2018), writing for the New York Times, criticizes social programs and philanthropic efforts that endeavor to "save one person at a time," assuming that the individual is the most important unit of change.

Noting that while it's possible to do good that way, he observes that "you're not really changing the structures and systems that shape lives." Still awaiting some mythic savior to change our structures and systems is not a blueprint toward our desired futures either. We need some foothold that can hope to grow a strong sense of what Marshall Ganz (2009) called a "public narrative." Brooks goes on to say, "It could be that the neighborhood, not the individual, is the essential unit of social change."

What is within the hands of people and what is within their power to change? In an economic model built on the myth of scarcity, to take this question seriously is to be ultra-radical, since it is all at once disruptive of technocratic and corporate interests. Yet even a precursory look beyond such interests reveals the thirteen irreplaceable functions of citizens in a democracy. We are the primary collective producers of

1. our health and well-being;
2. safety;
3. care for the environment;
4. safe food production and consumption;
5. local economic development;
6. raising our children;
7. aging well in place/locale;
8. building strong communities;
9. civic action toward deeper democracy;
10. response to natural disasters and emergencies;
11. the curation of knowledge and sharing of wisdom, culture, and heritage;
12. care for people who have been marginalized; and
13. our capacity to live creatively with the unknowable.

All thirteen are critical interdependent functions of community and civic life, and small local places are utterly central to their emergence. Small bounded places provide an ideal threshold wherein different associations, made up of citizens with varying passions for one or more but not necessarily all of these functions, can share the collective effort of civic life and wellness co-creation. In a neighborhood, for instance, with community-building support, such disaggregated associations can weave a subtle web, as an association of associations, so to speak, where the whole truly is greater and more powerful than the sum of its parts.

When such civic functions are regularly performed, while citizens and communities become stronger so too does democratic government. It is as though we are exercising a civic muscle each time we take on one of these functions together. There is no rule book as to how these functions should be carried out. In fact, there are no "shoulds" at all, and therefore no standards by which the quality of outputs might be measured. As my father always said, "If something is worth doing, it's worth doing badly."

All of these functions are within the domain of community-powered change. If people do not bring their collective power to bear on these functions, they will not happen. Therefore, these are "pinch points," to paraphrase author Peter Block, where we are confronted by our own democratic freedoms (2018).

Certainly, from an asset-based perspective, what nourishes community-powered change is the intentional will to identify, connect, and mobilize community assets, with people firmly in the driver's seat of this process. Some call this asset mapping. Others may recognize it as an organic iteration: ordinary people coming together to understand the challenges and opportunities before them and to devise and implement solutions—in short, to be coproducers of the future. It is a relationship-driven, internally oriented asset-based perspective. It is also not a panacea. On the road to justice, as ABCD Institute cofounder Jody Kretzmann says, ABCD is necessary but not sufficient. We need an ecosystem of methods and approaches to advance toward deeper democracy and communities where there is enough for everyone.

The challenge for institutions in supporting community-powered change then is to ask:

- Where are we replacing, controlling, overwhelming the power of people to be producers?

- How can we listen better to what people in citizen and community space think they can do, and what they think would be helpful from outside?

The challenge for communities is to stop being colonized by top-down institutional ways and grow power from the inside out.

Bringing Citizen Participation to Life

Some years ago John McKnight attended the annual Canadian Conference of Community Development Organizations. Several hundred groups were in attendance. The convener of the conference told him that the best community "developer" in all of Canada was at the conference and pointed toward a middle-aged man named Gaëtan Ruest, the mayor of Amqui, Quebec.

John introduced himself to Mayor Ruest and asked about Amqui. The mayor said that it was a town of about six thousand people on the Gaspé Peninsula amid the Chic-Choc Mountains, located at the intersection of the Matapédia and Humqui rivers. These rivers are the richest Atlantic salmon rivers on the North American continent, and Amqui is the regional center for fishing for these salmon.

Gaëtan invited John to visit his town, and a year later John was able to take him up on the invitation. He found that all the townspeople were French-speaking, and a great deal of the economic base of the community was from fisherpeople who came to fish for the rare Atlantic salmon. One day, as Gaëtan and John walked together down the street, two men approached the mayor. There was a long conversation in French. After they were finished Gaëtan explained to John what had happened.

The mayor said that the town had put nets on salmon streams in order to keep the fish near Amqui and accessible to the fishing guides. The two men reported that somebody was cutting the nets to let the salmon go upstream where they could poach them.

"That's terrible," Gaëtan replied. "What do you think we can do about that?" The men thought for a while and then suggested three things that could be done. "Is there anybody who could help you do those things?" Gaëtan asked. "Yes," they responded. "We know a couple of other fisherpeople who could help." Gaëtan said, "Will you ask them to join you to meet with me at city hall this evening?" They agreed.

That evening John joined Gaëtan at the meeting with four concerned people. The mayor had insisted that they meet in the city council's meeting room and he led a discussion of how the group could deal with the salmon poaching problem. By the time they were done, the group had specific plans and specific people committed to carrying them out.

Then Gaëtan asked, "Is there anything the city can do to help you with the job?" The participants came up with two ways the city could be helpful. "I am making you the official Amqui Salmon Preservation Committee," Gaëtan said. "I want you to hold your meetings in the city council meeting room because you are official. I want you to come to city council meetings and tell the council people how you are coming along."

The convener of the National Association of Community Development Organizations, previously mentioned, told John that the process he had observed in the council meeting room that gave birth to the Amqui Salmon Preservation Committee was repeated over and over during Gaëtan's long tenure as mayor. As a result, the convener said that in Amqui, hidden away in the Chic-Choc Mountains, almost all the residents had become officials of the local government and the principal problem-solvers for the community.

John wholeheartedly believes that every public official can learn a great deal from the mayor of Amqui. Gaëtan starts with the premise that the residents are principal problem-solvers, not the mayor or his officials. This means they have the best ideas about what needs to be done. It also means that they have the best knowledge regarding who can do what needs to be done.

Working on the basis of these assumptions, the mayor's functions involved:

- listening carefully to the problem definition and solutions put forth by citizens;

- convening residents to develop a plan of action involving them and their ideas;

- offering support for resident initiatives rather than assuming the city was the problem-solver in the community;

- making residents into official actors with responsibility and authority over their initiative; and

- creating an experience that will lead residents to feel they have ownership in the community.

Amqui flourishes because the mayor acts on three principles:

1. First, work with residents to determine whether they can act together to resolve problems using their own community resources.

2. Second, enhance collective citizen resources by providing supportive municipal assets.

3. Third, acknowledge there will be some problems that cannot be resolved with citizen resources, even if supported by government assistance. In these cases, the municipality must take full responsibility.

The sequence of these three steps is critical, if citizen participation and production is to be achieved. The first question must be, Can citizens define the problem, create solutions, and then implement them? The last question is what must the municipality do. This is a wonderful and all too rare example of a public servant and elected official who truly understands the value of citizen participation and how best to promote it.

Still, if communities are so invaluable to our socioeconomic and environmental well-being, and citizen participation so worthy of promotion, why are they and their local assets typically so undervalued and underpromoted? That is the question we turn our attention to in the next chapter.

* * *

Communities often grow their confidence and collective efficacy by using their primary assets—that which is local and within local residents' control—as their starting point. Then they proceed to liberate their secondary assets—that which is local but currently outside local residents' control. Using the morale and momentum that results, communities begin to figure out what they can do without help and what they can do with allies and outside support. From there, they ready themselves to take on the challenge of liberating external assets—that which is not local and not yet within their control. The end result is that when they encounter external challenges, they do so not as supine, deficient, passive clients of institutional, top-down change. They meet their challenges as strong, connected, vibrant citizens cocreating an alternative future.

Chapter 2

Black Swans, White Swans, and Ugly Ducklings

Why Top-Down Approaches (Mostly) Don't Work

It is impossible to control creation.

—Evelyn Scott

The Black Swan (Cygnus atratus) is a large water bird, a species of swan, which breeds mainly in the southeast and southwest regions of Australia. The species was hunted to extinction in New Zealand, but later reintroduced in 2013.

—M. J. Williams

WHY IS IT THAT the mayor of Amqui's ethic with regard to citizen action is so uncommon? To understand this we need to explore why so many people cast communities in the role of the Ugly Duckling and institutions as the White Swan.

To explain, allow me to first discuss the role of the Black Swan. The Black Swan theory developed by Nassim Nicholas Taleb (2007) is a metaphor for events that seem to emerge out of the blue but have a major historical impact. They are often retrospectively explained away by rationalizations and false logic, and so their significance tends to be missed. These events, though disproportionately significant relative to more predictable occurrences, do not play to standard scientific norms, or rules of probability. Such occurrences are therefore "outliers."

Heat Wave: The New Normal

Nowhere is the need for resilient communities more apparent than in the face of natural disasters. Heat waves, more so than hurricanes, floods, and freezing conditions, highlight this fact, underlining the need for community building at neighborhood scale to ensure sufficient resilience to withstand such climatic challenges. Heat waves, as with other natural disasters, also highlight the limits of health- and social-care systems to intervene unilaterally.

An example: in August 2003, a brutal heat wave struck Europe, killing an estimated seventy thousand people, most of whom were over sixty-five years old. The media and the public for the most part were oblivious until after the fact. In meteorological terms, this counts as a Black Swan occurrence. A high-pressure system produced the hottest summer weather since record-keeping began in 1873 and, when measured by mortality, the worst natural disaster in contemporary France.

According to official estimates, 14,802 people died in France during the first half of August 2003 as a direct consequence of this heat wave. There were many factors at play in France, and in particular in Paris, that did not play out in other European cities to the same extent. In London, for example, six hundred people died, compared to nearly six thousand in Paris. August is a time when most professionals in France, including doctors, go on holiday. As a consequence, the first to realize the scale of what was happening were French undertakers, who were being overwhelmed with bodies.

The number of doctors and other healthcare professionals on vacation was an important factor in that it reduced response time and capacity. But a variety of other factors were at work also, such as the population density and quality of housing in any given area. During the first two weeks of August in Paris, the people most likely to die were women over sixty-five who were living alone in substandard urban housing.

Other contributory factors included the collective impact of air conditioning on the cumulative heating- and cooling-down time of a city, particularly at night. Measuring the heat island around houses and apartment blocks proved that while "cities often function as the beating heart of the economy, they could also become the pressure cookers of a country" (Keller, 2015), as was the case in Paris for those two weeks. The extent of vegetation was also a critical factor: along with lower housing density, it explains why London experienced only a little more than 10 percent of the death toll in Paris, where green space is much less abundant than in London.

It is also important to remember that often people don't notice the effects of dehydration and so tend not to drink enough water. In addition, some medications can amplify the effects of extreme heat. Reduced mobility was yet another critical factor. Still, according to global public health expert Richard C. Keller (2015), the single biggest contributory factor for dying in a heat wave is living alone. It may be more helpful to interpret that critical factor in terms of the extent to which one is connected to a wider community. In that frame, rather than viewing the practice of living alone as the substantive issue, we see that it is the paucity of relationships with neighbors that kills within the context of a certain confluence of events. Put boldly, for the most vulnerable in a prolonged and intense heat wave, community connections, not access to services, are a matter of life and death.

Keller rightly points out that the heat wave of 2003 was as much a social as a health and epidemiological disaster. The interplay between quality of housing, economic insecurity, isolation, and health equity are well rehearsed, but when set against global demographic shifts and climate change, the immensity of the challenges facing public health and our neighborhoods becomes clear.

In a decade or so the world will be older and far more concentrated in urban areas; indeed, in the next five years, for the first time in human history, a majority of the world's population will live in cities. The speed at which the world grows older is mind-boggling: In the year 2000, 420 million people were sixty-five or older (6.9 percent of the world's population). By 2050, this cohort is projected to increase to approximately 1.5 billion, or 16.3 percent of the world's population. The world is getting older at a rate unprecedented in human history (World Bank Open Data).

Outside the Global South, aging combined with large drops in fertility means fewer workers to support growing numbers of retirees, pushing inflation up and tax revenues for public services down. Increased longevity sits side by side with other demographic "firsts" that are quickly exposing the financial limits of our medical systems and social services, and raising serious questions about their capacity to unilaterally improve health, provide social care, and promote general well-being.

The 2003 European heat wave provides a tragic reminder of the need to expand our concern beyond institutional and systems reform and direct our efforts toward building communities of place. This shift would be made with a view to supporting local people to identify, connect, and mobilize their own and their neighbors' assets in pursuit of a good life and enduring change. It is supported by Eric Klinenberg's (2015) study of the Chicago heat wave of 1995, which demonstrates clearly that survival is not about differences between one country and another but about how different neighborhoods are organized. In the summer of 1995 South Lawndale was the best place in the city of Chicago to be, since fewer people died there as a consequence of deeper social ties. In the summer of 2018, a realization across many parts of the world began to dawn: heat waves of this magnitude are no longer Black Swan occurrences; they are our new normal.

Ugly Ducklings

The way we view most social challenges today is deficit-based. We don't see the swan, black or white—we see the Ugly Duckling, particularly in economically marginalized neighborhoods. Hence, we tend to see tragedies such as the deaths from a heat wave in Paris or Chicago as a failure of systems and institutions, and further evidence of the need for more services.

Mapping people's journey toward well-being in this way is deeply problematic, especially if we harbor aspirations toward deeper democracy. It obscures from view the capacities that exist within and around people that can be used to secure what is required for a good life in any and all climates. While the map is not the territory, if communities of place are mapped as Ugly Ducklings, those that reside there internalize that map and so the actual terrain becomes distorted. Consequently, their responsiveness becomes dulled, sometimes with tragic consequences, as was the case in Paris in August 2003.

What once was a label simply mapped onto reality becomes "the way things are around here"; a half-baked perspective becomes a fact of life and the dominant culture. And so, just as an immature White Swan can come to be known and treated as an Ugly Duckling in the well-known fairy tale, communities and their residents can become known by the sum of their problems and not by their capacities and potential.

The work of Jody Kretzmann and John McKnight (1993) has revealed the disabling effects of mapping people by their so-called deficits or needs. In the late 1980s, John and Jody traveled across North America, visiting more than three hundred neighborhoods in twenty cities. In partnership with a core group of associates, they set out to understand the building blocks of healthy urban neighborhoods. Their four-year odyssey brought them into personal contact with thousands of people commonly labeled and defined by the sum of their issues, such as unemployment, teen pregnancies, poor housing and other problems.

John and Jody had the presence of mind to ask a set of questions that were different from the norm. They sought to understand what happened when, despite socioeconomic-political challenges, citizenship and community prevail in neighborhoods; they did not focus on why there were so many apparent problems. This research was essentially an ethnographical revelation of how economically marginalized communities become stronger and endure. Through this participatory process they gathered more than three thousand stories in response to questions like "Can you share a time when you and your neighbors came together to make things better around here?"

These stories revealed six key "community building blocks":

1. the skills of local residents;

2. the power of local associations;

3. the resources of public, private, and nonprofit institutions;

4. the physical resources and ecology of local places;

5. the economic resources of local places, and reciprocal exchange in more general terms; and

6. the stories and heritage of local places.

These building blocks, which John and Jody eventually called "assets," represent local residents' down-to-earth account of their engagement in producing and nurturing their health and well-being, maintaining their environment and local economy, raising powerful children, aging comfortably and actively at home, responding to natural or human-made disasters, and deepening democracy, justice, and wisdom.

These assets also served to challenge the prevailing approach to urban and rural development. Jody and John's work disputed the way the helping professions, funding agencies, and policymakers focused almost exclusively on the needs and deficiencies of individuals, families, neighborhoods, towns, and villages.

Their seminal work *Building Communities from the Inside Out: A Path toward Finding and Mobilizing a Community's Assets* (1993) captured the lessons of that four-year engagement. It also described the principles and practices of asset-based approaches John and Jody developed over earlier decades. Encouraged by record sales of the book, in 1995 they established the Asset-Based Community Development (ABCD) Institute, now located at DePaul University in Chicago.

More than two decades later, the ABCD Institute's archives are replete with practical tools and probing analyses of modern society. Taken all together they offer both a proscription and a prescription for modern society. The proscription: don't seek your good life in the marketplace. The prescription: in each of our neighborhoods reside those whose gifts and talents combine with ours to provide much of what we need to live well and prosper—if we can discover, connect, and mobilize them.

Today, the ABCD Institute and the principles and processes it espouses occupy a central position as part of a large and growing movement that considers local assets as the primary building blocks of sustainable community development. Central to the asset-based approach is the emphasis on community building that is citizen-led and relationship-focused. To achieve this, it is necessary to work in a place-based way and at neighborhood scale, with a focus on people's capacities, since people can't know what they need until they first know what they have.

White Swans

A central part of the challenge in revealing the White Swan behind the Ugly Duckling label of modern-day neighborhoods is that, while most of us call our neighborhoods communities, in practice they are not. Like the Ugly Duckling, they simply have not reached their potential; they have not matured—yet.

Communities are made up of groups of related people. Powerful and enduring communities create cultures where relatedness flourishes. The places where we live are all too often made up of unrelated people—neighborhoods of strangers. At most, we know the neighbors who live either side of us and across the street, whom we nod at each morning before getting in our cars to drive to work. For those who have sufficient mobility and social capital outside their own neighborhood this is a tolerable way to live.

However, for those with diminished mobility and social capital, neighborhoods can become prisons of loneliness, only a heat wave away from tragedy. Our neighborhoods are therefore places in need of recovery and maturation. That said, there is much to work with.

Our neighborhoods are in need of recovery not because they are Ugly Ducklings but because we have failed to do two things: to recognize them as swans and to nurture the conditions for each metaphorical White Swan to emerge in all its respective glory. The assets that reside there can be identified, connected, and mobilized into productive and inclusive action through community-building processes, the kind that we have been removing from the investment sheet of local governments for more than thirty years.

Restoring confidence in the power of community life and collective capacity is not the same as suggesting communities can or should go it alone, without the support of outside institutions. There are limits to what can be achieved locally, and in chapter 4 I will explore what outside agencies can do to support communities. Before getting to that, however, in the next chapter I want to detail some recent historical trends—especially in the area of propaganda—that have contributed to a shift in how communities address life's necessities. The next chapter explains the dynamics of the transition from community sufficiency to dependence on the marketplace. More particularly, where once neighbor-to-neighbor support was the first port of call and goods and services from the marketplace supplemented those supports, now a strong feature of modern consumer culture is that the necessities of a good life are not considered to be primarily in local neighborly networks, but instead in external programs and services delivered by specialist salaried strangers. In sum, what is necessary for a good life has been outsourced from citizen space to the professional world of service, having been intentionally commodified by a minority of arrogant elites and framed as "needs" to be satisfied by the market.

* * *

The White Swan represents maturing communities of place where the culture of reciprocity is palpable. Now where might we go to find one of those? From a policy point of view, I believe this should be *the* question of our time, and the hottest topic of all. The answer to this question is that communities are all around us, close at hand, awaiting the community building that will make the invisible assets within them visible in all their abundance.

Part Two: **Rekindling Community in a Consumer Society**

We can all reverse the Bernays curse and make the long journey from consumer to producer, but it requires a collective will, which is fundamentally countercultural. It is thus that deep democracy is cocreated and enduring social justice realized.

Chapter 3

The Bernays Curse

Countering the Seven Tactics
of Hidden Persuaders

Without community, there is no liberation.

—AUDRE LORDE

WE ALL KNOW A Freudian slip is when you say one thing and mean another. Or, as someone once quipped, "When you say one thing and mean your mother." Typically, it happens without conscious intent. Edward Bernays, Sigmund Freud's nephew, changed all that. In a way, he was to make Freudian slips an institution, for all the wrong reasons.

When he returned from Paris at the end of World War I, where he had assisted US president Woodrow Wilson to use propaganda to convince the masses that he was "bringing democracy to Europe," Bernays' main pre-occupation was how to use propaganda in the corporate world for mass manipulation, albeit for very different purposes.

Bernays played a pivotal role in popularizing the ideas of Sigmund Freud in America. He combined Freud's ideas with those of Gustave Le Bon and Wilfred Trotter on crowd psychology with a view to becoming a kind of psychoanalyst to troubled US corporations. It's fair to say he used his connection to Freud to "big himself up," and it worked. That said, he was a man of considerable talent in his own right and authored a number of seminal works in the field of public relations, the best known being *Crystallizing Public Opinion* (1923). This text was later cited by Joseph Goebbels, Reich Minister of Propaganda for Nazi Germany, as having had a significant influence on his thinking.

More important, Bernays was instrumental in transforming postwar America. Before Bernays, people had largely behaved as regular citizens, people who consumed goods and services mainly on the basis of necessity. Bernays' work transformed Americans to mass consumers who purchased goods and services on the basis of whims and wants. This form of mass manipulation set the template for the rest of the Western world for the last hundred years (Curtis, 2002). It was an inevitable progression from citizens taking care of their own to becoming passive consumers of "care" services.

The Rise of "Care" Services

The New Deal introduced by US president Franklin D. Roosevelt to combat the effects of the Great Depression of the 1930s was a series of programs and policies of relief, recovery, and reform. The New Deal provided much-needed employment, training, access to housing, banking regulation, union protections, and Social Security. None of those programs was about services.

But by the time the New Deal was framed, the new human service institutions that also emerged from this legislative framework were modeling themselves on the structures and strategies of corporate America and thinking of their "end users" as clients rather than citizens.

Bernays' knack for turning citizens into consumers became legend and was welcomed by the captains of corporate America, who feared that the assembly lines that ran nonstop during the war would grind to a halt. Bernays ensured that did not happen. Of course, he was not solely driven by capitalist ideals, although there's little doubt they featured significantly. He also believed that mass manipulation was essential in society, to control the irrational drives and "herd instincts" of the populace. Based on these beliefs he was able to rationalize the use of techniques of mass manipulation to influence not only purchasing but also voting trends:

> If we understand the mechanism and motives of the group mind, is it not possible to control and regiment the masses according to our will without their knowing about it? The recent practice of propaganda has proved that it is possible, at least up to a certain point and within certain limits. (Bernays, 1928)

Bernays termed this means of control the "engineering of consent," and he was absolutely certain that these techniques were both necessary and desirable. He thought it a logical consequence of order and civil society that the ruling classes would have to employ such techniques to quell and control the herd instinct. In essence he believed that if people were consuming as individuals, then these animal instincts, which had previously spilled over into war, would be satiated.

It may seem strange now to think that mass manipulation on this scale could have been rationalized as an antiwar device, but it was the post–WWI era after all. The second driver of mass manipulation was corporate greed, which to this day is a powerful force. The third was political; the message sent out by American politicians was that if you want to be a good American, be a good consumer:

> Economically we have a boundless field before us; that there are new wants which will make way endlessly for newer wants, as fast as they are satisfied. ("Hoover Economic Report Sees Prosperity Ahead for Nation," 1929)

Despite Bernays' pretense at purity, whereby he positioned himself as the prime defender of democracy, some of his activities were highly questionable and, from a Freudian perspective, narcissistic. Perhaps the most eyebrow-raising was his propaganda campaign to overthrow the democratically elected president of Guatemala, Colonel Jacobo Árbenz Guzmán. The tab for that piece of public relations was picked up by multinational corporation United Fruit Company (today's Chiquita Brands International). Bernays' campaign simply worked through American media outlets to brand Jacobo Árbenz Guzmán a communist.

The kiss of death having been given, the overthrow was "legitimately" assisted by the US government and was somewhat inevitable. Such is the power of spin. Bernays much preferred to manipulate the masses through news broadcasting outlets rather than standard advertising, since people's defenses were down when they read or listened to the news; they naively expected the truth.

The Hidden Persuaders

In 1957, *The Hidden Persuaders* was published and launched author Vance Packard's career. In the book, Packard laid bare the use of consumer motivational research and other psychological techniques by advertisers and politicians to manipulate expectations and induce desire for products and candidates. He identified eight "compelling needs" that the hidden persuaders could aim to fulfill:

- *Emotional security*: Promise comfort, happiness, security, and no bad feelings.

- *Reassurance of worth*: As L'Oreal reminds us, you should have it "because you're worth it!" And once you have "it," it will serve to symbolize to you and others that you are adding value and deserve your place in society.

- *Ego gratification*: Playing to our need for affirmation, ads regularly tell us, even before we make a purchase, that we have made the "wise choice," "right choice," "smart choice."

- *Creative outlet*: Famously, when Betty Crocker cake mix first hit the shelves, it was not at all successful until people were asked to add an egg to the mix. Today potential buyers are still sold products on the basis that they can personalize them and engage in a form of user-led creative expression.

- *Love object*: We all need something to love, and if you don't have that special love object, don't worry! The market will invent it and then convince you that you need it. This was typified by the Subaru Love Promise advertising campaign: "The Subaru Love Promise is our vision to show love and respect to all people at every interaction with Subaru. Together with our retailers, we are dedicated to making the world a better place." The promise to replace customer service with love at every interaction may make for good marketing, for some, but I suspect that most customers know that they are engaged in a transaction and will react with incredulity at such a declaration. While most advertising campaigns are not so bold in their claims to make you a love object, or create an object you can fall in love with, the underlying promises of love are easy to surface.

- *Sense of power*: One of Bernays' (1965) public relations stunts involved reframing cigarettes as "torches of freedom" for women. Cigarette sales among women went through the roof.

- *Roots*: Even in a world where the culture of "self" dominates, our identities remain intimately tied to our sense of place, our sense of where we come from. For example, McDonald's, which has perfected the art of standardization, takes care to include regional twists in its menus to demonstrate their deference to the "local." These are, of course, minor concessions, ploys to get us to feel better about buying that which is not of our place or made by our hand.

- *Immortality*: Marketers work hard to convince us that they are our number-one cheerleaders and allies in the fight to cheat aging and death.

According to Packard these eight needs are so strong that people are compelled to buy products to satisfy them. The difficulty arises when the products or services fail to deliver on the implied or explicit promise to address any or all of them, which they inevitably do; of course, people then feel dissatisfied. What follows this dissatisfaction is not the scene one would expect, where the consumer walks away never to return; instead, a form of addiction or compulsion becomes evident. As the American philosopher Eric Hoffer wisely reminds us, "You can never get enough of what you don't really want," so, as strange as it sounds, the marketplace is designed to keep us dissatisfied, because that's what keeps us coming back. By conflating material things with what ultimately makes us happy, we are persuaded to buy and become complicit in creating our own unhappiness. We handle our dissatisfaction by buying bigger, better, more—in a different color, size, configuration—but buying nonetheless. With strategies from built-in obsolescence to money-off coupons, the market keeps the trap going. The outcome of our engagement in addictive consumption is that eventually what we consume starts to consume us.

Reversing Bernays

People like Bernays and Packard's hidden persuaders are masters at maintaining the status quo and shoring up the "priestly classes." They do so through the use of spin to legitimatize this abuse of power. In a very real sense civic renewal is an attempt to "reverse Bernays," to make the journey back from being clients to being citizens. To that end community builders must encounter the world as it is, and that means being wise to their tactics.

The seven tactics most often employed by the hidden persuaders in our world, and to which community builders and citizens need to be most alert, start with creating a culture of self.

Tactic #1: Create a Culture of Self

It's the old rule of divide and conquer. If people rely on each other and exchange things, they buy less.

People organized into collectives are also more difficult to rule. Hidden persuaders use media and politics to convince us of the virtues of the indefensible, such as long commute times to work, atomization across family generations, single-use land planning, social stratification of housing, and on and on. Their primary message: you are freer on your own. The culture of self is now more than a century old and is typified in the immortal words of the Frank Sinatra song "My Way."

Just as narcissism turns a river into a mirror, consumerism turns a community asset into a self-serving commodity, which in due course turns on us. It is the job of hidden persuaders to convince us that happiness can be commoditized in keeping with personal preference and that success is therefore commensurate with one's capacity to grow one's purchasing power. Independence becomes prized over interdependence, and over time a culture of narcissism replaces a culture of community.

Tactic #2: Turn Productive Villages into Dormitories for Consumers

Village economies have a proven track record for promoting economic self-reliance and sufficiency (Graeber, 2011). We know intuitively and now evidentially that village economies are more effective when it comes to environmental sustainability and sustaining the health and well-being of their inhabitants. These competencies are the enemies of an open economy, which is predicated on making people dependent on "your" products, goods, and services. To grow national GDP, we need people to buy the idea that a good life exists outside the village, in the marketplace. We are now so invested in this idea that we have become significantly indebted in order to personally compete for consumption rights.

According to Karl Polanyi (1944), the Austro-Hungarian economic historian and author of *The Great Transformation*, one of the most influential books of the last century, village economies historically operated mostly on a principle of gift, not money, exchange, and were therefore better placed to become repositories of fair wealth redistribution. In effect, they ran contrary to the values that underpin a culture of narcissism.

Hidden persuaders are experts at dealing with such "cultural contradictions." Why let the truth get in the way of a good story? The spin they use convinces us that our home places are rustic, backward, populated by amateurs and witch doctors that want to limit our freedom and hold us back. "Fake news" has been a feature of our lives for a very long time.

The message of the hidden persuaders: "Look to the hills, the bright lights, the big city; there's gold and freedom and no one to hold you back. That's where you'll find yourself and make your fortune. And on the days where you're feeling sad and lonely, they've got some really good therapists who can help. And if you can't afford a therapist? Don't worry, the city has lots of services for 'the poor.'"

Hidden persuaders also use the argument of scale to great effect: "How are we to reach everybody and ensure that everybody's needs are met if we stay small and local? To efficiently and effectively reach everyone we must go to scale." They even try to convince us this is a form of radical inclusion and equality.

Many of our economic, housing, environmental, health, and social-care policies are harmful to village life and community cultures but inversely beneficial to commercial interests and the cult of individualism. The art of spin is in getting us to cut off our nose to spite our face while sustaining a smile, and so for the last fifty years policies that have eroded community life have gone through with little or no debate.

Tactic #3: Promote a Culture of Competition and Pursuit of Perfection

Villages are not, of course, perfect places; there are all sorts of feuds and fault lines to be negotiated. Notwithstanding, the primary function of the village is to provide a context within which a culture of community can proliferate and prevail. Such a culture is created through practices of hospitality and cooperation.

Consumerism abjures such cooperation, since it runs contrary to its principles. To borrow from Alfie Kohn (1986), author of *No Contest: The Case against Competition*, the rule of consumerism, which promotes competition over cooperation, is this: "For me to win, you must lose."

Hidden persuaders understand the importance of feeding that competitive urge, not only between individuals, but also to promote a sense of competition within our "selves." The pursuit of perfection translates into the annual exchanging of our smartphones and explains why *en masse* we have passively accepted that these days nearly everything we purchase has built-in obsolescence after a couple of years. We rationalize it as the price and pace of progress. Our pursuit of perfection has also fueled a cult of anti-aging, a fear of death, and an active hostility toward human fallibility and limits. This has translated into multibillion-dollar pharmacology and medical industries aimed at winning the "battle" against our finite humanity and an abdication of responsibility to care for those who don't measure up to our standards of perfection.

Tactic #4: Convince People They Can Buy Care

The hidden persuaders have worked hard to assuage our pangs of guilt around outsourcing the care of our own imperfectibilities and the fallibilities of our families and neighbors; we transfer care for ourselves and others to those who, in the professional world, are suitably credentialed. We have most notably outsourced the care of older people, people on the margins, and labeled people of all kinds, on the assumption that what they need is located within institutional programs, not in community life. This assumption is a recent one in human history and is directly tied to our journey over the last century from citizens to consumers.

Marie de Hennezel (2012) observes that the commodification of care has become big business and carries with it a double charge. First, there is the overt financial charge for the program or intervention consumed, and second, the hidden charge paid in the currency of personal agency and social capital. Hidden persuaders perform a clever sleight of hand to take our attention away from this inherent contradiction. This tactic involves drawing our attention away from the right to self- and collective determination and toward our right to receive services and have our needs adequately addressed by those best qualified to do so. It need not be so, de Hennezel tells us:

> Something within us does not grow old. I shall call it the heart. I don't mean the organ, which does of course age, but the capacity to love and to desire. The heart I refer to is that inexplicable, incomprehensible force which keeps the human being alive . . .
>
> It is this heart that can help us to push on through our fears, and bears us up amid the worst ordeals of old age. (Hennezel, 2012)

Tactic #5: Make People Dependent on Goods and Services

Bernays perfected the techniques now ubiquitously used to confuse actual needs with product and service categorization. As a consequence, in the space of one hundred years, regular people have transitioned from addressing their needs by first inventorying their local assets to now having their needs assessed by strangers intent on persuading them that the only way their life will get better is if someone/something from outside comes into their life to make it better.

The basic message coming from commercial, public sector, and civil society institutions is "You need us, we know best. Consume what we have to offer and you'll be better." The premise behind this message would be "You cannot depend on each other; you and your neighbors are inadequate and insufficient in the face of your complex needs. You are not qualified to understand and solve your own problems. The worst solutions come from neighborhoods." Consequently common knowledge of how to produce is lost. Collective production first becomes a mystery, then a myth.

Tactic #6: Discredit Associational, Amateur, and Civic Life and Space

The function of associations is to act as a vehicle to amplify and multiply our individual capacities, skills, and passions. They perform this function by creating an ambient context within which gifts can be exchanged and, accordingly, positively compounded. Associations can only function within a nonhierarchical gift economy, which is to say an egalitarian cooperative environment that is deeply relational, not transactional.

In that kind of ideal environment, freedom and democracy can flourish, but associational life is highly susceptible to external counterforces. Hidden persuaders understand this, and this is exactly what Nazi propagandists used to undermine freedom of association and expression in Germany. If you can turn the Scouts into Hitler Youth, while simultaneously making the trains run on time and restoring people's financial security, you can rule a nation—and corrupt a generation.

Tactic #7: Remain Hidden, Even to Yourself

Imagine if you could persuade yourself that you are not operating in an imperial, patriarchal manner by wearing what John McKnight once called the "mask of love" (1984). You could rationalize almost any form of manipulation from this position. The best hidden persuaders are, therefore, hidden even unto themselves. They have convinced themselves that they are operating in people's best interests, using their superior positions and intellect to "nudge" the unsophisticated "herd" toward their better selves. The mask has become the face.

In the next chapter we travel to an island paradise to explore what happens to indigenous cultures when outsiders come in uninvited and then abruptly leave.

* * *

To reverse the Bernays curse and take on the hidden persuaders of our world we would be wise to heed the words of Brazilian educator and philosopher Paulo Freire: "It is not enough for people to come together in dialogue in order to gain knowledge of their social reality. They must act together upon their environment in order critically to reflect upon their reality and so transform it through further action and critical reflection" (1970).

We counter the tactics of hidden persuaders, not so that we can be better-serviced consumers, but so that those whom the hidden persuaders have defined as the problem can secure the power to redefine the problem. We can all reverse the Bernays curse and make the long journey from consumers to producers, but it requires a collective will, which is fundamentally countercultural. It is thus that deep democracy is cocreated and enduring social justice realized.

Chapter 4

Paradise Lost

Cargo Cults and Austerity

Awake, arise, or be for ever fall'n.

—JOHN MILTON, *PARADISE LOST*

TANNA IS AMONG THE remotest islands on the planet. Prior to World War II, its inhabitants had few encounters with the outside world.

That all changed with the arrival of American soldiers, who set up military bases on nearby islands. They arrived en masse in ships and planes brimming with cargos of medicine, clothes, food, and equipment to sustain the troops across the Pacific. They also arrived with their military customs, their uniforms, radios, and a myriad of other behaviors and regalia previously unseen by the inhabitants of Tanna.

How do people in these situations make sense of such incursions into their daily lives? In the absence of any industrialized, technological points of reference, they use the points of reference that are available to them. In this instance, a significant proportion of the Tanna natives concluded (quite logically) that since the soldiers weren't actually doing anything productive to bring the cargo to them—no craft of any kind was being employed, nothing of any kind was being produced, yet stuff kept falling from the sky—they must have been engaged in acts of ritual magic that caused them to be favored by the gods.

On Tanna the American soldiers regularly shared items of cargo with the local inhabitants. Then, on May 8, 1945, the war in Europe ended; a few months later, on September 2, 1945, Japan surrendered to the US. While the rest of the world celebrated, the inhabitants of Tanna were bereft. The soldiers systematically left and with them took the "cargo." Not surprisingly, after the soldiers left, in an effort to invoke similar favor from the gods, many of Tanna's inhabitants took to imitating the militaristic "rituals" of their visitors.

The name "cargo cult" is used to describe those imitations even though it is a pejorative one. The term impugns the motives and intelligence of the island inhabitants and carries little critical comment about the behaviors of those who landed on the island and then abruptly left, having forever altered its culture. The behaviors on Tanna are, in fact, completely understandable, even predicable. What they teach us is how nonindustrialized communities respond to outsiders, and also the inherent dangers of outsiders carelessly sharing their cargo in an effort to be "helpful."

The Cargo Cults Narrative

When you listen closely to some of the narratives that have grown up around economically marginalized communities in the face of austerity, they are not all that dissimilar to some of the underlying judgments that Westerners make about cargo cults. It is not uncommon to hear such patrician and bigoted sentiments against economically marginalized people as these:

1. They have developed an unhealthy dependence on outside aid; they need to learn to stand on their own two feet and stop looking for handouts.

2. They are fundamentally oriented toward materialism and have lost connection to the wholesome traditions and values that have helped people get out of poverty or at least live a sustainable life for generations.

3. Their lack of sophistication and education has caused them to misread the situation and to place unrealistic and unsustainable expectations on the benevolence of outsiders, and now they are passing this dependency culture on to their children.

4. They are being guided by local leaders who are abusing the situation for their own selfish ends: knowing the cargo will never come, they still use their charismatic leadership styles to convince their followers otherwise.

5. They are feckless: while they wait for the cargo they could at least engage in more productive activity, but they do not, proving that in fact they are fundamentally lazy.

In short, it is all their fault.

The *Oxford English Dictionary* defines a cult as "a relatively small group of people having religious beliefs or practices regarded by others as strange or as imposing excessive control over members: a network of Satan-worshipping cults." I wonder if, given similar circumstances, we're not all susceptible to becoming members of a cargo cult. At a stretch you could even get some mileage out of arguing that consumer society is a mass cargo cult of a sort. Watch people in shopping centers, or on public transport: their behaviors are not all that dissimilar to the natives of Tanna imitating the US army march. Or consider the level of adoration given to pop culture celebrities, movie stars, and the like. We too have our own John Frum (the mythical figure that the Tanna people have worshipped for decades). Performing meaningless ritualistic acts in the hope that someday your bounty/cargo will land is not a bad description of the function of a client in a consumer society.

Scarcity vs. Abundance

Tanna is an example of a so-called primitive society that, prior to the arrival of the "cargo," can be viewed as affluent. It can be anthropologically proven that the inhabitants were competent in the art of organizing abundance (Baudrillard, 1998; Sahlins, 1974) and making the invisible, visible. Conversely, the American soldiers and those who commanded them can be viewed as organizers of scarcity, and so making the visible, invisible.

The Tanna people at one level can be said to have suffered from absolute poverty in that they had few, if any, personal possessions prior to the arrival of the American soldiers. They did not work in the industrial sense of the term, made no economic calculations and did not amass a store of goods of any note or import.

But what inoculated them against the consequences of such scarcity, which would see them face untold hardships in the industrialist, productionist, money-based world, was that they were not of that world. Instead, they organized their world as a village-based gift economy, where "time" was not commodified and waste made no sense. They shared what they had with other members of their community and consumed what they had immediately, or at least before it "spoiled." They fundamentally trusted in the abundance of natural resources (Graeber, 2011).

Western cultures, in contrast, are racked with anxiety at the prospect of insufficiencies that may befall them if their personal capacities fall short. Consider the concept of affluenza as popularized by Oliver James (2007). Affluenza intentionally conflates *affluence* and *influenza* to highlight the growing and harmful effects of consumerism on people's well-being. James defines affluenza as "a painful, contagious, socially transmitted condition of overload, debt, anxiety, and waste resulting from the dogged pursuit of more." This is not a plea to go back in time, nor a revisionist look back to bygone days through rose-tinted glasses. Instead it is

1. an effort to appreciate the capacities for cultural adaptation that many of our forebears demonstrated so as to learn from them;

2. an inquiry into how we may better adapt to our current contexts; and

3. a bid to assume a less high-handed view of the past by comparison with modern times.

In so-called advanced societies, how many paychecks away from destitution are any of us? The answer, as well as the extent to which the state in question provides social protection, is in large part contingent on how willing and able our families, social networks, and communities are to provide a buffer (social capital).

In hunter-gatherer societies that community buffer was the norm, the baseline from which everything else was made possible. Indeed, if you look closely at how many economically marginalized communities in the US, Australia, and Europe organized themselves in the 1930s and 1940s to weather the Great Depression and the war years, similar characteristics were plain to be seen—although, given the industrialized context, they were not as apparent as in hunter-gatherer societies. Indeed, the spirit of '45 in the United Kingdom, which saw the introduction of their National Health Service system (a universal health service free at the point of need), was predicated on ensuring all democratic states took care to add support to that baseline, not replace it (Beveridge, 1942).

When the soldiers arrived on Tanna, they simply could not see that abundance.

Instead, all they saw were the perceived deficits and the associated needs of the inhabitants, and so they sought to address those needs by sharing items from their "cargo," and they felt good about doing so. Thought of in these terms, the focus shifts away from the native inhabitants and on to the "imperial outsiders," who arrived with this covert message: "We have the cargo, you just have deficits and ignorance; we can help you."

Little did any of these outsiders, or indeed the policymakers and planners who sent them, know what the consequences of their well-intended actions would be. In all likelihood nobody gave them a second thought. The soldiers mapped Tanna based on their values, which were largely grounded in their own anxiety around scarcity of resources, which they in turn projected onto the local people they encountered. These soldiers undermined, with Hershey bars and good intentions, the indigenous compass that had been used to find, connect, and mobilize local assets since the dawn of humankind.

Clearly, the presence of the American soldiers on Tanna and other islands had profoundly harmful effects. Eventually, in the shadow of these well-meaning white-faced outsiders, local people came to see themselves as insufficient and began to believe that the only way they would be fulfilled is from outside in. They grew ever more doubtful of their indigenous capacities, and the more they saw of the external assets of the "cargo," the harder it was for them to see value in the assets within and around them.

Eventually their assets became invisible even to them, and their multigenerational capacity to make visible the invisible atrophied. In place of a reliance on the abundances within and around them emerged the belief that things will only get better when someone with special powers (the Great One, the Big Man) comes from the outside to make them better.

Cargo Cults and Disabling Professionals

Might there be some useful parallels between the phenomenon crudely referred to as "cargo cults" and the disabling effects of professional helpers? In much the same way—albeit for different reasons—that American and Japanese soldiers set up bases on islands in the Pacific, with the introduction by Franklin D. Roosevelt of the New Deal, professional helpers moved into economically marginalized communities across Europe and the United States. They too (for the most part) could not see the assets that existed in abundance in these communities.

So, what has this all got to do with modern occurrences of austerity? In late 2008 there seemed to be a broad consensus that we were passing through uncharted economic waters; we were several years into what many bureaucrats were calling "austerity," and what some in civil society referred to as fiscal retrenchment, of a kind and to an extent not seen before. In response, much effort by various governments was going into weaning "poor people" off dependence on the "cargo." Increasingly, we heard policymakers and professionals who once handed out funding and set up programs—in much the same way American soldiers handed out Hershey bars on Tanna—insisting that communities use their own assets.

These austerity measures are layered on top of more than fifty years of a deficit approach to helping people that is most manifest in the harm done to the six building blocks of community:

1. Most people have come to define themselves and their neighbors as consumers and clients, not producers and citizens.

2. Associations (unpaid people in groups of three or more coming together by consent to define problems and possibilities, create solutions, and take action) shrink in the face of the growing credentialed classes who are paid to provide services, often for what once was provided through associational life. Accordingly, people come to believe that wisdom is digitally encoded or housed in a university, health production is the purview of the medics, and care for people with high-support needs is the sole domain of social service professionals. They also believe that their prosperity is contingent on the whims of megacorporations and that our safety is in the hands of law enforcement officials.

3. Institutions established to safeguard the common good have come to look more like businesses. They are more concerned with issues of market share, client base, and service delivery than with local democracy and the common good. Clientelism has replaced the ethic of service, and people's needs have become confused with service categorizations and pathologies.

4. Ecologies have fallen outside the influence of indigenous peoples. Monsanto is emblematic of the extent to which the corporate world has come to colonize our lands and our lives.

5. Our economies are more defined by debt than by gift exchange (Graeber, 2011); meaningful discussions about wealth distribution and practical antipoverty initiatives are pushed aside in order to advance discussions about service-based economies, which are contingent on centralizing decisions about public goods rather than enabling people to make their own decisions and purchase or create their own services locally. Solutions to the challenges of wealth distribution, such as Universal Unconditional Basic Citizen Income, are badged as fringe ideas in an effort to sustain what is now predominantly a service-based economy.

6. Our cultural heritage comes to reside in museums or in annual civic celebrations. Culture is put in its place alongside the other competing interests of modern daily life. Hence the stories that have the potential to bind us have no sense of present or future; they tell instead of a time that has long passed and evoke melancholia where once they spurred us toward collective action.

Modern-day "cargo" takes many different forms, such as cruise ships that dock near islands like those in Papua New Guinea and consequently displace ancient traditions of connection and exchange.

For example, Kula, also known as the Kula exchange or Kula ring, is a ceremonial exchange system conducted in the Milne Bay Province of Papua New Guinea. The Kula ring was first studied by the famous anthropologist Bronisław Malinowski, who described in detail the intricate network of exchanges of bracelets and necklaces made of shells and other adornments across the Trobriand Islands. His study in the 1920s and subsequent anthropological research and debate about gift economies help us understand that this shell art and the exchange of these necklaces and bracelets were, and to a small degree continue to be, part of an essential system of exchange (the Kula ring) that affected every aspect of island life. This exchange system is linked to power, protection, connection, and one's standing (reputation) across these islands and in each village. One's standing is determined not by money but by the number of yams you have and how many Kula connections you have been able to negotiate. That is what makes you the "Big Man" of the village: the more you have the bigger you are.

Today, as more cruise liners arrive on these islands—bringing with them their cash to pay local villagers for their performances of traditional dance, tours around their island, and local crafts—the Kula exchange is displaced and replaced by the cash economy, and local culture becomes a performance art to support tourism and not a way of life. As well as hidden cultural costs, there are also significant environmental costs with tons of waste being dumped into the open sea by the cruise ships.

Sympathy or Empathy?

A less obvious example of modern "cargo" are some traditional charity-style food banks in industrialized cities that provide food parcels to "the poor and hungry." Many of these food banks, though well intentioned, possess unspoken hierarchical divisions between the helpers and those that are receiving help, which result in the people receiving food parcels often being stigmatized, while those volunteering to hand out the parcels are feeling good. These practices expose a series of unfortunate and unintended consequences, all largely driven by good intent. What is apparent in all such instances, from handing out Hershey bars to distributing food parcels, is that too often they are driven by sympathy, rather than genuine empathy.

If empathy were the driver in food banks, for example, we would not be able to tell the difference between the helpers and those receiving help. People would be known for their capacities, and issues of food sovereignty and local nutritious food production and consumption would be fused with ensuring no member of the community goes without or feels diminished when they receive a gift. Examples of an empathetic approach to food can be found among locals in the South Central Neighborhood in Singapore, through a response they call "We Wish You Enough." In the Singapore approach neighbor-to-neighbor conversations take place about how they can all organize their capacities and resources to ensure everyone has enough to eat and generally have a good life. The Real Junk Food Project in the UK and other countries, where food is repatriated from local supermarkets on a daily basis before it goes to landfill, is another example. Here community meals are shared with neighbors, which provides the context within which the necessities are shared, other gifts exchanged, and life's challenges explored as a community of people with wants and offers.

A critique similar to the one made against food banks can be made of most current welfare systems, in which there is a superior-inferior relationship dynamic between the helpers and the "helped." It is a sympathetic model, which means that as we see further cuts in public services and as neoliberal ideals become mainstream, it will increasingly lack not only empathy but even the most elementary features of sympathy. People in receipt of welfare payments are all too often stigmatized with labels like "sponger," "benefit queen," and the like. Not only do they find themselves caught in a welfare trap where it is economically better for them and their families to stay on welfare than to find alternatives, but they also find themselves being stigmatized for the way society has set them up.

The contrast between sympathetic and empathic ways of helping is as important as it is disruptive and is ably demonstrated by cultures throughout the world. (I will explore more empathetic ways of supporting local economies in chapter 7.) Most recently, while I was in Singapore, I experienced culturally embedded empathy in a Chinese New Year tradition, called *yu sheng* or *lo hei*, in which family members bring ingredients to a shared pot and stir in sweet sticky sauce. They then have family members recite the symbolic meaning of each of the ingredients.

The name of each ingredient is usually a homophone of a word that is part of an auspicious saying; for instance, *yu* is the pronunciation for both the words "fish" and "abundance," the latter being part of the greeting *nian nian you yu* ("May you have an abundance [of whatever you desire] every year"). As the ingredients are added, diners recite the corresponding saying, with exaggerated tossing of their food using chopsticks. It's said that the higher one tosses, the happier one will be, which comes from another homophone—in Cantonese, *lo hei* means to "toss" and *hei* also means "happiness."

The belief is that the ritual creates the conditions for prosperity and health for the year ahead.

They are correct in this belief insofar as such rituals call forth empathy between family members, deepening the ties that bind, and that is the foundation of health and prosperity: health is clearly determined by social bonds, and prosperity, or adequate wealth, is not so much about what you know or who you know as it is about who you know who knows who you *need* to know. This is the same principle that underpins the Kula exchange.

The world needs more collective empathy and the rituals and practices that call it forth. But what we're getting instead is sympathy. Sympathy increases proportionate to the speed at which our rituals disappear and often arrives with an associated set of rules and standards that must be followed. While empathy binds like the sweet sticky plum sauce of the *lo hei* ritual, the ingredients that provide us with the sustenance and the energy to be productive must be connected in our communities if we are to be well. Sympathy, in contrast, divides us and turns us into consumers. It divides the helper and the helped, the haves and so-called have-nots, the good guys and the bad, the rich and the poor, the needed and the "needy."

Here is a simple way to assess whether you are practicing sympathy or empathy: sympathy means the helper doesn't need anything from those whom they help. Empathy upends this relationship, creating a bond of interdependence between both parties. The helper needs the helped as much as the helped needs the helper. Those who practice empathy understand their liberation is intertwined with those they serve, and so they move beyond classic helping into a shared pursuit toward liberation.

Empathy invites people who have been labeled as "needy" back into community life because their gifts are needed and because we need them to be whole. Sympathy has the effect of creating dependence between those perceived by some as "needy" and the "needed," often at the expense of interdependence at the center of community life, which is what collective empathy creates.

Sympathy creates soup kitchens and traditional food banks; empathy creates community kitchens, where the harvests of local foods are prepared by neighbors, where everyone's gifts are needed to create the feast. In the community kitchen you can't tell the difference between the helper and helped because they are interdependent. The person labeled as homeless is actually the chef, and that person is as worthy and as needed as the middle-class volunteer eager to help. It is in this space that together they practice a version of *lo hei*. And it is there that they get better at being human together.

In such spaces people may begin to ask challenging questions: "Why do we have five empty homes for every homeless person in our city?" or "Why can't we figure out how those who want more friendship and companionship in their lives can be connected with those who have it to give and need a place to live?"

Yet, as we are seeing in the United Kingdom, with the deepening of fiscal entrenchment (often referred to as austerity) come more and more cuts to traditional services, and if existing sympathetic institutions, after encouraging dependency for decades, clumsily flee economically marginalized communities—all the while insisting that such communities now have assets where once they claimed they had none—then they will heap further harm on those communities and so completely discredit their professions and organizations. Such communities are of course not without assets; in fact, as I have argued up to now, they have an abundance of them, as did the people of Tanna, so they are not plundered places or Ugly Ducklings, so to speak. They still are places with capacity, even though that capacity is often undervalued or unseen; to borrow from Wendell Berry's aphorism "There are no unsacred places; there are only sacred places and desecrated places," such communities have been desecrated.

The central point here is that the assets of these communities have been obscured, overlooked, and often actively demeaned; consequently their gaze has been turned upward, toward the skies and away from where they live and what they have. Just as the people of Tanna continued to look to the skies long after the cargo planes were gone, so many marginalized communities believe the best solutions to their problems come from outside in. Restoring culture and the commons begins when those who have done this kind of harm to the culture of communities acknowledge this cultural trauma and learn to serve while walking backward in a way that reveals community abundance, not abandonment.

There is what might be described as a hydraulic-like relationship between institutions and communities. As with hydraulics, as we press down or reduce the influence of the institution, we must ensure that the functions of the community are simultaneously restored and increase in value and authority, so that as one goes down the other goes up. This hydraulic metaphor highlights a repatriation of functions (which the institutional world appropriated) from the institutional world back to citizen space. This is no less than a process of decolonization. The rationale for this relocation of authority is not about saving an institutional system money; rather, it is about saving people from the system, which is to say, deinstitutionalization.

The next chapter considers how best to reduce institutionalization by increasing interdependence at the center of community life. It also shows that just as institutions can increase interdependence by pushing back against their systems' red tape and imperial impulses, the reverse is also true. The systems can pull rank and draw cultural functions away from citizen space, just as a syringe would draw blood from a body, and rebrand community functions as necessary institutional services and programs. Pulling the institutional piston up creates a suction effect that denudes social capital and culture, deflating the power of communities, all the while inflating the status of institutions, so that a counterfeit care emerges and a careless society is created. Human necessities become service needs, culture is replaced by bureaucracy, and the belief that change happens best from top down and outside in becomes the prevailing narrative.

* * *

The people of the Southwest Pacific are often referred to as the People of Paradise (Attenborough, 1960). For the people of Tanna, the arrival of well-meaning outsiders replete with their "cargo" began for them the journey toward "paradise lost."

We are not as far removed from our neighbors on the island of Tanna as we may at first assume, and the more economically or socially isolated we are, the closer we are to them, because in the final analysis what makes the rich richer makes those labeled as poor poorer, and those who experience social isolation even more alone, no matter where we are on the planet.

Chapter 5

Too Small to Fail

Lessons from E. F. Schumacher, Stan Hallett,
and Marian Tompson

We didn't mean to start an organization. We just wanted to help our
friends. Of course, we had to name our group because it was the orga-
nized American way to do things, but we couldn't have a name that had
the word "breast" or "breast-feeding" in it.

—Marian Tompson, founding mother,
La Leche League International

IN THE PREVIOUS CHAPTER I introduced the analogy of the hydraulic effect
to explain the optimal relationship between institutions that are reducing
disabling dependency on their programs by proportionately supporting the
increase of interdependence in community life.

To explain the hydraulic relationship in more detail, we need to go
back to the 1600s when the French scientist Blaise Pascal discovered that
if you put fluid within a contained space, pressure applied on one point
transmits equally in all directions. So in practice if I press my thumb on
just one point on a rubber ball with water inside, but with hundreds of tiny
pinpricked holes all around the ball, water will spring from all those holes,
even though I applied pressure to just one point.

Another way to visualize this dynamic relationship, which became
known as Pascal's Law, is in Figure 5.1, which illustrates how a small amount
of input on one side can create a significantly greater impact/output on the
other side. What we will see in the examples shared in this chapter and the
next few to come is how this delicate relationship-building process can be
nurtured or undermined.

Stepping away from the physics for a moment, in real-life societal terms, what I am constantly seeing is that when professionals find more appropriate community alternatives to their institutional top-down solutions, the inputs are less costly in money terms and cause less negative impact on social capital and quality of life. Community alternatives to custodial prison sentences are a good example. Compared to the financial and emotional cost of incarceration on the person and their family, not to mention the wider community, the value of an authentic opportunity for a person who has committed a crime to make a solid contribution to their community in a restorative and supportive context cannot be overstated. I completely accept this is not a feasible option in all instances but would argue strongly that it is in most. (Community alternatives to incarceration are discussed in more detail in chapter 10.)

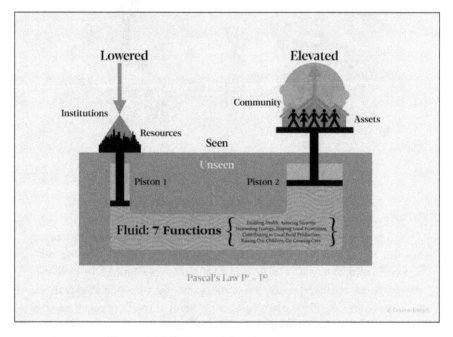

Figure 5.1. When institutions elevate communities

Figure 5.1 demonstrates the ideal hydraulic relationship between institutions and communities: the institution uses its resources to relocate authority to communities, hence elevating and supporting communities (capacities, resources, and functions) to their rightful position in a democracy by serving while walking backward, so to speak.

The corollary is that when the emphasis is on institutional solutions and drawing assets and functions into institutional space and away from civic space, the institution is elevated and citizen space is lowered and devalued; costs go up and the sustainable impact on society goes down, as illustrated in Figure 5.2.

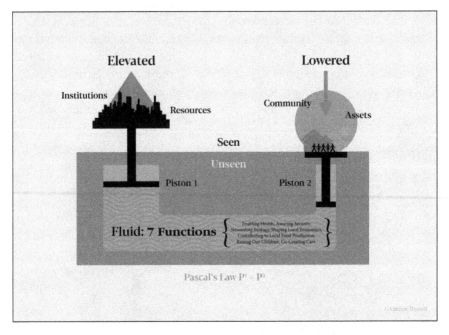

Figure 5.2. When communities outsource their functions

Figure 5.2 also illustrates how the community inadvertently creates downward pressure when it outsources community functions to the institutional world, as a result elevating institutions while simultaneously lowering the status of citizen space. This is the same phenomenon at play in the mainstream marketplace when citizens fall afoul of the Bernays curse; they outsource citizen functions to the marketplace.

The displacement of functions from the community to institutional side in the transition between Figures 5.1 and 5.2 demonstrates an inversion in roles: the professional role was once defined as that which happened after and as an extension, supplementary to the primary work of citizens acting collectively (Figure 5.1); Figure 5.2 illustrates our current narrative, which defines the role of citizenship and collective civic effort as that which happens after the expert work of professionals is complete. It is no surprise, therefore, how many people confuse human necessities with service categories—so much so that the necessity of a listening ear becomes the need for a psychologist, the necessity of a friend who likes me for who I am becomes a requirement from my progressive doctor to issue me a social prescription, the necessity of a daily walk becomes the need for physiotherapy, and so on.

Citizen space is constantly shrinking in modern life, and what once was addressed by families, kin, neighbors, and friends is now being outsourced to institutions, and accordingly monetized. Bewitched by the Bernays curse and the seven tactics of hidden persuaders (see chapter 3), we have allowed a distorted perception of community life and its capacities to take hold in the zeitgeist. The role of communities has become deflated and that of institutions inflated beyond all reasonable proportions. Banks are considered too big to fail; similar attitudes have become mainstream with regard to our human services systems. The prevailing narrative suggests that bigger, better resourced, more professionalized, institutional systems equate to better outcomes for all.

Yet public trust in these institutions and their systems is at an all-time low. The limits of giant systems have never been more apparent; from the banking crisis of 2008 to the current opioid crisis, evidence abounds that institutions cannot unilaterally make us better. Nevertheless, it is as if we are speaking out of both sides of our mouth, with one side looking for less bureaucracy, the other for more institutional intervention, as if these were unrelated matters. We urgently require a new, better, and more congruent story. The time has come to make small the new big.

Too Small to Fail

Imagine living in a world where the default position was "That's too small to fail!" Such a world may be on its way. There is a growing narrative in support of localism and indigenous living. The belief that civil society grows proportionate not to the extent people's needs are addressed by institutions but by the strengths connected and expressed by citizens is "trending," so to speak. This trend could easily adopt Fritz Schumacher's epigram "Small is beautiful" from his groundbreaking book by the same title (1973).

In the late eighties, Stan Hallett, a close friend and colleague of John McKnight's, drew a vital comparison between the work John and his colleagues were doing in neighborhoods and the approaches to the "intermediate or appropriate technology" that E. F. Schumacher had been promoting in the Global South. Like John, Schumacher considered outside aid—in his case, Western aid—to be woefully inadequate, as the money intended for economically marginalized people typically did not filter down to them.

Schumacher contended that what "the poor" needed was "tool aid" and "know-how" that would enable them to use their local assets more effectively. For John McKnight, what "the poor" needed was sufficient income to make the same choices as professional helpers, not professional therapy or ameliorative alternatives to income.

In helping to better understand what was emerging from John and his colleagues' work and how it contrasted with other community-building efforts at the time, Stan coined the term "grants economy" to sum up the common belief within many communities that "if you can't get a grant for it, it can't be done!" Stan recognized how a grants economy plants a concept of money in people's minds and sets a predictable pattern in motion. In a grants economy, you start out with a lot, and at the end you've spent it and have nothing. At that point you conclude that what you need to continue to develop as a community is another grant.

Stan also noted the contrast between the early research that John, Jody Kretzmann and their colleagues had undertaken versus the community research traditionally carried out by universities. Stan said to John and his colleagues, "Your research findings don't grow out of grants. I haven't heard about grants in any of these neighborhood stories. So, this is the reverse of a grants economy: it's an asset-based economy." Clearly an asset is the opposite of a grant; in fact, Stan's observation is where the term "asset" came from in the name asset-based community development.

An asset is something that starts small and, if connected well, ends up larger. It's a multiplier of what people have. It means that something little grows to something bigger—not huge but bigger.

Properly understood outside the framework of the banking industry, assets are the local resources that, when correctly connected, will create much more together than they do apart.

With assets seen this way, it becomes clear that the most important thing to attend to in community building is connections, since the assets are always there, though they may be hidden in plain view and complex to bring together. But when two assets that were not connected get connected into a productive relationship, that's when things start to change.

Stan joined the Center for Urban Affairs in the early seventies. It was the era when Schumacher's book *Small Is Beautiful* was very influential. *Small Is Beautiful* described "appropriate or intermediate technology" as an alternative to the expensive, polluting, modern machine-age options. "Stan's thought paralleled that of Schumacher," John McKnight observed not too long ago (Russell, 2017). "He created and taught us a powerful abbreviation: FESWAW. It stood for Food, Energy, Soil, Water, Air and Waste."

Respecting FESWAW

Food, energy, soil, water, air, and waste were the six essentials of life in Stan's way of thinking, and each was related to all the others. Modern technology prevented the productive use of each essential by constantly disrupting their interrelationships. "Appropriate" technology was a way to use tools so they respected and supported the primary life-giving FESWAW relationships.

Stan also thought there were two kinds of tools. One he named a "unitility" and the other a "multility." His example of a multility was a greenhouse built on the top of a flat-roofed two-flat apartment on Chicago's West Side. On the West Side, thousands of two- and three-story buildings had flat roofs, which Stan thought to be both wasteful and presenting a great opportunity. He persuaded John and his colleagues to build a simple greenhouse from a kit on top of one of the two-story buildings.

This simple handbuilt greenhouse, made of plastic panels hung on a wooden framework, had many "outputs," Stan observed:

- It captured the heat escaping from the roof, using it to warm the greenhouse.

- As it captured the heat and held it on the rooftop, the greenhouse reduced the necessity for more heat in the building, thus reducing energy costs.

- It captured the sun, thus adding to the seasonal growing capacity.

- It produced nourishing food.

- It produced income from the sale of surplus food.

- Older local residents, who often had been raised in rural areas in the South, began to come to the greenhouse and grow food. This activity revived them physically, mentally, and spiritually, enabling more healthful lives.

- A local school began to bring young students to learn about agriculture and energy conservation.

In these ways, a simple tool made of basic materials produced energy savings, nourishing food, income from sales, health for seniors, and education for students. Stan said the greenhouse was a good example of a multility, because it had low inputs and high outputs.

The illustration Stan used to contrast with the greenhouse was an electric toothbrush. It required copper from Montana, steel from Brazil, rubber from Sumatra, oil from Saudi Arabia, costly and polluting systems to get these materials to a place of manufacture, complex machines to process and assemble the materials, and hours of labor at every stage.

Having created a machine with prodigious inputs, its output was the energy saved by people who no longer wanted to move a brush up and down, back and forth across their teeth. The electric toothbrush was the perfect example of a modern tool with high inputs and low outputs—a unitility that broke FESWAW bonds around the world.

Another gift from Stan was naming the community-building work that John and others were doing. Stan said that they were basically involved in promoting the "associational world." In Stan's way of thinking, an association was a small group of citizens whose joint work was a multility—low inputs and high outputs. In other words, every association is a set of connected people whose collective effort is based on the multiplication of the gifts and capacities of each member. It is a set of natural relationships where the whole is greater than the sum of its parts. It is the social equivalent of appropriate technology.

Clearly there are strong links between Stan Hallett's thinking and Schumacher's. Schumacher for his part was heavily influenced by Leopold Kohr, as was Ivan Illich. Central to Kohr's thinking was the idea of "proportionality: proper to this place and this place alone" (1957). Proportionality, according to Illich (1973), was a primary organizing principle that helped people understand the cosmology of the premodern world. In nonmathematical terms, it framed the way things and people fit together and, through their interdependence, gave form and shape to each other, so that one kept the other in balance.

Tipping the Scales

Many industrial technologies simply do not enable people to live in a balanced way—quite the opposite, in fact. Cars and screens of various hues are just two of the more obvious examples of where this misalignment plays out. And so books such as *Small Is Beautiful*, Illich's *Tools for Conviviality* (1973), and McKnight and Block's *Abundant Community* (2010)—and the movements that have grown up around them—are all in search of greater balance between humans and systems. They advocate for the setting of limits in the relationship between humans, their ecology, and the technological world, including the techniques of professionals, beyond the industrial model for everything from classrooms to boardrooms.

Building on this critique, the asset-based community building approach to civic renewal not only highlights the need to understand the irreplaceable functions of citizens and their associations but also points to the fact that in addressing local and global challenges there is an optimal starting point: neighborhoods. Sadly, civic and community functions are grossly undervalued and overwhelmed by consumerism. They have been eclipsed by institutionalism and professionalism. Current organizational structures and ideologies operate like the curtain that concealed the counterfeit Wizard in L. Frank Baum's novel *The Wonderful Wizard of Oz*. For civic assets to flourish, the limits of institutions and their professional wizards must be revealed.

As noted already, there is a necessary hydraulic relationship between processes of deinstitutionalization and interdependence. The reason this is so is that although systems are dynamic and emergent, power relations between institutions and communities tend not to be. As institutionalism goes down, interdependency at the center of community life must go up, and vice versa. If such optimal hydraulic relationships do not exist, then typically what happens when people are deinstitutionalized is that they are relocated to independent living options, which in practice ends up as lonely living, since they are without neighborly connections. So, more often than not, people who have been institutionalized end up being placed in smaller institutions surrounded by people with the same diagnostic labels and told that they are living in a "community care" setting. But in actual terms it is a congregated care setting. These are places filled with good people and good intentions but with few, if any, connections to near neighbors and wider community resources. The result is, in effect, similar to Gertrude Stein's observation in *Everybody's Autobiography* (1937) about the fact that her childhood home in California no longer existed: "*There is no there there.*"

Trends in breastfeeding since before the 1950s and the power dynamics between the medical professions and the breastfeeding movement offer a perfect illustration of the push-pull hydraulic effect that exists between citizen space and institutional space. As young mothers, Marian Tompson and seven of her friends from neighborhoods in Chicago started breastfeeding their children in the 1950s; they could not possibly have known what lay ahead for them, or how their actions would inspire the world. At that time the infant-formula industry, backed by the majority of pediatricians and general medical practitioners, marketed formula as being superior to breast milk in providing the nutrients that babies needed to thrive. Most women were unduly influenced by professionals and marketers to stop breastfeeding, or never start, and purchase formula instead. Over a period of years, the function of breastfeeding, performed naturally for millennia by young mothers, often with the support of older women, almost ceased.

When Marian and her friends sought out other mothers for support, they discovered that breastfeeding was all but a dying art. Sixty years later, thanks to Marian and thousands of women like her, breastfeeding is making a comeback. The movement and organization that she helped found—La Leche League International (LLLI)—is now active in more than eighty-seven countries throughout the world.

This is a story of recovery, similar in sequence to the succession process that happens after a period of deforestation that results from mono-cropping. As with many other social movements like it, La Leche is intentionally small and local, but a proliferating force for change nonetheless. Like an act of revelation, it takes what seems to have disappeared and makes it visible and vibrant once again by connecting what was already there and multiplying it.

When I asked Marian how La Leche had spread so widely and yet remained true to its hyper-local neighborhood beginnings, she shared two nuggets of wisdom. First, she said, "We kept everything mother-sized," which is to say they kept things doable, simple, local, and led by mothers, since their shared purpose was not to grow a big institutional framework but to grow a supportive association centered on nurturing their children. Second, she said, while in many respects "we did take on" the formula industry, their movement was not solely in opposition to the industry. They did not assume a Saul Alinsky–style community organizing approach, which tends to favor more direct confrontational tactics. Because they were primarily in favor of breastfeeding their power grew out of their association, not the extent to which they reformed the institutions in question. When you are in favor of something, you don't need to grow evidence to proliferate; you need to grow trust, membership, practice, and know-how, and those can only be achieved at human scale, small and local. But ultimately it was that power of association that was to "take on" and gain ground over megacompanies like Nestle and profoundly influence attitudes within the medical world to this day. The struggle continues.

The next chapter offers a critique of development, to reveal how large-scale development initiatives such as the green revolution have othered people by gender and have split people and ecology, with devastating ecological, cultural, and economic effects, so that development has created a new form of scarcity.

* * *

The wisdom voiced by Stan Hallett, E. F. Schumacher, and Marian Tompson is worth even more of our attention today as we reflect on how to live on a planet that we are fast consuming to the point of ecocide. If the conclusion that small is beautiful and cannot be allowed to fail is the material of poets and romantics—not of economists and politicians—then our political, economic, and environmental versions of reality urgently need more poets and romantics. But the wisdom of breastfeeding mothers would be even better.

Chapter 6

In Critique of Development

Choosing Sufficiency over Greed

Abundance is necessary for the successful practice of gift giving. Exchange competes with gift giving by capturing the abundance, channeling it into the hands of the few or wasting it, thus creating scarcity for the many.

—Genevieve Vaughan

THE REAL DIFFERENCE BETWEEN abundance and scarcity is so counterintuitive when in the grip of a consumerist, neoliberal outlook that we often fail to see the contrast clearly. A shorthand way to reveal the difference is to compare a bike and a car. Bikes run on muscle, save you money, and are relatively harmless to local ecologies (a metaphor of a sort for abundance living); cars run on money, make you flabby, and harm local ecologies and global ecosystems (a reasonable metaphor for what scarcity living ought to mean).

Referencing Stan Hallett's thinking cited in the previous chapter, abundance living does no harm to FESWAW, while scarcity living does. Hence choosing sufficiency (living with enough) over greed (always wanting more) is at the heart of the distinction between the two concepts and ways of living. What the contrast between the bike and the car offers in memorability it lacks in nuance, and so to thoroughly understand the potency of sufficiency and abundance as a generative and integrative perspective and way of living I propose we turn to the wisdom of thinkers and activists in the feminist movements, in particular those concerned with the gift economy and the wider thinking found within the field of integrative feminism.

A Global Shift

The following sentence, uttered by President Harry S. Truman in his inaugural address of January 20, 1949, heralded a change in the course of history for the Global South—what then would have been inappropriately though popularly termed "the Third World":

> We must embark on a bold new program for making the benefits
> of our scientific advances and industrial progress available for the
> improvement and growth of underdeveloped areas.

Few apologists remain for this imperious approach to helping, yet shifts in approaches to development in the Global South are painfully slow. Echoing former President Truman's promise to rescue "underdeveloped areas" and Lyndon Johnson's 1964 "war declaration" on poverty, Robert S. McNamara (president of the World Bank at the time), speaking in Nairobi in 1973, declared war on global poverty—especially in the Global South. Nearly a half-century later, a growing body of public commentators, economists, and activists are reaching an uneasy consensus: this war, too, has failed—and some among them are going further to highlight, as did Illich, that this form of development has created a new form of scarcity.

Paul Collier's erudite analysis in *The Bottom Billion*, William Easterly's impassioned assault in *The Tyranny of Experts*, and Jeffery Sachs' commentaries on corruption provide usefully varied insights into the overall nature and scale of the failure. They cite a lack of emphasis on human rights, poor governance, corruption, and an overreliance on top-down technological solutions as among the many reasons for the current malaise.

But it is Dambisa Moyo, the Zambian-born author of *Dead Aid: Why Aid Is Not Working and How There Is a Better Way for Africa*, who gets to the root of why we have failed to end poverty. For Moyo the root cause is patriarchy. Her observations in this regard are pertinent on both sides of the hemisphere. Her commentary also illuminates the abundance that lies hidden behind the multilayered veil of consumerism, globalization, and technocracy. She mounts an elegant assault on the technocratic arrogance and scarcity mindset that is so deeply embroidered into the economic paradigms of industrialized countries. These have generated and continue to sustain an obscuring and perverse map of the Global South, especially Africa. In contrast to the prevailing deficit map, Moyo considers each of the fifty-four countries that make up the continent of Africa to be replete with all the resources, skills, and talents needed to ensure a flourishing future for all citizens of the continent.

Plowing a similar furrow to that of asset-based community development, Moyo starts with a different set of assumptions than those of most economists, policymakers, and politicians in that she views economically exploited communities in terms of their abundance, not their deficits. For her, the primary challenge relates not to the paucity of institutional solutions or the quality of solutions already implemented but to the extent to which institutions have become ersatz producers of health, wealth, and happiness—not to mention the extent to which they have displaced the abundance and irreplaceable functions of communities they purport they serve.

Hers is one more voice reminding us that the sickness idiom that perpetuates a view of people not as citizens with producing capacities in the areas of health, wisdom, justice, and sustainable livelihoods but as passive, broken consumers of predetermined goods and services is all at once ubiquitous and utterly unsustainable. This is true not just in the Global South but across the world.

The Story behind the Story

The promise that development would create a rising tide for all on the jetstream toward a modernized, technologically advanced society, especially for the most "underdeveloped areas," was written over and over again on a counterfeit bill of goods. More than seventy years have passed since President Truman's fateful address, and it is clear that what has actually resulted as a consequence of "development" is ecological disaster with no livable alternative. For example, local communities have been made to witness vast deforestation and soil erosion on a scale unprecedented in human history, not to mention erosion of cultural and kinship patterns.

Vandana Shiva, an ardent activist against Monsanto, in her various publications calls our attention to the facts about the story behind the story of "development." Reporting from the trenches, so to speak, she highlights what Illich called the iatrogenic impact of institutional overreach. In her first book, *Staying Alive: Women, Ecology and Development*, she relates the journey of the Chipko movement (also known as Chipko Andolan), which started in 1973 as a nonviolent effort to resist deforestation, first by private companies and later by the Indian government. While the movement started in India, in Reni village of Chamoli district, Uttarakhand, it gave birth to a powerful form of ecofemism (since women were its mainstay) with global echoes and local expressions evident around the world to this day.

For members of the Chipko movement the forest was their source of soil, water, and pure air; for foresters it was a source of revenue. Chipko won their first major victory in 1976 when they convinced the government to stop private companies deforesting the upland forests. Soon after, though, state-run companies took up where private interests left off. With state-sanctioned deforestation also came militarization, and Chipko members who resisted deforestation faced police and prison time in order to save their forests and way of life. Nevertheless they persisted, with rituals of love for the forest such as daylight lantern vigils in the hope that deforesters would see the light and other peaceful forms of protest.

Chipko had male members, but it was primarily a women's movement. As Vandana Shiva notes, it was women who worked the forest, who created and owned the songs and rituals, and who understood the sacred nature of the place. And it was women who had the embodied experience of deforestation, as many daily descended as many as ten miles down the Himalayan hillsides in pursuit of safe drinking water in the valleys.

Deforestation happened in the name of progress/development, but it resulted in the erosion of the agricultural base of that region. Himalayan hills are set on high gradient slopes, where rains come three months of the year; before deforestation the organic material from the forests acted to naturally maintain and retain the water flow. That same organic material was essential for sustaining livestock. As deforestation became critical by the early eighties, flooding lower down in the valleys had become endemic and the distressed sale of livestock necessary. Acceleration of deforestation equated to the decline of agricultural productivity. Hence since the sixties, despite the continued effort of the Chipko movement, local women report that they were subject to a shift from self-sufficiency to dependency.

Growth-Created Scarcity

In *The Violence of the Green Revolution: Third World Agriculture, Ecology, and Politics* (2016), Shiva illustrates in the starkest terms what happens when FESWAW is damaged, as she reflects on the devastation the so-called green revolution wreaked around the globe.

The green revolution (GR) is the name given to a science-based effort at transforming Global South agriculture. In the end, the Indian Punjab was to be the most negatively impacted. Today one-quarter of the land mass used during the GR is desert; it literally has turned to salt (Patel, 2012).

In 1970, the so-called father of the GR, agronomist Norman Borlaug, received the Nobel Peace Prize for the development of "the kinds of grain which . . . speed economic growth in general in the developing countries." The supposed "miracle seeds" that Borlaug engineered were seen as the long-term solution to the food crisis that policymakers increasingly feared, in the face of rapidly growing populations and finite food sources. Far from being a panacea to avert violence in the face of food shortage, Borlaug's invention was to create the very opposite of what it intended.

Borlaug created the high-yielding variety of wheat in the fifties and within a decade secured significant investment from the Rockefeller Foundation. The Mexican government offered their country as the first pilot site.

In the dominant paradigm, technology is seen as being superior to society. Technology is seen as benign, a solution to society's problems; rarely is it seen as a potential source of new social maladies. "In periods of rapid technological transformation, it is assumed that society and people must adjust to that change, instead of technological change adjusting to the social values of equity, sustainability, and participation" (Shiva, 1991, 231–32).

The new seeds generated by technology were relentlessly thirsty. As a result, from Mexico to the Punjab, wherever the "miracle" seeds of the green revolution went, intensive chemical use and irrigation followed to improve soil fertility. However, what they yielded was the inverse of what was promised: where once there had been sufficient carrying capacity and land productivity, following the GR land scarcity was the standard.

Soil became a passive receptor of inputs to be later purchased in the markets. Inputs included seeds, which before the GR had been produced within the local ecosystem, acting both as food for humans and livestock and as a source of its own reproduction (it was the product of the soil and went back to that soil and produced grain as well as seed). The GR created an ontological split whereby the grain was no longer the seed and the seed was no longer the grain. As we'll see below, it also created a split between nature and culture and between genders.

The ecological costs and natural resource conflicts associated with the GR were rooted in the replacement of cropping systems based on diversity and affordable/cost-neutral internal inputs; now systems were based on uniformity and costly external inputs. This is a powerful example of Stan Hallet's model of unitility and multitility at play: the former sees low costs—simple, local inputs yielding diverse, cost-effective, and multiple outputs; and the latter sees high costs—nonlocal, multiple inputs yielding singular outputs, with limited productivity or counterproductive outcomes. The shift from internally resourced to externally purchased inputs did not merely change ecological processes of agriculture. It also changed the structure of social and political relationships; relationships based on mutual obligations and kinship patterns between members of a given village and the local ecology shifted to transactional relations between farmers and the market economy.

Shiva notes that this shift knocked local cultivators "off their minds"; the egalitarian ways that existed before the GR and the vitalizing roles of women as co-cultivators were wiped out by this development initiative.

Economically exploited local men turned to industrialized solutions, ne-cessitating new dependencies with banks, seed and fertilizer agencies, food procurement agencies, and electricity and irrigation organizations. In doing so they turned away from local capacities and uncritically accepted the very idea that underpins development as holy rite: development happens best from outside in, because your best life is in the marketplace and not within your family and community. Hence the GR was the proverbial wolf dressed in sheep's clothing: it was a neoliberal endeavor to marketize, colonize, and control food production at the expense of local culture and ecology mas-querading as "development" for "underdeveloped areas."

In sum, Shiva notes that development turned the other into a "not me," which set in train the battling between the sexes. Part of the development process generally speaking catalyzes the fragmenting of the mind, dropping people off their heads and shattering identities. The disturbance of the or-ganic/social existence and environmental degradation are part of the same thing. Development is a worldview, and the GR brought a new and fragment-ed worldview. Where local men turned to the marketplace because colonial men from the West encouraged them to do so, in the name of development, the seed was split, the family was split, nature and culture were split. In the final analysis, development created environmental, economic, and social deserts, and more than a few cargo cults and desecrated places.

Toward a Gift Economy

Women and the Gift Economy: A Radically Different Worldview Is Possible, ed-ited by Genevieve Vaughan, is a veritable repository of wisdom from feminists advocating for a shift toward the gift economy. Offering songlines to restore the commons and ties that bind without being binding in the restrictive sense, it speaks to how connections that have been severed can be reconnected: be-tween the gift economy, women, and the economies of indigenous peoples. The shift toward the gift economy is all at once a shift away from the world-view of the market that is destroying life on the planet.

One of the central arguments in *Women and the Gift Economy* is that a gift economy embodies a commitment and orientation toward care, as freely given gift, while market economies are oriented toward "exchange," in the transactional and privatizing sense of the term. The market then is based on a logic of self-interest because it requires an equivalent return for what is given, satisfying the needs of the giver as opposed to those of the receiver. Gift giving is different in that the gift circulates more so than in transactional exchange. Similar to the Kula tradition discussed earlier, some indigenous societies continue to practice gift giving, although they have now mostly been forced into the context of the market. But examples of gift giving can still be found in abundance in modern living: in parenting, in family members and friends caring for each other, and in campaigns for social justice. So, examples of gift giving abound in our society, even though they are often unrecognized or undervalued.

In commoditized societies the demeaning of such gift giving is most acute in relation to women. Free housework can be considered an unrecognized gift that women are giving to their families and to the capitalist system. But this is not to say that in order to value these contributions they should be monetized; to do so is once again to elevate the market economy over the gift economy as the only way to denote value. This opens the door to other forms of oppression and cultural trauma.

As Vandana Shiva's work reveals through the commodification of free gift areas—such as water, traditionally grown seeds, medicinal plants—globalization captures the gifts of the many in the Global South, monetizes them, and then channels them to the few who can afford them in the Global North.

One of the central contributors to *Women and the Gift Economy* is Angela Miles, professor of adult education and community development at the Ontario Institute for Studies in Education of the University of Toronto. Her work on integrative feminism, along with other feminists for the gift economy, is a vital contribution in deepening our understanding of how to restore the commons in ways that include all gifts and avoid drawing new fault lines that in turn generate more social fragmentation. Throughout her writings, she regularly notes that feminism is a politics affirming everyone's humanity through the affirmation and recognition of women, as well as the shifting of an anthropocentric view around sustaining and connecting life (Miles, 1996). Feminism therefore seeks to actively value the things in patriarchies that have been underresourced, pushed to the margins, and disrespected.

Feminism continues to be concerned about women being equal and autonomous and ending structured oppression and gender as a structure of power as opposed to simply differences between men and women. It is, however, far more expansive and nuanced than some of the reductionary ways in which it is sometimes characterized in that it is about more than equality in the world as we now know it. Instead, feminism is about moving toward a world where the values of integrative feminism are the norm. That means affirming women's values as social values with much to offer everyone, regardless of their gender.

What Does Integrative Feminism Mean?

To understand what integrative feminism means it is important to distinguish between equality-frame feminism and integrative feminism. According to Miles,

1. equality feminism wants as many women to be doctors as men, with equal pay across the board; and

2. it also wants equal responsibility for work in the home.

Integrative feminism wants the following:

1. Nursing and allied and ancillary healthcare personnel to be paid and respected as much as doctors. So it's a question of readjusting values and resisting not just inequality but also the basic definitions that are handed down and often received uncritically. It's not just saying women are as human as men are. It's about being clear about what we mean when we talk about human beings. What are the things that we feel are and should be defining of who we are?

2. To see a much deeper shift that affirms what has been female associated, not just claiming to be as good as men.

3. All people to take on binaries and dualisms—as well as hierarchies—so we move toward deeply egalitarian ways of living.

4. Gender to be seen as a structure power (power over).

When moving to transformative economics we must talk about changing the central paradigm, and that means moving from transactional exchange completely and not just unequal exchange. We have to be in a gift paradigm and we have to recognize that all of nature, all of our survival relationships, our whole social milieu, our ecosystem, the relationships we are born into are necessarily part of this shift.

In the next chapter I consider the hydraulics of modern-day consumer economies and argue for the need to elevate the neighborhood economy as an alternative to the disembedded, dislocated global economy.

* * *

According to Frédérique Apffel-Marglin (1985) the self is a tripartite construct in that the "self" owns the body and mind. In her theory the mind is transcendent and unsituated, separated and officiating over the body and nature. This view came from the commodification of the workforce.

Alienating labor had to be programmed to get work done, and so new habits had to be created. Building on Bentham's theory of surveillance, and in particular the panopticon and Foucault's interpretation of this, Apffel-Marglin extends Foucault's critique, arguing that new habits of industrialized peoples (desired by industrialists) had to be intrinsic and not feel oppressive. Hence she observes that rationalism became a sort of benign panopticon in its own right, and to this day we all routinely internalize rationalism as the high watermark of human achievement. The internalization of mind over matter is inculcated through institutions, not kinship or culture. Schools, hospitals, law courts, and the like are the mechanisms by which the surveillance needed is duly swallowed, and we become our own prison wardens within a commoditized world. Her analysis helps us understand that the hidden persuaders (see chapter 3) do not exist only within the marketplace; they exist within all institutions, whether for profit or not.

It is from institutions that the modern person learns to glorify science at the expense of indigenous living and nature. The internalizing of the panopticon of rationalism, where reason seeks to control the body and in particular the body of women—since the female body was seen as analogous to nature—has gotten us to where we are today. This is to say that hyper-rational modern economies are the opposite of the gift economy; in contrast to gift economies, modern economies are reductive, fragmenting, and profoundly alienating. The only plausible way forward is to search out and nurture new ways of valuing each other for our gifts rather than our exchange value. Having domesticated, demeaned, and doctored our bodies, especially the female body, we must now be clear that an equality between men and women that does not question and replace the predatory division between culture and nature will not serve or save us. That political movement must happen outside the surveillance by the institutional world of civic space, and instead within the freedom and power of citizen space. It must therefore happen in whispers and with guile.

Chapter 7

Economic Imperatives

Departing the Marketplace and Rekindling Local Economies

Whether you consider yourself an economic veteran or novice, now is the time to uncover the economic graffiti that lingers in all of our minds and, if you don't like what you find, scrub it out; or better still, paint it over with new images that far better serve our needs and times.

—KATE RAWORTH

THE PARADOX OF THE marketplace is that even when we are not wanted as producers, we're needed as consumers. The dominant culture promotes forms of production and consumption that discourage people from developing the capacity to look after themselves and each other. Independence from services and interdependence in community life are actively discouraged.

At its core, the modern "marketplace" is perfectly organized to give more to those who have the most, by taking from those who have the least—hence the increasing differential between the rich and the economically marginalized. As wealth gets firmly lodged in the hands of ever fewer, the conditions for a rise in totalitarianism in industrialized countries ferment. And, indeed, as the economy becomes more disconnected from society, the rise in unemployment, indebtedness, and inequality becomes inevitable.

Still, the root of this political and social disease is not the economy per se. As Karl Polanyi argues in *The Great Transformation: The Political and Economic Origins of Our Time* (1944), the fundamental issue is that the economy is no longer embedded in society. Adding insult to injury, it is furthermore true to say society has become actively marginalized by economic imperatives.

This marginalized position is both the problem and the necessary starting point for awakening community and rekindling democracy and local economies. To borrow from community organizing parlance, "The master will never use his own tools to tear down his own house." The change has to come grassroots up and involve us as consumers stepping back into our own inherent power as citizens. It has to come not from outside intervention but from mobilizing our own assets and re-functioning our associational life as did Marian Tompson and her neighbors in the early days of La Leche League.

Mobilizing from the Inside Out

There are three categories of assets that can help us to mobilize from the inside out, not to reform economic systems but to decenter the economy, to recenter community, and to enlarge the commons. These are:

- *primary assets*, which are local and within community control;

- *secondary assets*, which are local but not in community control; and

- *external assets*, which are neither local nor in community control.

When it comes to growing civic power there's a fundamental choice, and the choice relates to sequence. Do we start with a focus on changing external forces, or with our primary assets and work outward from there? Is it wise, for example, to put so much energy into attracting the next big company to our towns/neighborhoods at the expense of growing small, indigenous enterprises?

These are questions of orientation. If one's orientation is in the direction of sustainable growth, then there are strong ecological, economic, social, and political arguments for promoting an approach to economic development that starts from inside out. The inside-out orientation sees economic development and community building as mutually reinforcing of asset-based community driven efforts. This is precisely the approach the Nebraska Community Foundation (NCF) is using to fulfill its organizational mission: "NCF was established in 1993 by a group of visionaries determined to empower communities throughout the state to grow and prosper." Through philanthropy, they support communities/hometowns to develop strong local economies, high quality of life, and abundant leadership and citizen participation. In the recent past Nebraska's biggest export was their young people. Young Nebraskans were—and many still are—migrating from small towns to other states to go to college and find work. But with the help of NCF the residents of many of these hometowns are fighting back. They are "turning up their dream switch" with a view to figuring out how they can reverse the trend by discovering, connecting, and mobilizing local assets to create more vibrant economies and communities (NCF, 2016).

Conservative estimates by NCF suggest that if things kept going as they were, citizens of small towns across Nebraska stood to lose in excess of 60 billion USD over the next fifty years capitalizing their children's departure (NCF, 2011). Nebraska citizens were literally financing their own societal and economic demise. They were living in a "leaky bucket" that had local assets spilling out of towns and regions. The approach to plugging it is to cultivate grassroots responses that enable people to use what they have to secure what they want.

Reorienting $60 billion so that it grows local communities, as opposed to capitalizing the state's death by a thousand cuts, seems like a no-brainer. But until someone does the research and points out what's actually happening, it is difficult for people to clearly see the options before them. When the figures suggest that within the next fifty years your state will come close to dying if change is not brought about, they have the effect of grabbing people's attention. Clearly, no white knights are likely to come charging over the hill, so with NCF's backing, citizens in towns across Nebraska are stepping up to generate change from inside out. Families with three children are adopting a fourth: their hometowns.

For example, Mary and Margaret Linhart of O'Neill, Nebraska, worked at the post office in nearby Verdel for most of their lives. In 2008, when Mary Linhart died, few people were aware that she and her late sister, Margaret, held a small fortune that could change the lives of high school students in north-central Nebraska for years to come. An endowment Mary created through her handwritten will now totals more than $1.1 million.

Helen Martens was an elementary school teacher in the O'Neill and Emmet school systems for thirty-five years and a substitute teacher for another ten years. She was passionate about ensuring that every local child have an opportunity to learn about rural life. From that passion she hatched the Shamrock Friends 4-H Club and the Boots & Saddle Club. When she died in 2010, she left a legacy gift now valued at $1.25 million to continue her life's work and have incredible impact on the lives of young people in the town of O'Neill.

Few would have seen Rudy Elis—a bachelor farmer from Vedigre whose daily attire was a work shirt and overalls and who didn't believe in handouts—as a philanthropist. Yet he left an estate gift now valued at $1.9 million that has helped businesses grow and families to return to the O'Neill area.

Each of these individuals led an ordinary life, yet by creating combined endowments through NCF within the last decade, these three people have created a legacy that has enabled the reinvestment of $780,166 in grants, building a brighter future for their neighbors in their former hometown of O'Neill. The cumulative effect of such efforts acts like a cradle within which the lives of young people currently living in these hometowns can be nurtured. And they serve as a magnet to young families from out of town who yearn to raise their children in a place that still believes it takes a village to raise a child.

The work of NCF can be understood as a form of what E. F. Schumacher referred to as appropriate or intermediate technology (1973). What they do is not about top-down service delivery. They are not about providing relief; they are about facilitating community building, and they recognize that the only people who can build community are the people who live, sleep, and work there.

Across the world there are many great examples of grassroots actions like the NCF that have enabled communities to grow a sufficiency economy that is light on the planet and promotes well-being. Let me share one from my own recent experiences.

In August 2016, Peter Kenyon and I took a 600-kilometer round trip from Kalamunda, a suburb of Perth in Western Australia, to Kulin, in Western Australia's wheatbelt. This area is the breadbasket of the country but also the place where the paradox of the market is most apparent. We drove past small town after small town, where populations are decreasing, before we came to Kulin, where the population has nearly doubled over the last ten years.

Kulin is a community with real fight in its collective belly. In response to being literally bypassed by construction of a major roadway, following a community conversation about "life after a bypass" the first thing they did was to create what they call the "Tin Horse Highway." This is an alternative route that draws traffic off the main road and into the center of Kulin. People who see cartoon horses pictured on road signs get intrigued and choose in sufficient number to take a detour into the town, where they stop and spend their dollars. And why wouldn't they? It's a town that offers the "Grey Nomads" a place to park their motor homes, have a free shower, and explore a great place to eat and play.

Kulin is also known for the Kulin races, which attract thousands of people every year. Not to mention the Blazing Swan Festival. When the local children and teenagers in Kulin said they'd love a waterslide, the community found a way and sourced a secondhand waterslide from Queensland for $90,000 AUD, then figured out how to have it transported.

Kulin has also made it known that it's a Vietnam veteran friendly town. And it has reached out to kids whose lives have been blighted by abuse and dislocation from family. They have created Camp Kulin for these kids and in many ways embodied the African adage that it takes a village to raise a child. The camp is a place where kids who have no one are adopted by an entire town.

In Europe we can find oodles of similar examples; my favorite is the Italian region of Emilia-Romagna, where co-ops produce a third of that area's GDP (Duda, 2016). Emilia-Romagna has a population of nearly 4.5 million people, and from an economic perspective it is very special. About two out of every three people are co-op members. Co-operatives are part of the DNA in the region, and now they are beginning to morph into a new market: the provision of social services. This is the single biggest growth area for the co-operative movement in the region. Could it be that with the social values of the co-op movement, its members have the capacity to create more cost effective and care-filled alternatives to more traditional large and bureaucratic institutions?

To answer this question, we must first more deeply analyze what we mean by the economy and figure out how we might rekindle a more local, village-based expression.

Toward a Neighborly Economy

Critics of modern economics affiliate themselves to two main schools of thought:

1. One wants an alternative economics.

2. The other wants an alternative to economics.

The basic assertion of the modern-day economics of consumerism is that people are born needy and the means of satisfying them are inherently scarce. Scarcity is the linchpin of the consumerist model, whereby commercial institutions promote "scarcities" that they claim they are best placed to provide.

The general assumption that human needs are best met from scarce resources and not from abundant community resources has fueled the relentless expansion of the consumptive economy and the consequent erosion of environmental and societal resources.

The anthropologist Marshall Sahlins challenged our view of what counts as affluence when, in his *Stone Age Economics* (1974), he claimed that Stone Age people constituted the "original affluent society," in that they had more than sufficient means to meet their modest needs. So-called primitive societies, he argued, should not be understood as failed attempts at being civilized; rather, they should be understood for their incredible adaptive abilities to learn how best to prevail, in any given place and time, through the co-creation of cultural ways of being.

Kate Raworth, the Oxford economist, argues in *Doughnut Economics* (2017) that our economies are not closed market systems engaged in reinforcing the "produce/consume" ping-pong between households and industry. Instead, our economies function within and are interdependent on our cultural and associational lives and the environment we share. When we draw on the planet's resources, like oil and water, to produce things that ultimately end up as waste, we all at once destroy our environment and our economy. Raworth's work lifts up the inherent value of the commons and the need to re-embed economies within local communities. Her critique of the use of gross domestic product (GDP) as a benchmark of advancement is also useful and joins in with an ever-growing chorus of dissent. Measuring economic progress using GDP, she notes, not only obscures negative sabotaging impacts on us and the places we live in and love but also counts them as net gains for the economy, while also ignoring the widening gap between people who are economically networked and those who are economically exploited.

Raworth's critique of using GDP as a measure of economic health echoes that of Senator Robert Kennedy, who, while running for president in 1968, observed,

> [Gross domestic product] does not allow for the health of our children, the quality of their education, or the joy of their play. It does not include the beauty of our poetry or the strength of our marriages, the intelligence of our public debate or the integrity of our public officials. It measures neither our courage, nor our wisdom, nor our devotion to our country. It measures everything, in short, except that which makes life worthwhile, and it can tell us everything about America except why we are proud that we are Americans.

It is clear from Raworth's work, and that of legions of other economists who are paying attention, that the trickle-down theory of economics is a fiction and the continued assertion by many legislators to the contrary is a deceit.

While her way forward resonates in many areas with the core philosophy espoused through these pages, it is not to Raworth's theories that I turn for a model of an alternative economy, but to Peter Block (2016). His straightforward analysis of the value of what he calls the neighborly economy is a compelling and accessible way of ensuring that those who are most economically marginalized can be connected to the resources of the commons and wider economic possibilities.

Block notes that a dominant narrative, made up of socially constructed beliefs, creates four expressions of modern economies:

1. *Consumer economy*: Whatever you have is not enough. Whatever you need can be purchased. Life included. I believe I am not enough, my family and neighbor are not enough, but I also believe my good life can be purchased in the marketplace.

2. *Industrial economy*: Speed, scale, efficiency, replicability, and productivity rule. It animates my day; I come to believe I have to be bigger, faster, richer. I and what matters to me become commodified by the industrial belief system, and I start believing that things are only of value if they can be standardized, duplicated, and mass produced.

3. *Knowledge economy*: Convenience, virtual connections, and big data are the solutions.

4. *Philanthropic economy*: People on the margins are broken and we have the moral obligation to fix them. Most of these forms of help start with a deficiency mindset in relation to the people they are trying to serve.

The alternative is the neighborly economy, which is framed by a new narrative that is grounded in local culture and vernacular beliefs. It is distinctive from the dominant narrative in three main ways:

1. *Neighbors have a job to do*: Livelihood, health and well-being, raising children (ours and our neighbors), stewarding local food production, and addressing loneliness.

2. *Social capital is the primary currency*: Trust and cooperating with local strangers gets the job done.

3. *Persons are defined by their gifts*: This represents irreplaceable value to the neighborhood.

In departing the modern marketplace, we must have something compelling to move toward—a better story, so to speak. For Block (and for me), the better story for us and our planet is the neighborly economy. To appreciate how it differs from the way the modern marketplace operates, consider how communities exchange tangibles and intangibles among their members.

In the nonmonetary world, there are three forms of exchange: 1) the exchange of intangibles, 2) the exchange of tangibles, and 3) the use of alternative currencies. In the commercial world, there is a fourth form of exchange: money.

Exchanging Intangibles

Through the long history of human exchange between kin, clan, and neighbors, exchanges have primarily been about the circulation of gifts. It is said that a gift is not a gift until it is given; it is also true to say it is not a gift until it is received. Abundant communities nurture a culture of giving and receiving; such exchanges tend to be entered into in a relational rather than a transactional way.

Exchanging Tangibles

This form of exchange involves bartering or swapping tangible resources—a pig for five chickens, for example, or six households on a street sharing one lawnmower.

Alternative Currencies

Like exchanges of tangibles and intangibles, alternative currencies enable local choice and control. During the Great Depression, for instance, many small towns created alternative ways of paying their debt by introducing local currencies as an alternative to the beleaguered US dollar. A popular modern example is Timebanking, where members of a time bank use their time as a form of currency; each hour of contribution is equal to all others regardless of what is contributed.

All three types of exchange occur within and strengthen the commons (shared civic space) in that they increase gift exchange, they deepen associational life, and they encourage hospitality. These three practices of a productive, sustainable neighborhood create abundance. Like Stan Hallet's FESWAW (chapter 5), gift exchange, associations, and hospitality (GAH) are the interactive fabric of a good life and a good economy. Hence one can evaluate the strength of a neighborhood economy by the synchronicity of GAH.

Money

The final form of exchange is money-based, and while it is an important feature of community life, I consider it to be the least useful of the four exchanges in producing collective well-being, because it operates on the basis of scarcity, not abundance. Money is seen as a scarce resource because it is about debt; in effect, it is a promissory note or an IOU. It also tends to operate outside the commons (civic realm), in the realm of private property, in that it does not promote gift exchange, associational life, or hospitality in the way the other three forms of exchange do. Money can often undermine the other forms.

That said, money exchanges, when kept local, can play a powerful hand in nurturing community well-being. Credit unions, worker-owned cooperatives, and shop-local initiatives are all good examples. We also know—based on what we have learned from our friends who are vulnerable to not having their gifts recognized and received—that when people have income in place of services and programs (e.g., personal budgets), they can use that resource to enable themselves to become more interdependent and increase their choice and control.

We Have Work to Do

David Graeber in *Bullshit Jobs* (2018) notes that not only was John Maynard Keynes incorrect when, in 1930, he predicted that technological advances would increase leisure time by reducing work to a fifteen-hour week, but, in fact, the very opposite has come to pass. We have also seen a significant increase in ass-covering, risk avoiding, and box-ticking, Graeber argues, plus an exponential increase in what he calls "bullshit jobs."

Graeber wonders why it is that capitalist institutions that prize efficiency, measurability, and scalability, not to mention value for money, permit so many faux jobs, the likes of which once abounded within the bureaucracies of the old Soviet Union. He deduces that if it's not an economic strategy, then it must be a political one; the prevention of revolt, perhaps?

People work to contribute, to find meaning and make a difference; expecting people to do things that feel inauthentic or unnecessary is dehumanizing. Graeber paints a picture of a society that has lost its way and forgotten its primary functions: first, to enable citizens to cocreate shared visions of preferred futures, and second, to be the primary producers in making those visions apparent and tangible. He proposes a number of solutions to navigate our way out of this modern malaise, chief among them being Universal Unconditional Basic Income.

It seems, though, that most states would rather sustain bullshit jobs or current welfare programs than support Universal Unconditional Basic Income. There are many arguments for and against basic income. And our attitudes with regard to how people are "valued" in society lie hidden behind all of those viewpoints. When, for example, we believe that people's "value" is derived from their employment status, we naturally struggle with the idea of giving people a basic income because it seems we are giving them "money for nothing." When we hold such beliefs about how people derive their value or how we value people, our fear is that basic income will promote laziness or fecklessness. In essence we are in thrall to one or more of the four economies that Peter Block invites us to depart from.

If, instead, we started the conversation within the belief systems that define the neighborly economy we would speak of citizen contributions and gift exchange. We would intentionally shift away from market language, opening up a new conversation as we head toward the realm of abundance and depart the realm of scarcity.

The argument for paid jobs, whether we're telling people to get one or we're demanding the state create more of them, is leading us toward a political brick wall. We need to reverse course and ask, What is all this for? Ivan Illich reminds us in *The Right to Useful Unemployment* (1978) that there is important work to be done in our communities that is of profound value. Indeed, it is so valuable that if we were to lose it, its loss would do huge harm to the social fabric and collective well-being of our people and our ecologies. His prophecy may well be materializing today in the form of chronic loneliness, the opioid crisis, and a range of other public health challenges.

The consumer mindset holds that the good life is to be found in the modern marketplace, but you've got to work to earn your share. Within this belief system, work means paid work. Yet historically, this is quite a new perspective. For most of human history one's good life was interdependent with the well-being of one's neighbors, and work was primarily about what you contributed to your family and community. Work was handmade, homemade, and homespun—not a bullshit job in sight.

These two perspectives—work as paid, with one's salary then spent on private property, and work as gift exchange, with at least some of one's gains then invested into the commons, toward the well-being of one's neighbors and oneself, as is happening in Nebraska with the support of the NCF—are clearly divergent views. These competing beliefs lurk behind the modern basic universal income conversation, and they need to be discussed. In engaging in such a discussion, it is important to recognize that the intended outcome is the most important focus: creating an economic floor. Basic universal income is one means of getting to that outcome. The conversation then must first and foremost be about the value of creating an economic floor so that all people can be valued.

A Question of Policy?

If we want to ensure that those who are economically marginalized are supported, then we ought to look at what has previously been done to advantage the advantaged and do that for everyone. One of the things that has advantaged the advantaged over time is that the vast majority of them have had an economic floor from which to launch themselves and to act as a safety net when they fall. The second advantage is that they move in a vast sea of people who are intensely economically networked.

That being the case, let's consider how policies might value and connect people in better ways than are currently in place. Perhaps in modern economies the best we can do is to ensure that when we truly value others, we start our encounters by seeking to reveal their intrinsic human capacities, not their market "value." I believe this is the most transformational starting point. From there we would support them as being of value to others, and support others to value them.

When governments introduce policies that inherently value people they find creative ways of making people even more valuable in their local economies and communities. In turn, people return the compliment by contributing to the building of stronger local, regional, and even national economies. By contrast, when governments introduce legislation and consequent programs that devalue people, they inadvertently create systems that stifle inventiveness and trap people in cycles of state dependency and long-term unemployment.

A practical example of how people have been appropriately valued is the United States G.I. Bill of Rights. The Servicemen's Readjustment Act of 1944, known informally as the G.I. Bill, is widely considered—across all political spectrums, around the world—to be one of the most successful pieces of legislation ever passed. It enabled low-cost mortgages, low-interest business startup loans, and cash payments for educational return at all entry points, as well as provided one year of unemployment benefit for returning soldiers. Canada saw similar results for its programs of support for World War II veterans. Few would argue that this investment in the human abundance of servicemen and women and their families and communities has done anything but contribute enormously to the overall wealth of both nations to this day.

At the core of both pieces of legislation was the recognition that citizens are the primary inventors of a better tomorrow. Veterans were valued, and so the way benefits were given to them made them of value to their local economies and communities. In turn, veterans were enabled to contribute to growing the future economies of the US and Canada at their own pace and in their own way.

The central role of a democratic government and the policymakers that frame legislation is to support citizen-led invention, most certainly not to stifle or do harm to it. That support can come in many forms, and wealth redistribution is by far the most important. Currently service provision, though an important means of wealth distribution, dominates over all other possibilities.

The G.I. Bill was far from perfect, no more than the Mincome experiment introduced in the 1970s in Manitoba, Canada. Mincome was an experimental Canadian guaranteed annual income project that operated between 1975 and 1978 (Hum and Simpson, 1991). The project was funded jointly by the Manitoba provincial government and the Canadian federal government under Prime Minister Pierre Trudeau. The purpose of this experiment was to assess the social impact of a guaranteed, unconditional annual income, including whether a program of this nature would cause disincentives to work for the recipients and, if so, to what extent. Notably, the mothballing of data for many years was followed by the digitalization of the data, which is a veritable treasure chest of evidence regarding the impacts of guaranteed annual income.

What the G.I. Bill and Mincome provide is evidence of what happens when you take a different approach to support. In these instances the state is acting as an extension of communities, not as a replacement for them or solely as the human service side of the economy, to provide income or its equivalent in place of services and programs.

There is an important paradox to draw out here. In the marketplace, fallibility and human fragility are rarely embraced. Leave your problems at home or take sick leave if you must, but don't let them affect your performance. The implication is that to do so is to reduce your market value.

Family and community are meant to be spaces where we can bring our fallibilities and fragilities, as well our frivolities, joy, creativity, sexuality, and spirituality. And our suffering. Work—that is, paid work—is not so open to such things. For the most part, paid employment is about the ethos of the factory, not the family; it is organized to ensure the few can control the many. This doesn't mean that places of work are bad or malign; they just are not the soft and fuzzy organizations that the brand promoters might have us believe. Fail to hit your targets and you'll soon find out which side of the factory/family line you're on, and on which side your bread is buttered.

Genuinely supporting those who are economically marginalized and exploited is not about getting them into jobs; it is about creating the conditions within which they can fully participate in all aspects of a good life inclusive of sustainable livelihoods. It is about engaging them in the work of citizenship with their neighbors, maintaining a sustainable livelihood as they do so and ensuring that their family and community can be nourished. This cannot happen if policies continue to further dislocate people from economic opportunities. The G.I. Bill and Mincome connected people to each other and economic opportunities in extremely innovative ways.

As Wendell Berry (2012) would say, "Do unto those downstream as you would have those upstream do unto you."

While time banks, land trusts, credit unions, and community building will certainly do much to enhance local gift exchange and connection in the neighborly economy, they would certainly be more impactful if every citizen enjoyed the security of an economic floor and the support of a community builder who could bolster the growth of a neighborly economy.

The next chapter considers the impact of major global and demographic shifts happening in many parts of the world, the growing influence of older people's voting patterns, and the worrying disconnection between older people and their younger, typically nonvoting fellow citizens.

* * *

The only credible antidote to the damage of modern marketplace economics is the community abundance approach. By abundance I mean that which never gets used up, no matter how much of it is used. Or, more to the point, that which grows the more it is given away. It is the direct opposite of scarce, privately owned commodities. Examples include friendship, song, dance, love: the cultural base of abundance.

Our intercultural and planetary futures depend not on industrial market share but on friendship; not on market bonds but on the ties that bind (trust). The future rests not on power or privilege but on relationships and contribution to others. Here scale matters, as Polanyi, in his seminal work *The Great Transformation*, points out: there is a world of difference between a local village or even regional marketplace and the modern markets we see in industrialized contexts. The former is embedded within local culture and community life, while the latter has become dis-embedded from and eclipsing of local culture—and therefore it often acts in extractive, predatory, and dehumanizing ways toward communities and the human beings that revolve around their economic orbit. Here the offer of the marketplace is analogous to the master offering dependence, not the servant offering service.

That is why the concept of abundant communities is so vital to our shared economic futures. It recognizes the huge reservoir of individual, associational, cultural, economic, and ecological capacities we have in every community, just waiting to be discovered and fruitfully connected. It all at once shifts the narrative from one of mass production to the production of the masses, while also relocating the locus of change from scaling up to scaling back and down to the local and regional. This is the jubilant truth that underpins the principles of Jubilee, where debts are forgiven, land is returned or gifted, and once again we become our neighbor's keeper.

Part Three: **Rekindling Well-Being in a Sickness-Making Society**

Imagine a world where every institution, whether within the sphere of commerce, government, or civil society, had an active policy to reduce dependence on their service, by increasing interdependence in community life. If such a world were ever to exist it would be radically different from the one we know today.

Chapter 8

Pulling Back from the Edge

Growing Old in the West

You can choose not to be interested in politics,
but you can't choose not to be affected by it.

—PENNY WONG

PROVIDING BETTER AMBULANCES AT the bottom of the cliff to intervene when people are chronically ill instead of setting up fences at the top to promote a preventive approach to ill health and a health-creation posture toward wellness is a half-baked and wasteful endeavor for policymakers and practitioners alike. Like Wile E. Coyote's plans to confront the Road Runner in their cartoon world, it is not a blueprint for a complex, integrated, and functional society. Nowhere along the life course is the futility of such policies and practices more apparent than in old age.

What if we had the means by which, with older people in the lead, families, communities, and agencies could cocreate better fences before the precipice and ensure that a good life is nurtured well before people reach the "edge"? To ensure that people age well and age their own way, why not an approach that focuses on identifying the wide range of assets that could be used to support older people? Would that not be more fruitful than current approaches, exclusively concerned as they are with the needs and deficiencies of an increasingly aging population?

Aging well across the life course—in one's place, in a way that feels productive, surrounded by family, friends, and neighbors—is everyone's business and is worthy of greater attention than is currently being afforded this simple, powerful ambition. The central crisis of modern welfare states is our failure to build hospitable, competent communities where young and old can age well and contribute their talents, skills, and knowledge, while receiving the contributions of others in kind. Software—gentle, intelligent, human power—is needed, not the hardware of machinery and ambulances.

In policy terms, we are spending too much time seeking hardware answers to questions at the bottom of the cliff. Here are two more pertinent, software "top-of-the-cliff" questions that should concern us:

1. What are citizens uniquely competent to do to lead an aging-well movement?

2. How can agencies/institutions support such citizen-led action?

Working at the Top of the Cliff

There are ten domains within which senior citizens are uniquely competent, and if civic agency is not exercised in them then there is no viable, service-based alternative, regardless of how well resourced such services may be. No matter how many Acme Company solutions the Coyote employs, he is always undone by the cunning and agility of the Road Runner. Similarly, aging well and dying with dignity require more than services and fiscal investment; they require the special capabilities of individuals and their communities—their experience and their cunning.

The ten domains of senior competence are health and well-being, safety and security, environment, nurturing the local economy, mindful food production and consumption, raising powerful connected children, building resilient communities, civic action for deeper democracy and a more just society, responding to emergencies, and coproducing knowledge and sharing wisdom. Focusing our work within these domains is useful for broadening the narrative about what we need to age well.

First Domain: Health and Well-being

The most significant factors determining one's health are the extent to which we are positively connected to each other, the environment we inhabit, and local economic opportunities (McKnight and Block, 2010). The benefits of focusing on a health-seeking, well-being agenda versus a disease model are undisputed (Foot, 2009). However, allegiance to the "sickness" model continues to dominate the way most health practitioners and policymakers drive the health agenda (Harrop et al., 2007).

Balancing person-centered care services with an explicit community-building agenda is not new; many savvy public health professionals have worked this way throughout their careers. That said, asset-based community building approaches are not sufficiently embedded in mainstream thinking and practice to allow them to reach their tipping point.

Currently, the aging well, well-being, and health relationship has clients/patients passively receiving services from professionals/experts. Still, a paradigmatic shift to a relationship between citizens, community builders, and service providers working to cocreate each other's well-being is possible.

For example, I once worked in the Dublin Docklands area of Ireland to facilitate an asset-based community development approach to aging well in place that illustrated the possibilities as well as the challenges of attempting such a paradigm shift. Relationships there were often fraught with conflict, as disgruntled recipients of state-funded services voiced their frustrations to public servants in the vain hope that change would result, while professionals defended their approach. Older people spoke in stories, professionals in facts and figures.

To chart our way out of this blame cycle, we worked with older people to "draw" a new map of the territory with which they could look at issues of health, firstly with their neighbors and then in time with the professionals in a more equal, fresh way. This altered perceptions from the half-empty to the half-full part of the glass, so to speak. There also emerged a deeper understanding among citizens that better health outcomes were not the unilateral responsibility of professionals but required that they enter into relationships with their neighbors to deepen association and with professionals to do with them what communities could not do alone, based on a co-creation model.

Second Domain: Safety and Security

In the Dublin Docklands project, older people and the professionals both agreed that safety was a priority. Early discussions relating to safety focused on Acme Company–like solutions such as more police and surveillance cameras. The issue that bothered older people the most, however, was low-level antisocial behavior, which demonstrated how deeply security was intertwined with feelings of isolation and loneliness. The Dubliners were not alone in experiencing those feelings.

More than 56 percent of residents in another asset-based community development project, based in a former regeneration neighborhood in Limerick, Ireland, said they were concerned about older neighbors living in fear but were unsure of what they could do to help. When we connected those residents' instincts toward neighborliness with their skills, knowledge, and capacities, a range of meaningful, citizen-led initiatives emerged, many of which improved the quality of life of older people in the neighborhood.

Robert J. Sampson's research (2012) suggests that the main determinant of our local safety is collective efficacy, which in simple terms relates to

- how many neighbors we know by name; and
- how often we are present and productively together with one another in the public areas outside our houses.

This research points back to the need for greater relatedness at the street level, something that falls outside the realm of service provision; it is uniquely within the competence and control of people in the neighborhood. That neighborliness should be considered a linchpin of a community safety strategy may seem counterintuitive. However, anyone who has spent time working at the neighborhood level knows firsthand the correlation between isolation and safety (perceived and actual) and understands the life-altering impact of building a social support network.

Increasing numbers of professionals are cognizant of these choices and are opting to put their energies into community building before serious problems arise. These professionals are playing catch-up with a growing body of local residents in neighborhoods around the world who are rekindling the capacity in our home places to live well to the very end of life and to die at home surrounded by family, friends, and neighbors.

Third Domain: Environment

Aging-well objectives do not exist in a separate orbit. Silo thinking that places environmental concerns, aging well, and economic and social development in separate spheres challenges our communities by fragmenting their capacities and relationships and compartmentalizing expensive professional efforts. By intentionally thinking about aging and environmental sustainability as interrelated, for instance, we contribute to the progress of both agendas and expand those agendas to encompass many others.

We are all aware of our elders' sensitivity to scarcity. Our parents and grandparents knew the value of keeping—in drawers, sheds, and attics—a menagerie of things like buttons for a time they might be useful again; not for them the unsustainability of built-in obsolescence or a throwaway mentality. Older people may reeducate us toward a less wasteful, make-and-do philosophy; they are living examples of the knowledge that you cannot know what you need until you first know what you have. Older people are able guides to their younger neighbors navigating the landscape of ever-deeper periods of austerity. They are the wayfinder toward enough; they know the songlines that help us lead satisfying lives within the bounds of sufficiency.

Fourth Domain: Nurturing the Local Economy

As we saw in the stories from hometowns in Nebraska in the last chapter, most small and medium enterprises that are now the mainstay of local economies around the word were hatched from within local communities, often from the odds and ends found in drawers, garages, attics, and basements, along with a blend of creativity and necessity. Necessity is the mother of all invention. Small, local startup enterprises tend to be blind to age but hugely rewarding of time invested, sustained commitment, and micro investment— three assets that many older people have in abundance.

All is not rosy, however. The financial clout of older people is siphoned out of local communities, both to the benefit of distant communities and to the benefit of commercial forces. For example, the number of British citizens living in or possessing a second home in France is estimated to be half a million. About 27 percent of them pay taxes to French local authorities and so may be considered residents; this represents a loss of their accumulated pensions and social capital from their original locales in Britain (Lichfield, 2011). The second migration of older people's money is to commercial care homes, often distant from the place where their "residents" earned the funds.

In both cases, people worked hard for a secure retirement, and just when they might be able to exercise that power in their communities, they depart. They become consumers of residential care services, which cannot provide the benefits of a respectful, integrated neighborhood, or they parachute into an environment in which they are strangers with money but no relatedness to the society in which they have chosen to live.

It is not surprising that the hills of Tuscany are nicknamed Chiantishire; in Spain, it's Costashire; in France, Dordogneshire, etc. Those places are home to many British pensioners who have traded the cash value of a home and their lifetime bonds with neighbors for a life in a homogeneous, older, English-speaking community, separated from continental European cultures and societies (Guha, 2010). What's more, some have seen their financial position decline. For example, many British people who made the move to Spain now find that, due to the devaluation of Sterling against the euro over a decade and the complexity of British social security rules, they are relatively less well off than had they stayed in Britain (Jones [2011], Kett [2011], Fueyo and Perez [2011], and Marques [2011]).

Aging well is not just important for older people; it is vital for the economic and wider well-being of everyone. Our elders are not just nice to have around for their wisdom and their voluntary contribution to society; they are prime investors in our local economies.

Fifth Domain: Safe Food Production and Consumption

Urban pea patch and community gardens, which appear to be enjoying a renaissance over the last decade, are not just spaces for individuals to produce their own food. They are social and educational spaces where gardeners can pass the time in the company of their neighbors. There they get exercise, exchange ideas, seeds, and gardening techniques and, finally, enjoy the outputs of their efforts—freshly grown produce.

These spaces once were worked by older citizens; this demographic has been leavened by the greater participation of younger gardeners lately. Plants may cross-fertilize to improve their strains in these places, but more and more, in the exchange of knowledge and experiences, a new cross-fertilization is taking place: a cross-generational transfer of wisdom and respect for nature, the environment, and the food we put into our bodies.

Sixth Domain: Raising Powerful, Connected Children

The Intergenerational Foundation has conducted research that highlights a very modern childhood phenomenon: the average UK child has only a 5 percent chance of having someone aged over sixty-five living in their area; this is 10 percent less than children of the early nineties. Even more disturbing is the finding that the level of segregation between the generations has almost doubled during the same period. Our dysfunctional economies are driving this demographic polarization, and it's getting worse. This trend has created what we casually think of a "youth culture," but actually it is the creation of a new market segment, which is to say the absence of culture.

Children need to grow up in communities where they can safely connect with productive adults of all ages. Some children and families need professional support, but they also need the power of other people within their communities: as the African proverb reminds us, "It takes a village to raise a child." Another proverb reminds us that children who do not receive the care of the village will burn it down to feel its warmth.

Associations such as sports clubs and bands are spaces where old and young can come together for common purposes, be they physical development, to represent one's place, to enjoy leisure time in a convivial environment, to "apprentice," as it were, as a young adult, or all of the above.

Associational life is the critical ingredient in aging well; beyond family, our connections to informal social networks, from faith groups to social justice campaigns, are key determinants of how long we live and how often we are sick. Associations that embrace and blend all generations bestow richness on young and old alike. Divisions between them dissolve when young and older people focus on assets and contributions instead of needs and problems. The joy and challenge of raising our children is too expansive and critical to be carried solely by families; it truly is a village challenge. The solution to family breakdown is not in parenting courses but in community connections. Rekindling democracy starts with the recognition that our children, our "kinders," are the civic sparks that we must nourish, and that our intergenerational associations are the nurseries where they learn to be citizens.

Seventh Domain: Building Resilient Communities

One of my favorite Western movie plotlines is the conflict between the older, wiser men and the younger braves of a Native American tribe as they confront the encroachment of white settlers, backed by a superior armed cavalry and large posses of civilians, onto Native lands. At some stage in the film, as the elders aim to sue for peace with the "decent" army officer, the most hotheaded brave interrupts the negotiations, makes a speech and departs, leading the young warriors on a guerrilla campaign that they then lose.

These movies are strong allegories of change. The old chiefs represent the wisdom the older generation brings to society; they are like trees that bend with the wind, knowing that to resist the gale means they will be toppled. The young may confuse that with gutlessness, and sometimes it may be hard to tell which is which, but older citizens who have seen it all before are less likely to panic or to cut and run.

Communities can learn from this spirit that confronts change and absorbs the best of it while retaining the best of what came before—it is a spirit that resides in our older citizens' DNA. The name for this is *resilience*. Here resilience should be understood as the capacity of the community to endure in the face of an external threat, as well as their ability to learn together how to prevail in a place while staying present to all its challenges and possibilities. In other words, resilience is the ability to cocreate a culture that welcomes the gifts of all ages and respectfully adapts to the local ecology.

*Eighth Domain: Civic Action
for Deeper Democracy and a Just Society*

Civic action for social, environmental, and economic justice keeps govern-ments accountable and democracy meaningful. Study after study in all de-mocracies shows that older citizens vote in greater proportion than other cohorts of the electorate; they have a greater desire to register their voices when called upon at election or referendum time. For example, according to census data, in the 2016 US presidential election, 71 percent of Americans over sixty-five voted, compared with 46 percent of millennials. In 2017 the referendum to decide if Britain would leave the European Union showed just how polarized the generations have become: age eclipsed class and in-come as an indicator of voting patterns, with the older generation leaning toward Leave and the younger toward Remain. Brexit portends an ever more common and worrying trend evident in all industrialized countries, where older and younger generations blame each other for the social and economic maladies of the day, as they become more dichotomized along the right-left political spectrum. Industrial societies have become more age segregated than at any other time in history, and proportionately more polarized; those with least to lose in the long term (but a lot to lose in the short to medium term) turn up at the voting booth, while those with most to lose in the short, medium, and long term stay at home. Civic action for deeper democracy and a more just society seems further away than ever before.

This is an inversion of how older people as a demographic would have voted in the past; historical voting patterns of the older generation would not have been so starkly oppositional to those of younger generations. The question is, What has brought about this change? There are many possible answers but the fact that the generations are being socially, economically, and geographically dislocated and segregated plays a very significant role.

It is likely that, for some time to come, older people will continue to vote more often and in greater numbers than their younger counterparts, with grave consequences for our planet's future, for freedom of movement, and for wage levels for younger generations. When we exile our older people from the social capital they worked so hard to build, we do more than force them to vote to protect their pensions; perhaps we also inadvertently cause them to forget what the right to vote in a democracy is all about: the well-being of the many, not just the few. Refreshing this memory is not a matter of voter participation; it is instead about participation in civic and community life, with all age groups and diverse perspectives. Our future democratic well-being is therefore contingent not just on campaigns to get out the vote among young people, or to move toward a post–fossil fuel era, or other such worthy ambitions, but on listening campaigns that enable us to reconnect people across all ages and perspectives in a public conversation about how we can all age well together. Having such a conversation will necessitate that we climb an empathy wall that is increasingly dividing us by age and ideology.

Ninth Domain: Respond to Emergencies

Nowhere is community power more apparent than in the face of emergencies; when put to the test, we dig deep, self-organize, and respond. The main reason community power becomes so apparent then is that emergencies often strip away day-to-day institutional supports or at least inhibit their responses. A character in the last line of Samuel Beckett's 1953 novel, *The Unnamable*, says, "I'll never know, in the silence you don't know, you must go on, I can't go on, I'll go on." To go on takes spirit. Beckett's doubting, weary, yet defiant expression of the human spirit is embodied in our senior citizens. It is what the Japanese call *gaman*, meaning fortitude in times of unbearable challenge. Older people have had a lifetime of learning how to endure; they are the repositories of stories about going on when the outcome is unclear, undecided. We are living through such times.

Tenth Domain: Coproducing Knowledge and Sharing Wisdom

Knowledge and wisdom are most at home in the domain of associational life; they do not fare well when restrained by curricular boundaries or commercial self-interest or technological matrixes. Birmingham, England became the heart of the Industrial Revolution in large part because people there, chasing ideas and asking searching questions of science and technology, found co-conspirators in the associational life of that unfashionable town. The midwife to one of the greatest transformations in the global economy in the last millennium was the Lunar Society of Birmingham, a club for the free exchange and debate of ideas on science and the scientific method which produced some of the greatest inventions of the day (Uglow, 2002).

We are firmly in the age of the learning society; learning organizations and digital learning commons pay tribute to and pave the way for breakthroughs in collective intelligence. Though freshly packaged in digital form, such concepts are simply new iterations of something the people behind Birmingham's "Midlands Enlightenment" happened on by chance in the eighteenth century. Today, we are more intentional with our efforts.

Stephen Denning (2011), a former World Bank knowledge worker, calls these Midlands Enlightenment salonlike conversations "springboard stories"—stories that cause ideas to spring to mind and in turn to change perceptions.

Older people in particular consistently tell springboard stories. These tend to be narratives of a time when the community came together to make things better. The stories are always true, and some actually happened; they are always told by a someone possessing an innate community-minded intelligence and able to mobilize neighbors by connecting them to the know-how of community building. They say, "We have achieved this before, this is how we did it, let's do it again." These storytellers/innovators/connectors convene micro-enlightenments every day; in-tune community builders will find them and offer them support, or just cheer them on.

Post Office as Springboard

Recently, an Irish friend of mine told me of his mother's one-person campaign to save her local post office. A recipient of an old-age pension from the Irish state since 1993, she has consistently refused the social welfare office's requests to alter the method of payment from book payments at the local post office to a direct transfer into her bank account. She is convinced that their real agenda is to save money at her and the local community's expense. She argues, convincingly, that if all payments were made this way, then the post office would lose an important economic function and move closer to closure. So, her Friday routine involves collecting her pension at the post office, making some purchases there, visiting the church for mass or, when it is her turn, cleaning the church. Then she visits the credit union to deposit money into her and her daughters' and grandchildren's accounts, making that local financial institution stronger and educating younger people in the ways of financial management.

His anecdote is a familiar one, and it serves as a reminder of the importance of social networks and associational life to aging well across the life course, as well as of the vital contribution that older people make across all ten domains, a contribution that lies hidden in plain view.

People of all ages need to give and receive care. Unfortunately, too many older people are dying of loneliness in a sea of untapped care and compassion. They are dying feeling alone and useless; no institution can cure this. Our neighborhoods are awash, however, with people who care deeply about the welfare of their older neighbors but have fallen out of the habits of neighborliness and mutuality, the channels through which such care is expressed. Older people are crying silently; caring neighbors are too diffident. They need to be brought together.

If people are isolated in a sea of potential neighborliness, and are even more isolated in a sea of institutionalized care, then we need to concern ourselves as a society more with the building of hospitable communities and less with the building of hospitals and the provision of hospital and nursing home beds. The software of hospitable communities trumps the hardware of hospitals when it comes to loneliness and isolation. The value and challenge of this point will be lost if it is taken as a sweeping judgment on nursing home care, when in fact the point here is that in the absence of hospitable communities that support families and their mothers and fathers to age well at or close to home, institutionalization and/or isolation are inevitable, not optional.

This chapter illustrates the interconnectivity of our lives across the life course. Speaking of aging in isolation of all the other domains leads to the same problems that the medical model has run into in elementalizing the body instead of accepting it for what it is—a holistic system, not separate treatable organs. In other words, it leads to siloed thinking in terms of policy and practice, which in turn results in specialism that struggles to work collectively and segregation and congregated care settings as standard. That is why in the next chapter I argue that we need to shift our conversation from single issues revolving around specific target groups, such as older people or people in recovery from addiction, to viewing the village as the primary unit of change. It doesn't just take a village to raise a child, it takes a village to do most anything of value, including, of course, aging well.

* * *

In the final analysis, a community that has not created intentional space for older people and their contributions is a community that is lessened in health, security, and prosperity and, in one way or another, is populated by individuals heading for an ambulance at the bottom of a metaphorical cliff. Only citizens can build a good life behind the fence-edge, well away from the cliff face. Is it not time to pull back from the edge, to recognize that there is more to aging well than services and more at stake than money? If so, is it not also time for those working professionally with older people to balance service provision with community building?

The Wile E. Coyote versus the Road Runner comparison cannot be dismissed as flippant. Focusing exclusively on the "hardware" of machinery, hospitals, medicines, and votes is, ultimately, as pointless as the Coyote's fascination with Acme Company products to capture the Road Runner. Community-building approaches offer an alternative vision. While ever respectful of the need for clinical hardware and institutions, they encourage us to look at the "software" of individuals, associations, and the limitless energy of social relationships. It is a process capable of harnessing the underutilized and untapped cunning of all people in society—and who could be more cunning than our senior citizens?

Chapter 9

It Takes a Village

In Search of Medical Heretics

I believe that the community—in the fullest sense: a place and all its creatures—is the smallest unit of health and that to speak of the health of an isolated individual is a contradiction in terms.

—WENDELL BERRY

IN THE FALL OF 2015, I was in Evanston with John McKnight. One of the things we did while I was there was play poker with his poker group—a group that has been playing poker since before I was born. John joked that these days before they start every game they have an "organ recital." Someone will report how their heart is doing since their operation, then someone else will share how their eyes are beginning to fail but how they've discovered these great new lenses, and so on.

As the first hand of poker was being dealt, that's exactly what happened. The organ recital played out before my very eyes, and I smiled to myself. But as the banter took hold and the game advanced, what became clear was that these wonderful men were not talking about their ill health any longer, if they ever had been. In fact, they were being healthful. In between the chips, beer, and banter, we were dealing out more than cards; we were actually making each other better through conviviality and genuine care. That's how we work as humans.

A Medical Nemesis

Health is not solely a medical issue; it is primarily a social and political one. The modern medical approach tends to minimize this idea, making the isolated individual the primary unit of health. Social critic and philosopher

Ivan Illich was at the forefront of arguing for a collective health and well-being approach and challenging medical hegemony. He maintained that beyond a certain institutional scale or intensity more medicine is making us sicker. Hence public health requires a dramatic shift away from a focus on individual deficits, lifestyle diseases, behavior change, and health-promotion approaches toward genuine community building and significant political investment in the health creation of local communities.

In his most influential writing on the expropriation of health, *Limits to Medicine: Medical Nemesis* (1976), Illich contends hospitals that claim sole dominion over health at worst accelerate the demise of the sick, and at best create disabling factors that slow up recovery. With regard to his cautions in relation to the overreach of hospitals, consider by way of evidence the rise of methicillin-resistant *Staphylococcus aureus* (MRSA) in hospitals around the world.

While Illich was opposed to institutionalism, he was not against institutions per se. Rather, he challenged attempts on the part of institutions to monopolize functions related to the production of health and well-being, death, safety, wisdom, and justice. These social goods, he contended, were not commodities unilaterally produced by institutional systems and thereafter consumed by individuals. Instead, he notes in *Tools for Conviviality* (1973), there are certain irreplaceable functions that natural communities must perform to be well and to prevail culturally. And, if they do not do those things, then there are no institutional tools or systems that can appropriately replace those civic functions.

Illich argued that the production of health and well-being is not a case of either/or (community or institutional) so much as a question of which comes first. He contended that an institutional inversion had taken hold, through which the community role is what is left after the institutions and their professional helpers have done what they think they can do better or more expertly. Illich contested this inversion and argued for its reversal: the institutional/professional role should be defined as being what is left after the community has done what it can and wants to do.

Not all health professionals respect the integrity of the community domain; their primary agenda is to treat perceived problems with institutional solutions, not to precipitate and defend community capacities. They often compound this error by redefining people's needs as deficiencies and relocating social and political challenges to the realm of individual responsibility. In so doing they are in effect operating within an economics of scarcity, where health is viewed as a scarce commodity of which they are the sole purveyors, and their market is millions of isolated, passive individual consumers. Impact within this paradigm is measured not by increased health and well-being but by the absence of disease. In the grip of this scarcity model communities lose the capacity and connectivity to perform their health-producing functions, and in turn the state fails to effectively address collective health issues.

Illich's thesis then can be summarized as follows:

- Health is not a product.
- Citizens/patients are not customers.
- Doctors and medical professionals are not tools.
- The hospital and doctor's office are not factories.

Embedding such a perspective in society could be achieved in two possible ways:

1. Advance an alternative economic model to underpin health and medicine.
2. Advance an alternative to economics to underpin health and well-being.

Illich chose the latter. The alternative in his mind was an anthropological one, similar to Marshall Sahlins' argument in *Stone Age Economics*. Illich considered communities to be "abundant" in a myriad of subtle ways, which the "trained eye" tends to miss. The abundance he was referring to are the local assets that already exist within communities: the local people, their associations, exchanges, culture, and ecology.

For citizens and professionals to adopt this abundance perspective (the antithesis of the scarcity/deficit model), three fundamental insights are required:

1. Institutions are not benign and can in fact do harm while intending to help. Awareness of institutional counterproductivity and a shift from scarcity economics to a community abundance perspective are both needed to mitigate institutional overreach.
2. To ensure right relations between citizens and professionals, we must start by increasing interdependency in community life and decreasing institutionalization. The state and its respective institutions must create a dome of protection around community health production and act as a barrier against any commercial interests that would do harm to citizens' health. The state must also be prepared to invest in enabling citizens' health. Most importantly, though, the state and the helping professions that act on its behalf must be prepared to serve

while walking backwards; in other words, they must commit to de-institutionalizing people's lives while simultaneously precipitating re-communalization. This is the primary task of an ethical professional.

3. Health is often viewed as a scarce commodity that sick people consume and medical professionals unilaterally produce. To contradict this view and the associated behavior-change, lifestyle-disease narrative, we must come to recognize that communities when productively connected have innate health-creating capacities.

In the same way that the steel industry needs iron ore, the medical industry, as currently constituted and regulated, needs sickness. Collective civic resistance against such institutionalized interests will ensure better health and well-being for all.

The Quintessential Medical Heretic

The day after the poker game in Evanston, John and I had lunch with Marian Tompson, the founder of La Leche League International. Her story is well known and is summarized in chapter 5. What is perhaps less well known is the story of the doctor who was Marian's number-one cheerleader and supporter: Robert S. Mendelsohn. A highly qualified pediatrician, Dr. Mendelsohn was La Leche League's medical authenticator, if you like.

During the sixties and seventies, Mendelsohn began to consider himself a "medical heretic." He later recalled the process in the book *Dissent in Medicine: Nine Doctors Speak Out*:

> In the late 1960s, my patients began to return to me with the diseases that I had previously created. The first group of patients were the ones with cancer of the thyroid gland, because, when I was trained at Michael Reese Hospital as a pediatric resident, I learned that the proper treatment for tonsillitis was X-ray therapy. Together with hundreds of other doctors, I prescribed X-rays for the tonsils. This led to an epidemic of tens of thousands of cases of thyroid cancer. The second group of patients had permanently yellow-green stained teeth from tetracycline given for the treatment of acne. The third group were the DES sons and daughters. When I was a medical student at the University of Chicago, I participated in the DES experiments in which we gave women that female sex hormone diethylstilbestrol in a fruitless attempt to prevent miscarriages. It didn't work, but it did leave us a generation of sons and daughters with tumors and malformations of the reproductive organs . . .

> When I first recognized those events in the late 1960s, I thought that perhaps that was all past history in medicine. Doctors today must have learned from their mistakes . . .
>
> But, when I look today at diagnostic ultrasound, immunizations, environmental pollution, amniocentesis, hospital deliveries, allergy treatment, and practically everything else in medicine, it is obvious that doctors haven't changed at all. They are simply making a different, new set of mistakes. (1985, p. 8)

Mendelsohn practiced medicine at a time when patients knew little about the side effects of medications or the risks associated with various treatments, and certainly had no access to their medical records. Those were matters for doctors and nurses and hospital staff; they were certainly of no relevance to patients or the general public. At that time doctors knew best, and patients knew little that was of any relevance. Throughout his writings (three books and hundreds of syndicated articles) as well as television and radio appearances, Mendelsohn was a fierce advocate for patients and citizens and spoke ardently against medical hegemony.

Speaking on daytime TV programs like *Oprah*, he criticized popular drugs like Valium and Prozac and raised awareness of their harmful side effects. He highlighted the problem of the overuse of antibiotics, long before it was popular to do so. He embodied one of the most important features of what I term civic professionalism: he expressed public opposition to many of the practices of the medical system of which he was part. What's more, he spoke out loudly in defense of the freedoms and well-being of his patients and the public in general.

As a pediatrician, Mendelsohn saw firsthand how the medical professions were inadvertently "medicalizing" their patients, to the extent that people were losing choice and control over their bodies, lives, health, and well-being. And he saw how, in turn, "patients" were walking zombielike into those psychological chains. He concluded that people were increasingly turning to professionals to deal with issues best addressed in community life or through family support, and he was passionate about bending this trend back on itself. Consequently, in an effort to be an effective doctor, when people brought their children to see him he'd ask, "What would your grandmother have done about that?"

In sharing his memories of Mendelsohn with me, John McKnight noted, "I began to see that his assault on medicine as a practicing doctor was what a responsible professional would do. Bob was a professional trying to answer the same question we are, but at the opposite end: what am I really needed for?" (Russell, 2017).

Mendelsohn understood that community assets were decisive in determining our health and well-being and that there was no medical, scientific, or curative proxy for those assets. Accordingly, he asked himself a lot of probing questions about the appropriate roles and functions of medical professionals. In particular, he explored how he and his colleagues could ensure they did not do harm to the health-producing capacities of their patients and the communities they served.

In practice, he did this by conducting a very simple, organic but effective neighborhood impact assessment. The answer to the question "What would your grandmother do?" revealed what might be displaced if he, as a doctor, were to prescribe an inferior pharmacological alternative. Since the grandmother's function is irreplaceable, there is no adequate proxy in the medical world; "medicalizing" people who are not biomedically ill but who need social supports is a wholly inappropriate, inadequate, and poorer approach to health and well-being, in much the same way that formula is an inferior substitute for breast milk. In fact, it is even worse since it goes beyond offering substandard synthetic alternatives to natural solutions and instead offers that which could cause harm.

Returning to the analogy of the hydraulic relationship between institutions and communities, Mendelsohn is one of our greatest guides of this effect: he knew how to press down on the health piston to move his system back far enough out of the civic realm to create much-needed space for the breastfeeding movement to grow.

Cocreating Health

This sort of hydraulic heresy is needed in all domains of change—professionals must learn to learn to step back so that people and their communities can step forward into their citizen power—but nowhere is the need more apparent than in the field of mental health.

Consider the way our culture generally approaches mental health. Dinyar Godrej (2012) reminds us that good mental health is rooted in the community and is not the unilateral responsibility of the individual. In other words, people with mental health challenges are not to blame, nor, alone, are the professional systems that endeavor to care for them. The determinants of mental health are threefold and interrelated:

- biological factors, including genetic makeup;
- life circumstances/events of the person living with mental health challenges; and

- the impacts of the wider political, social, economic, and environmental spheres (e.g., consumerism, lead poisoning, inhumane policies, and so forth).

Godrej rightly argues that our focus has been largely on the first two determinants, and even then we tend to be overly diagnostic and consequently far too prone to medicalize issues.

The ratio of investment in "talking cures" as against chemical ones reveals a trend toward viewing people with mental health issues as in need of chemical intervention and consequently toward the exponential growth of prescription drugs and new diagnostic labels. Currently it is estimated that one in nine adults in the US are on antidepressants (Yan, 2017), and the *Diagnostic and Statistical Manual of Mental Disorders*, Fifth Edition (DSM-5), published in May 2013, contained a massive expansion of labels around what is currently considered to be within the domain of mental illness.

This a very complex set of issues that have more to do with market forces, the imbalance of power across society, and the need to properly regulate Big Pharma than with patient care and general mental health. The central point here is made best in the words of Andy Young: "Good mental health is rooted in social cohesion, not in the individual" (2010).

The challenge for us all is to try to navigate a very narrow strait between "normalization," which tries to deny the existence of the issue in the first place, and the overuse of diagnostic labels and professionalized interventions, which all too often distance people with mental health challenges from their families, friends, communities, and the economy, and often leave those outside the professional system feeling like they have nothing of value to contribute.

This challenge is further compounded by the fact that while it is generally accepted that we all need community connections to stay well and to recover, when we become unwell the common practice is to become isolated, whether by our own withdrawal or by others distancing themselves from us.

Many of our communities of place have become atomized, so much so that people are more likely to be watching an episode of *Friends* than they are to be making friends with a new neighbor. In line with these trends, we are growing ever more impotent in our ability to collectively cocreate our mental health.

If we accept that community cohesion is decisive in mental health, then we need to get serious about addressing the social fragmentation of our communities—and indeed, we can be more confident than ever in that assertion thanks to the findings of the Marmot Review (Marmot et al., 2010). Professor Michael Marmot in his groundbreaking report on health inequality in the United Kingdom looks beyond economic costs and benefits toward a goal of environmental sustainability. The review contends that creating a sustainable future is entirely compatible with action to reduce health inequalities through promoting sustainable local communities, active transport, sustainable food production, and zero-carbon houses, all of which have health benefits.

The central question then must shift from "How do we deal with an individual with mental health challenges?" to "How can we support somebody with mental health challenges by growing our shared community together with them, so that we can all contribute to each other's mental health and well-being?" Another question for professionals and policymakers falls out of this one: "How can we as policymakers and practitioners ensure that we support communities to become more competent in creating a place where people with mental health issues can thrive, and be there as backup when specialized supports are required?"

Mental health is not a product of pharmacology or a service that can be provided solely by an institution: it is a condition that is more determined by our community assets than our medication or access to professional interventions more generally. There are functions that only people living in families and communities can perform to promote mental health and well-being, and if they do not do those things, they will not get done, since there simply is no substitute for genuine citizen-led community care.

A Story from Ayrshire, Scotland

In 2014, the Nation Health Service (NHS) Endowment Fund for the Ayrshire and Arran NHS Trust provided funding for an asset-based community development project in Ayrshire, Scotland, to explore how peoples' assets and skills can be supported to develop solutions to community challenges. In practice the money was used to employ six ABCD community builders in neighborhoods in North and South Ayrshire, with some additional funding from the Scottish government to support an independent evaluation. From the beginning the independent evaluators followed and evaluated the Ayrshire project, focusing on the neighborhoods of Fullarton, Harbourside, and Castlepark in North Ayrshire, and in South Ayrshire on Lochside, Wallacetoun, Dalmilling, and Craigie.

Across seven communities a team of locally based community builders have been actively supporting residents to exchange their skills and talents to improve their local communities, in the hope that by increasing social connectedness in this way, the mental health and well-being of the local population will improve.

The May 2018 Evaluation report to NHS Ayrshire and Arran observed,

> The significant increase in mental health and well-being in North Ayr is perhaps the most important finding of the evaluation. This has been the core goal of the project since the outset. Coupled with this finding from the household survey, the personal stories of residents who have benefited from being connected up with local activities illuminate "how" the health of individuals is being improved, e.g., fewer visits to the GP; stopping prescription drugs; and being "signed off" by clinical specialists. (Social Marketing Gateway, 2018)

The report is peppered with wonderful examples, quotes, and reflections from residents on their community-building journey. Here is a comment from one resident, who speaks openly about her mental health challenges and the well-being benefits she experienced from actively contributing to the well-being of others in her neighborhood:

> I'm helping people, but at the same time they're helping me. The key is that this is purposeful.
>
> There's been a huge impact for me because last week my CPN (community mental health nurse) and my carer signed me off because they feel I've come on so much since doing this [connecting with other residents and doing things together with my neighbors]. Before this I had hit a wall and there was nothing to motivate me—I had no reason to get up in the morning. It's a massive deal for me to be signed off by both of them because it makes me feel like I'm more in control of things—there's a light at the end of the tunnel now, whereas this time last year I was thinking, "Which bridge will I jump off?"—seriously. I've even got friends coming up saying to me, "I can't believe the difference in you" and "We're so pleased you got into this." I'm quite happy to sit in the house in my jammies all day, every day—got my dogs, cats, and my son (who's special needs, so can be quite hard-going) who can run out and buy me chocolate. But this has been something to take me out of that life. I'm helping people, but at the same time they're helping me. The key is that this is purposeful—it's all very well people saying, "You need to get out more and do stuff" but when you're absolutely down low you need the draw of purpose.

From Parrots to Coffee Grinds

In Harbourside one day a few year ago, Shaun, one of the ABCD community builders there, was walking around the neighborhood when he noticed a man walking toward one of the houses with a parrot on his shoulder. Shaun approached him and asked him, "What's the story with the parrot on your shoulder?" The man explained that he was going to see the residents living in the house, people with varying degrees of mental health issues. "They like the parrot!" he said.

Shaun knew of the house but had never visited there. He held his nerve and stood with the man and his parrot as he knocked on the door. He asked the person who answered the door if he could come in and speak to the person in charge and effectively charmed his way in. As the manager sat with Shaun and they both explained their roles, it was clear that the house manager wanted to figure out how to support connections between the people he served and the wider community as much as Shaun did. Shaun then asked him a brilliant question: "What have you got so much of here that you could give it away?" After a few moments of thinking about it, the manager shared two things he felt could be shared. The first was their back garden. The second was the magnolia-painted walls, which, a few months later, became canvases for local artists and the residents of the house, as a direct result of that conversation.

The garden was soon adopted by a local gardening enthusiast with an interest in developing a community garden. Eventually, she was joined by a number of the residents of the house and their neighbors. Then something magical happened: one of the people who lived in the house, a man with a range of fears about being in public spaces and meeting new people, became passionate about the garden. He started walking every day to the local coffee shop to collect coffee grinds, because they make excellent fertilizer for the garden. Slowly, he came to know and be known by the manager and the staff of the coffee shop and to be noticed by the wider community. This turn of events shows how people and places that have been rendered invisible and divided in most communities can become connected with the right support. Because of Shaun's gentle asking, he found local residents who are connectors themselves willing to broker people in from the margins to the center of community life.

The connections—between local artists, gardeners, buildings previously closed to the wider community, business owners, staff, and people vulnerable to not having their gifts received—have changed the nature and rhythm of Harbourside in all kinds of subtle but transformative ways. Not surprisingly, people directly involved are experiencing a boost in their mental health; the village is better off. What is somewhat surprising is the extent to which the positive impact on mental health has extended across the neighborhoods to benefit the entire population—a strong indication of culture change.

No Them and Us

This example of a village approach to mental health points up a challenge to us all, both professionally and civically. It present us with a fresh manifesto for coming alongside people with any health issues and their communities as facilitators or precipitators of the bridge building between them. That manifesto is about realizing there is no "them" and "us." This is about all of us!

So, here are some lessons we can draw from Ivan Illich, Dr. Mendelsohn, and the community-building work of Shaun, his colleagues, and the citizens of North and South Ayrshire, in finding the right balance between community building and expert, individualized approaches to health issues. We might call them precepts for professionals and systems that wish to cultivate appropriate relationships that do not disable the people they serve. Here, in effect, is a professional's guide to community building:

- Start with the assumption that the primary assets for people's enduring personal, social, economic, and environmental well-being are already within the communities they live in and that the work of external agencies is to help reveal those assets and support local people to link them up in a way that makes best sense to them.

- Recognize that external professional resources will largely be wasted if the internal health capacities and assets of people and their local community are not discovered, respected, and then developed in a citizen-led way. This is a necessary prelude to effective relationships with outside resources if unhealthy dependency and waste of resources is to be avoided.

    Therefore health professionals, within their Hippocratic oath, must articulate a precaution, a commitment to "do no harm" to civic agency. Outside resources (even where they are less ample than before) that overwhelm, control, or replace efforts of local citizens and their associations across the life course will harm and undermine the necessary civic efforts of people and their neighbors. So conduct a neighborhood impact assessment of what unintended harm your well-intentioned interventions may cause before parachuting in a service or going on what Darren McGarvey (2017), in his book by the same title, refers to as a "poverty safari."

- Ultimately, all enduring progress in the domain of health and well-being is contingent on understanding limits. What are you not going to do to be helpful?

- Citizenship does not cease when one dons a white coat and stethoscope. We need more medical heretics. Dissent among medical professionals is critical to democratizing health care. As author Peter Block reminds us, "If we cannot say no, our yes has no meaning" (2018).

Even the approach called "social prescribing," which is enjoying huge popularity in Europe and Canada, falls prey to the medicalizing trap (Williams, 2013). In social prescribing, people who are not biomedically unwell are redirected by doctors and allied health care professionals into social activities. Seen in its best light, it is a good faith attempt to get to the root of personal, social, economic, and environmental issues that seemingly present as clinical symptoms when viewed through the sickness idiom. In this regard it is an approach with some merit, but it fails to take into account the power dynamics that exist when a medical professional prescribes what a "good life" might be. It also medicalizes well-being.

The role of the effective doctor in supporting someone who is not biomedically ill, but rather is socially isolated, is to connect them with people like Shaun in Harbourside. It is important for doctors to realize that their medical systems are not benign and in all sorts of ways sabotage the innovation they intend to encourage. In effect, their systems produce antibodies against innovation. To counter these, the doctor must ensure that nonmedical community alternatives to interventions are as far from their institutions as possible. Hence the best way forward is to form alliances with locally embedded community organizations and support them in disruption, heresy, and active promotion of nonmedical, community-based solutions. I would strongly encourage a doctor who is interested in promoting citizen participation to model the mayor of Amqui and Dr. Robert Mendelsohn by actively cheering on the promotion of social models and asset-based community development approaches. The small, locally rooted community and voluntary groups are best placed to engage in such mischief and disruption; in contrast, the larger the community and voluntary organizations are, the more likely they are to produce sympathetic mirror antibodies to the medical system to shore up the status quo. The learnings from our wayfinders, including Marian Tompson, are clear: go local, resource well (but make money the bait, not the fish), relocate authority and then get out of the way.

We need to be cautious, since community building is not simply about referring people to different programs; instead, it is about disrupting power within professions and relocating authority to citizens who are uncredentialed by vested institutional authority and their associations. We must therefore take heed of what Dr. Mendelsohn teaches, especially when it comes to power relations and how pernicious medical hegemony is. We would also do well to heed Dr. Atul Gawande, who delivered the 2014 Reith Lectures, BBC Radio 4 and is the author of *Being Mortal* (2014).

In Gawande's final Reith lecture, titled "The Art of Well-Being," he acknowledged the reality of overmedicalization and noted that health systems are becoming a threat to societal and individual well-being. Before social prescribing can be effective, doctors must engage in medical proscribing. Proscribing is being clear about what they can't and won't do. Doctors can't, for example, connect people back into community life, if they themselves don't know those communities. Many of our doctors do not know the communities where they work any longer, because they do not live there. And one hopes doctors won't prescribe medications for people who are not biomedically ill in any case, so perhaps the innovation is to be found not in changing the prescription but in recognizing that we don't have a health problem; we have a village problem.

Prescribing, in stark contrast to proscribing, is about telling others what they ought to do. Doctors and their patients must be equally willing to become reacquainted with the health-producing capacities of citizens and communities, which is tantamount to saying doctors and patients have to stop being doctors and patients and first start being citizens together—citizens who only tap into medicine to safely do that which can't be done by communities. The next chapter details the practices of an institutional radical and considers what such a radical would prohibit and promote in their practice and institution to ensure more collective citizen vision making, community-driven efforts and social invention.

＊ ＊ ＊

Well-being in a sickness-making society cannot happen solely from a doctor's prescription. It requires that we go hunting for health-producing capacities at street level. It means that we must actively support local residents to identify, connect, and mobilize their own health-creating assets and that professionals redouble their efforts to do nothing to overwhelm, control, or undermine them. It is important therefore to recognize that most assets of this kind have no health label; they are the effects of social capital. In other words, there are two kinds of assets that are consequential to health: those that we see as healthful and those that we don't. It is the contrast between the group that aims to take off pounds sensibly and the quilting group. Clearly both are health-producing.

With community building and willing medical heretics, wellness will no longer need to be scripted by a doctor (*prescribed* means "pre-written"); from womb to tomb, we and our neighbors will become the primary authoritative authors of our own and each other's well-being, with our doctors and medical allies adding their medical knowhow only when need be and with a view to accelerating us toward the good life and collective well-being.

Chapter 10

Rekindling Well-Being from the Inside Out

Learning from Institutional Radicals

*Innovation is the result of a process that brings
radical ideas to create positive change.*

—Natasha Tsakos

Between 1990 and the summer of 1992 I trained to be a Roman Catholic priest. Two marriages and five children later, it's clear that was not the life for me. There were some early clues, however. For example, I've always taken the view that the word "celibate" was a typo; they—whoever "they" are—really meant to say "celebrate." It was a view that didn't wash with my confreres, and so I left. On the day of my leaving an older priest said to me, "You know the great ones die young, the good leave, and the rest stay . . . go well." And he smiled, as did I, and that was that.

The seminary experience taught me a lot about the limits of institutions, and so by the age of twenty I learned that the words "institutional" and "radical" do not easily sit together, nor should they necessarily.

There are radicals who work effectively within the bounds of institutions, however, and the person I would hold up as one of the most exemplary is Jerome Miller. His memoir, *Last One Over the Wall: The Massachusetts Experiment in Closing Reform Schools* (1998), recounts his experience as a reformer turned radical and is, in my view, essential reading for radicals who find themselves in the gap between institutional and community worlds.

Jerry's Story

In the late sixties, Jerome (Jerry) Miller was an associate professor of criminology in the School of Social Work at Ohio State University. He was well known for his radical views on reforming penitentiaries and reformatories for young people and adults alike. For example, he thought that sending kids to a reformatory was the worst thing you could do to keep them from becoming repeat offenders. He was at his most vocal around the time a series of scandals was breaking about the child abuse and brutality in the eleven reformatories for young offenders in the state of Massachusetts.

Massachusetts governor Francis Sargent took the view that what was needed was a "root and branch" reform of the whole system, and in 1969, after interviewing a number of likely candidates, his people settled on Jerry as the best reformer for the job.

The thing is, Jerry wasn't a reformer, he was a radical—he believed that institutional reform misses the point.

Jerry was quick to introduce good practices from the world of criminology into the Massachusetts system. He stamped out brutality, heralded in a wide range of new training programs, and employed some of the most talented professionals in the state. You might say that for the first two years as head of the juvenile correction system he reformed the reformatories, and consequently they were among the best in the United States.

After two years of reform Jerry was keen to assess the impact of these changes on the lives of the young people they served, using the rate of recidivism as a baseline. When he looked at recidivism during the regime of abuse that predated him compared to levels seen under his stewardship, he discovered that little had actually changed for the young people, except for experiencing less abuse while incarcerated.

He rightly recognized that the absence of abuse is not an outcome, it's an ethical baseline, and he also recognized that there were few, if any, tangible positive outcomes to speak of. All of the institutional reform, the professionalizing of the staff, and so on, had done little to change the reality for these young people when they stepped outside the correctional institution. The quality of the programs had improved the quality of life inside the institution for the young people the programs were aimed at, but had no effect outside. Reform of the institutions was clearly not the answer.

Jerry had brought the reformatories to the peak of their competence and still they proved impotent in the face of the challenges they purported to address. Faced with the realization that reformatories were at best ineffectual and at worst harmful, he systematically closed them down. In doing so, he set his face against institutional reform and began to seek solutions outside the world of systems completely.

Up to that point, year on year the Massachusetts Department of Youth Services was spending in excess of $10,000 incarcerating and failing each of these young people. At that time, Jerry noted wryly, that was enough to send a kid to Harvard, provide a generous weekly allowance and pay for weekly therapy sessions. Jerry began actively seeking out community alternatives to these wasteful and failing institutional programs.

Initially, he pursued arrangements that he felt might work well for the young people within the reformatory system. Just one example of a range of alternatives he explored: at the University of Massachusetts, he experimented with an initiative whereby previously incarcerated young people and college students became roommates and lived together for an extended period of time. The logic was pretty straightforward: as they got to know each other, it would become clearer to each of them what they could do together.

Jerry's radical nature showed itself most clearly in how he was able to invite innovation from others. He was far less interested in designing creative initiatives, such as the roommate experiment, than in creating the context within which people could come up with their own community alternatives to systems-based responses. Essentially, he invited regular people to think about what they would do to help these young people recover and get more deeply connected—something that didn't involve incarceration. Significantly, he had some resources that he was prepared to invest. So, the message contained the postscript "And I'll pay for it."

One of the standout stories involves Pan American World Airways and a "round the world" ticket. Pan Am was one of the first airlines to offer a round-the-world ticket in the early eighties, and it triggered an idea in the mind of one of the college students who was rooming with a kid from a reformatory. The student convinced Jerry to pick up the tab for both his and his roommate's plane ticket, plus travel expenses, and the kids disappeared for a year traveling around the world. Can you think of any senior public servant who would have said yes to such a proposition? Jerry did, and it was cheap at twice the price. The cost was around $3,000 each for the tickets, plus about $5,000 in spending money. So, for $11,000 two people's lives were transformed. It was an outlay that was on average cheaper than incarceration and considerably more successful and humane.

Not surprisingly, the idea did not take off. The resistance mainly centered around the belief that such radical approaches would have made a significant number of professionals redundant. Of course, the objection was not so plainly articulated; instead, other "industry experts" argued that the risks of such an approach were intolerably high. It is always the case that mistakes made in community are more apparent and less acceptable than those made by the system.

"Jerry made clear to me that [Ivan] Illich was right," John McKnight told me in an interview (Russell, 2017). "Institutions start out doing something constructive and then they level out, decline, and then reverse themselves and become crime-making reformatories. People who want to reform reformatories are therefore the great 'mis-guiders' of society. The progressives, the institutional reformers, are the final authority for keeping what doesn't work going—or as Mike Green would say, 'They've never figured out that doing more of what doesn't work won't make it work any better.'"

Seven Habits of Institutional Radicals

Jerry's story, and learning how he thought, is the most practical, applied experience in institutional radicalism I have seen. For example, Jerry had two rules:

1. Start with those who are deepest within the system—the most disempowered, the most disabled, the most violent. If you can show that you can do better for them outside the institution than inside, then it's easy after that. "He didn't do what most people do and cream off the people who are the least problematic," McKnight told me.

2. You never make a plan, because that in itself will stop you. They'll figure out what you're going to do and because they'll be against it they will mobilize the forces that want to keep the system going the way it is. So, act quickly and then act in a way that mobilizes the community's resources. (Russell, 2017).

Of course, Jerry is not the only institutional radical the world has ever known. Like many others he made a habit—or a practice, you might say—of doing certain things. Like other radicals, he practiced what I call the seven habits of highly effective institutional radicals.

Habit #1: Get Out of the Way

There are certain things that only communities can do; beyond a certain point, institutions become useless, and a community response is the only viable one.

When young ex-offenders leave an institution after a period of incarceration, the shock is not how many repeat their offenses but how few do.

Little or no intentionality goes into thinking about the return to community life for these young people. In fact, considerable barriers are placed in the way of family, friends, and community; the system makes it nearly impossible to sustain interdependence between the person who has been incarcerated and their community. Institutional radicals understand that institutions forget that they have been hatched from the nest of associational life and, through arrogance and an overeagerness to help or regulate, often get in the way of community alternatives.

Radicals heckle and disrupt their systems, mobilizing the hydraulic effect: pushing the system down and institutional resources out, so that more community can pop up. Like protective lionesses they patrol the boundaries between institutional life and community and snap at the heels of those who would seek to grow the influence and hegemony of the system, much like Robert Mendelsohn did in support of Le Leche League International (see chapter 9). To this end, they lead by stepping out of civic space or serve while walking backward—not doing for individuals and communities what they can do by and for themselves and each other. In simple terms, they get out of the path of collective citizen effort.

Habit #2: Reduce Dependency

The mantra of institutional radicals is clarion: if we are to reduce dependency on our institutions, we must increase interdependency in community life. These revolutionaries are driven by the belief that extended time in their institution, whatever it might be, is time lost from making a life. "Get a life, not a service" is their motto; they see services as being there only in reserve, while they believe community and free association is the preferred front line of social change and well-being. They do not measure their success by the number of clients they have in their programs but by the extent to which they have built community and, accordingly, reduced dependency on their services. This may seem counterintuitive, and so it should: it's a radical idea!

There are many ways of increasing dependency on services. From the outset, needs analysis is about the best, since it confuses service categories with human needs and simultaneously convinces those who are being analyzed that their capacities are irrelevant—only their needs matter. And so the most disruptively innovative step a radical takes is to move from needs analysis to a participatory asset inventory that is led by communities themselves. Radicals know that we can't know what people need until we (and they) first know what they have.

Habit #3: Increase Interdependency

Deinstitutionalization is not a new concept. In 2014 I spoke to some seven hundred social workers at the Swedish National Social Care Convention, many of whom had led the drive to close institutions across Sweden more than twenty years earlier. But they told me that for many, community care is tantamount to lonely living. The lesson here? Radicals don't just shut down institutions; they are intentional about promoting a greater level of interdependency between the people they serve and the community at large. Here again we see the relevance of the hydraulic effect: when you push down institutionalism in one place, something must come up somewhere else. A radical in this instance would seek to support people leaving institutions to build up interdependence in community life; a more traditional reformer unaware of the effect may simply release a person from the institution into another program and fail to understand the need to also actively support community building.

Habit #4: Be Authentic about the Limits

Systems and institutions are not designed to care. People care; systems produce services to a standardized format and are structured to enable the few to control the many. Radicals get this, accept it, and move on; they do not try to reform the system to do what it can't. A radical is also a pragmatist who accepts that institutions have functions, and so do communities. They are clear that institutions cannot and should not replace the functions of individuals, families, and communities.

To illustrate this, consider: What is the service for loneliness? There isn't one! If you think that befriending programs are the answer, then I hate to break it to you, but you're not a radical.

Habit #5: Be Clear and Vocal about What Community Can Do

Radicals understand that communities have irreplaceable functions, and if the community does not do them, they cannot be done by any other. Radicals are clear, therefore, around what it is they believe communities must do to be the change they seek. Their voice is a revelatory one; they often see what is invisible to most and invite it into expression.

Habit #6: Do No Harm

Radicals understand the harm they can do; they know that helping hurts as well as heals, and they see clearly the iatrogenic effects that their systems regularly bring about. Their prime directive is, therefore, to do no harm to the individual agency of the people they serve and the community capacities that can serve to grow interdependence beyond institutional boundaries.

Habit #7: Don't Reform; Re-function

Radicals are not invested in reforming their institutions and their systems. They understand that form follows function and that most institutions have never figured out their function, and therefore are formless. Many public sector institutions and some civil society organizations have lost sight of their function to serve the public good. Local governments throughout the world, for example, have become so focused on the provision of public services that they have failed to attend to their function as stewards of local democracy. Consequently, they have come to treat people as consumers or clients of their services and not as citizens with authority at the center of local democratic life.

In the radical's view, we do not need reform; we need re-function. Institutions, which were once hatched from associational life, have become bloated and arrogant. Their function actually is to do what we cannot do in associational life—no more, no less. Yet they regularly colonize our lives and the lives of our neighbors by trying to manage, regulate, curricularize, and otherwise control free space.

Restoring the function of our systems is the work of radicals and, in essence, is an effort toward halting the expansion of the institutional world into the associational world. Another motto of the radical is this: Institutions, know your place.

The next chapter considers the vital question, Where does most social change emanate from? There I argue that the measure of a good society is not the quality and number of its leaders but the depth of associational life and the extent to which strangers are welcomed.

* * *

Imagine a world in which every institution, whether within the sphere of commerce, government, or civil society, had an active policy to reduce dependence on their service by increasing interdependence in community life. If such a world were ever to exist it would be radically different from the one we currently occupy.

As in every walk of life, there are outliers in the institutional world, people for whom life's challenge is the growth of community alternatives to their system-based responses. They are people deserving of the name "radical," and some even manage to bring their institution along with them—or, should I say, they manage to get their institution out of the way.

Democratizing our justice systems, health care, social care, and education is not about citizens having "a say": it's about citizens—specifically those at the receiving end—having "the primary say." This is not a design issue, it's a power issue; the key questions to keep in our sights are (a) who decides? and (b) who produces? Ultimately, justice, health, and learning are not institutional problems; they are political and social responsibilities, awaiting collective citizen response.

Institutional radicals understand that authority needs to be relocated to communities, and they are inventive enough to play the field between their institutions and the communities where they hunt for hope. Imagine what would happen if they more consistently teamed up with highly connected people in community life. Together they'd eat the status quo for breakfast. And you know, that's not so radical a proposition.

Part Four: **Deepening Community**

Local democracy is not a product to be consumed but a way of living that must be cocreated by citizens.

Chapter 11

Generating Change and Innovation

The Leadership Question

*The best and the most beautiful things in the world cannot be
seen or even touched. They must be felt with the heart.*

—HELEN KELLER

DOES GREAT SOCIAL CHANGE always require a great leader or innovator?
Most assume that having the right leader or innovator critically determines whether change happens or not. And so, we spend time waiting or
searching for the next great leader to galvanize our response to some dire
event or crisis.

Moments of great social leadership, while important in their own
right, exist on a continuum of social change; they are often emblematic of
the efforts that they manage to convert or precipitate into more widespread
change. Sometimes these moments of leadership conceal what comes behind to fuel and sustain enduring change.

At the front end of this continuum for social change is a significant
but seemingly invisible buildup of energy through the work of community
connectors in the process of community building. Chapters 15 to 18 share
lessons learned about this community-building process from across the
world. It is the energy of community connectors that provides the necessary
momentum to precipitate sustainable change.

Social change does not launch itself from a standing start; it does not
hatch itself fully formed from the "I Have a Dream" podium. Its wellspring
is much closer to home; its nest is associational life in local neighborhoods.
Behind iconic leaders like Dr. Martin Luther King Jr. are millions of so-
called ordinary folks, in thousands of neighborhoods, who are invisible to
the unintentional eye.

Still the supposition that leaders lead, some with great vision or in-novation, people follow with great energy, and change comes out the other side, remains axiomatic. That's what we have been brought up to believe—that parents make their children, teachers make their pupils, bosses make their employees, and so on. Asset-based community building reverses those equations and argues that the opposite is the case.

People who organized and engaged in community building in their neighborhoods, towns, and villages were the "cause," and the "I Have a Dream" speech was their "effect." The speech that was dramatically and ceremoni-ously foregrounded was in part a precipitous act, but the most precipitous acts were those that happened in the background: they were small, local, and disaggregated. The March on Washington for Jobs and Freedom on August 28, 1963, was a revelatory act, a speech act that demonstrated the collective power and voice of millions of back-home conversations, meetings, actions, and sacrifices. Of the millions of people who made up the membership of the civil rights movement, 250,000 stood shoulder to shoulder as the summer of 1963 drew to a close; one in four among them were white people, and they stood in solidarity with their fellow citizens of color. The senior leaderships of the civil rights movement understood that words don't make meaning; people do. This is why still to this day surviving elders such as John Lewis continue to emphasize that the collective vision for the movement was and continues to be "The Beloved Community."

Leaders and Connectors

The conventional view of leadership, and how social and economic change happens, has meant that far too little attention has been given to wise stewardship and even less to "connectorship." In the same way that a dy-namo's capacity to generate electricity is contingent on a critical buildup of kinetic/mechanical energy, leadership that results in enduring social change is fundamentally dependent on connectorship, and the steward-ship that precipitates it.

The dynamo is a simple generator that is used to convert mechani-cal energy into electrical energy. It is a useful metaphor for the style of en-semble leadership or stewardship that converts sweat equity to the Beloved Community; it also provides us with a very useful metaphor for thinking about social change.

This way of thinking about generating energy and converting it into power is the opposite of how big, centralized energy providers/generators think. They do not see local people as generators of energy, but rather as consumers of it. Even if they did, it is not in their immediate economic interest to enable people to produce their own energy.

The primary purpose of big energy providers runs contrary to the ethos of local and personal energy production and exchange; they excuse this fact by arguing that what big energy offers meets the needs of countries competing in the global market: scalability, efficiency, and mass impact. By contrast, the dynamo commits to convert existing local energy to useful power in a way that is driven by the owner; it's a very local, personal, and fundamentally reciprocal relationship. The contrast of the bicycle and car comes to mind (chapter 6).

The business case for big energy is one that most policymakers find compelling, and yet neither the evidence base nor good environmental stewardship accords with their misplaced certainties. The popular argument for a central energy grid goes as follows: economic growth and the well-being of a nation cannot rest on local disaggregated dynamos; we must have the appropriate infrastructure to be a nation-state. The view that a central-ized power base from which emanates a national energy grid is essential for nation building has become an ideological certainty against which dissent is discouraged. The exact same argument is used to defend the centralization of governments and the globalization of markets and information. But as I've said, this seeming "certainty" doesn't stand up to challenge, though few dare challenge such holy writ.

Typically, arguments for the use of centralized power have been effec-tive in paralyzing most counterarguments, since to argue against it is to be anti-progress, and parochial, and in some instances even unpatriotic. Yet there are those who dare to ask the very reasonable question, How can we possibly know what energy or power we require from outside until we know what energy or power we have ourselves first?

Energy activist Greg Pahl has observed, "More than ninety percent of the electricity we use to light our communities, and nearly all the energy we use to run our cars, heat our homes, and power our factories, comes from large, centralized, highly polluting, non-renewable sources of energy" (2012). Harmful to us and our planet, this centralized giantist model is exacting un-sustainable and intolerable costs, and it must change. The Institute for Local Self-Reliance shines a torch and shows an alternative route and modes of production, all of which are local, small-scale, disaggregated, and sustainable. Pahl argues communities can plan, finance, and produce their own local, renewable energy that is reliable, safe, and clean. This expression of power shifts the narrative considerably—from one where citizens and communities are consumers of energy that is produced outside their communities to one where they are ethical producers of energy from inside out.

Whether related to energy production or caring for our shared free-doms and responsibilities (a practical manifestation of democracy), if citizens are to remain the most powerful people in a democracy, then in addition to consuming energy and power, literally and figuratively, from external sources, they must be able to produce it, too, and ideally produce it first. There are certain things that are best powered up by communities. Moreover, if we're going to wait to resolve all of the world's major challenges until the necessary national infrastructure is in place, or the infrastructure that is in place is fit for purpose, then we will consign billions of people to enduring economic exploitation and disease.

To put this in context, consider the World Bank's drive toward the electrification of the Global South. The initiative is being hailed as one of the largest antipoverty drives the world has ever seen. But is it? Achiev-ing such a goal on the scale proposed will involve massive environmental and social upheaval. Hydro-damming to the intensity required will displace millions of indigenous people, driving the most mobile among them out of subsistence farming and into the cities—and into urban poverty.

Social Inventors as Conductors

Most of the intractable social, economic, and political challenges we face will not be resolved by centralized power and, in fact, are often made worse by such top-down intervention. I believe that many enduring social chal-lenges will succumb to more localized connected efforts, especially when those efforts are nurtured and stewarded wisely and inclusively by citizens themselves. This doesn't mean that help won't be required from outside. But as we've already seen through the green revolution in the Punjab, for example, helping can harm as well as assist.

So, how can we help in a way that doesn't transform people from productive active citizens into consuming passive recipients? The key is having a radical conductor.

My work in East Africa brings me face to face with two of the world's most significant challenges: malaria and AIDS/HIV. Clearly, affordable drugs have been of central importance in addressing the ubiquitous spread of AIDS/HIV in Africa, but they will not succeed on their own. And what will? What is the equivalent of the conductor here? Here's where Trevor Baylis and Manu Prakash can help.

Trevor Baylis and Manu Prakash are two innovators who have a lot to teach us about offering help from the outside in a way that does not create unhealthy dependency and ultimately sap citizen energy to produce change and grow power. They believe the people who use their innovations are the landlords and they themselves are the servants.

Baylis was a British inventor best known for inventing the wind-up radio. The user winds a crank for several seconds to power the radio, eliminating the need for batteries or external electrical sources. Having seen a TV program on the spread of AIDS in Africa, which emphasized the importance of spreading information and education, Baylis immediately went to his workshop and developed the prototype for the radio.

Like all great inventors, once he truly understood the question, the answer quickly followed. He needed to invent something that could carry information across a continent with poor infrastructure, in general, and poor energy infrastructure, in particular. "The key to success is to risk thinking unconventional thoughts," Baylis once said. "Convention is the enemy of progress. As long as you've got slightly more perception than the average wrapped loaf, you could invent something" (Pink, 2012).

Another example of thinking and acting on unconventional thoughts is Manu Prakash, who invented the origami-based paper microscope. It is a bookmark-sized piece of layered cardstock with a micro-lens—and only costs about 50 cents in materials to make.

In his 2012 TEDGlobal talk, you can see Prakash's "Foldscope" being built in just a few minutes. Prakash's ambition is for the ultra-low-cost microscope to be distributed widely to detect dangerous blood-borne diseases like malaria. "I wanted to make the best possible disease-detection instrument that we could almost distribute for free," he said. "What came out of this project is what we call use-and-throw microscopy" (Newby, 2014). While his ultimate goal is to end malaria, Prakash, like Baylis, believes the best means of doing so is to put the technology—in as low-tech format as possible—in the hands of the people themselves.

These inventions provide us with a wonderful metaphor for the kind of innovation we need to address many of the social challenges of our day. Consider these characteristics:

1. low tech by comparison with other "gadgets" available to communities;

2. reliant on the energy of local people to function;

3. does not disturb local autonomous action;

4. can channel an important message/information for change, e.g., community grows from inside out;

5. cost effective relative to the proliferation of more complex solutions that do not engage the energies of the community;

6. mobilizes existing energy in a way that generates more connections and more power over time;

7. remains accountable to the local people;

8. can be switched off or thrown away;

9. does not claim to speak on behalf of local people to outside agencies or act as an interpreter of external messages; and

10. enables people to see and hear the facts without telling them what they should see and hear.

I would contend that the equivalent of the wind-up radio and Foldscope, in social innovation terms, are connectors working at the neighborhood level. They are the conduits of local community power and help create the channels through which energy can flow and deep democracy can flourish.

In chapter 12 our attention turns to what is possible when collective citizenship power becomes culturally rooted.

* * *

A powerful and beloved community is determined not by the quality or tenacity of local leaders but by the depth of connectorship, evident in the associational life of the community, and the willingness of residents to welcome the stranger. When leadership or innovation is required to support the energy flow of authentic community building, as it often is, it is critical that those who are privileged to have such a role take care to ensure their contributions precipitate the deepening and bridging of relational power and collective effort. In other words, their contributions are backgrounded and the Beloved Community is always to the fore.

Chapter 12

Growing Collective Power

Power from the People, Power to the People

If I can't dance, I don't want to be part of your revolution.

—EMMA GOLDMAN

ONE OF THE MOST familiar rallying calls for social change is "Power to the people." Of course, power comes in many forms, and there are also many ways of viewing power and growing it. Two perspectives on growing power that seem to dominate are the competitive view and the cooperative one.

Competitive vs. Cooperative Power

The competitive view sees power as finite; therefore, if my boss has power, I don't. To have power myself, I must get it from the boss. If I can't, I am powerless. Essentially, my boss has power over me and I must compete to get my rightful share of that limited supply. It is a zero-sum game. In this model of power I am essentially a consumer and a victim.

The cooperative view sees power as infinite. It considers everyone to have some power of one variety or another, and it is by connecting disparate slivers of power together that power grows. In this model of power cooperation beats competition; I am essentially a power producer or coproducer.

As interdependent but free adults living in a democracy, we can choose which model we will operate from, which is to say that we can measure the depth of democracy by the relative freedom to choose between cooperation and competition. Cooperation is far more likely to flourish in a civic context than in a competitive one.

The contrast between competitive and cooperative approaches is clearest in how people interact with land and other people. Bill Mollison, cofounder of permaculture, reminds us that resources are typically mediated through two questions:

1. What can I get from this land, or person?

    Or

2. What does this person, or land, have to give if I cooperate with them?

"Of these two approaches," he says, "the former leads to war and waste, the latter to peace and plenty" (Mollison and Holmgren, 1981).

There are those who strip our assets and those who help us discover, connect, and mobilize them. We need strategies to engage both. To deal with competitive greed and dominant forces, people who are oppressed often use cooperative tactics among themselves to build solidarity, so that they can use more powerful competitive tactics to wrench power back from their oppressor.

The prize for that effort often comes in the form of additional consumer rights: the right to increased access to services, better quality of services, legislation to ensure better programmatic offers, and the like. But social change movements are not just about consumer rights; they are also about human rights, social justice, the right to vote, ending apartheid, fighting against totalitarian regimes, the right of women to have autonomy over their bodies. In this regard they offer a very important process for change and a highly effective one too. These are examples of campaigns that cry *"Power to the people."*

But, just as you would not choose a chainsaw to open a can of beans when you have access to a can opener, "power to the people" campaigns are not always the best tool for a given job. There are some things that they simply cannot do. Added to this point, wrenching power from a common nemesis is not the only reason people grow collective power: people also use collective power to educate their children at home, care for each other, have fun, celebrate and sustain their culture, protect their environment, grow local economic opportunities, and respond to natural disasters. This is what I describe as *power from the people.*

Power from the People

I believe *power to the people* and *power from the people* approaches are the estranged twins of social change. They have become separated from each other. Even polarized. Those in the "power to" camp see those in the "power from" camp as naïve, feeding into a "right-wing" agenda of "self-help, small state," while the "froms" see the "tos" as naively feeding into a disabling, overbearing state and market forces.

Unless we find a way of reuniting them we will not achieve enduring social, economic, political, and environmental change. John McKnight would say that doing one without the other is like fighting with one hand tied behind your back. I would add that sequence matters, and ideally growing power from the people as a starting point will lead to greater impact and deeper democracy for a greater aggregation of people. That's not to say that *power to the people* is not a legitimate starting point; however, I'm not convinced it's the most inclusive one.

One of the reasons for the estrangement lies in a fundamental misunderstanding on the part of the *power to the people* folk about citizen-led production. They see it as "soft power"; they are outwardly opposed to it because they fear it feeds into a "cuts to services agenda" or in some way lets the government off the hook. They consider it to be limp and ineffectual in addressing major societal/structural issues—something nice to do if you have the time but not likely to lead to change that matters. I'd like to gently suggest to those who take such a view that they are cutting off their nose to spite their face. In addition to using this narrative to navigate toward a post–fossil fuel/carbon era, as discussed in the previous chapter, can we not also leverage this line of thought to move toward a deeper democracy and economic justice? The primary site of power from the people and by the people is place or, more familiarly, neighborhoods.

The Soul of Community

My impression is that many people see neighborhoods as impersonal or ineffective groups (the Ugly Duckling phenomenon) and are therefore lukewarm and doubtful about local approaches to social change. While neighborhood-based change movements have their place in most people's minds, it's a small place. The general view is that they are good for the purposes of creating mutuality, and most accept the "be good to your neighbor, you'll need them some day" ethic.

Neighbor power is also great if you want to stop unwanted development; who wouldn't mobilize to protect their homes and neighborhoods? But the notion that neighborhoods are a central locus of wider socioeconomic change, where economic growth, health and well-being, justice, and democracy can be produced? Now that's a step too far! Or is it? Let's look at the evidence. According to a multiyear study by Gallup and the John S. and James L. Knight Foundation (2010), the answer to the question, "Can communities produce power that creates economic dividend?" is yes. After interviewing close to forty-three thousand people in twenty-six cities across the US over three years, the study found "attachment" is an important metric for communities, since it links to key outcomes like local economic growth (local GDP).

In the face of serious budget cuts, traditional economic stimulus strategies, like tax incentives for new businesses, have been taken off the table. In their absence, a lot of local councils are left scratching their heads as to what to do instead to stimulate local economic development.

There are a few local governments, however, that have been inspired by the findings of the Gallup/Knight Foundation research and are investing in "attachment" with a view to stimulating new economic potential. In other words, some cities are investing in community building not just to improve health and well-being across the life course and promote community safety, but as a means of economic development.

The driver is hard-edged economics, not the soft spongy stuff like quality of life or community development. The research evidences a relational—though not a causal—link between inclusive communities and economically vibrant communities. NESTA's Mass Localism discussion paper (Bunt and Harris, 2010) provides yet more evidence, this time from a UK perspective, that shows that local action can also have impact on big environmental issues.

These are big thoughts, and democracy, like economy and environmental issues, is typically thought of in equally large scale. Talk of democracy very quickly becomes a discussion about the functions of a nation-state, matters of social contract and the relationship between citizen and state. Before we know it, discussions about active citizenship are corralled into limiting dialogues about voter participation and activism at one level and volunteering at another. While volunteering is incredibly important and of immense civic value, it's important to emphasize that there's a difference between neighbor-to-neighbor civic action and volunteering. The key isn't volunteering alone, it's community building, of which volunteering is a subset.

Scale really matters here, because if people are to experience "citizenship," then that needs to register at a personal and associational level and emanate from there. This was the big message in a DEMOS report on the power of local people to influence democracy from the ground up:

> Community involvement has a recognized niche as a small but well-established area of government policy. But in reality, whole swathes of public service reform depend on whether or not people can be engaged in this way. Policies to improve public health, reduce fear of crime and boost people's skills—now

central to the promises of every major party—cannot succeed without the active involvement of millions of people. As our research shows, this involvement comes through practical relationships with certain kinds of organizations, not through some more abstract decision or form of communication. (Skidmore and Craig, 2005, p. 13)

In his TEDx talk, "Why Mayors Should Rule the World," political theorist Benjamin Barber (2013) argues that because of their capacity to influence locally led action, mayors are the ones that hold real power for change, not those in other elected positions of power. The implication is that mayors and the cities they serve will shape our futures.

Deepening this point, Jane Jacobs, author of *The Death and Life of Great American Cities* (1961), believed that a great city is, at its best, a federation of neighborhoods. Thirty years ago, in Seattle, a mayor came into office who understood the potential of this kind of from-the-ground-up democratic power.

In 1988, Mayor Charles Royer appointed Jim Diers to direct Seattle's new Office of Neighborhoods. The two subsequent mayors, Norm Rice in 1990 and Paul Schell in 1998, reappointed Jim. By the end of Jim's fourteen-year tenure, the four-person office had grown into a Department of Neighborhoods with a hundred staff. And Jim moved on to become a world-renowned author and speaker, founder of neighborpower.org and member of the faculty of the ABCD Institute at DePaul University.

The Department of Neighborhoods' mission was to decentralize and coordinate city services, strengthen communities and their organizations, and work in partnership with these organizations to preserve and enhance the neighborhoods. Until recently, the department managed thirteen Little City Halls that provide basic services to citizens and serve as meeting places for neighborhood organizations. It supported about four hundred community self-help projects each year through a $4.5 million Neighborhood Matching Fund that was recognized by the Ford Foundation and Harvard University's Kennedy School of Government as one of the most innovative local government programs in the United States. Another program of community empowerment initiated by the city aimed to support the collective planning efforts of residents in thirty-seven Seattle neighborhoods. They achieved this through a process of match funding, where the voluntary efforts of citizens in developing their neighborhood plan together were matched with funding to enable residents to contract their own advisors and secure technical assistance. This afforded participating neighborhoods a high degree of choice and influence—relative to those who experience the traditional top-down approach where city planners are in the lead—in the development of their own neighborhood plans and visions. The attractiveness of this collective citizen-led process was evident in the fact that thirty thousand residents from these thirty-seven neighborhoods engaged in the neighborhood planning process in ways they typically would not have when the city insisted on top-down planning in the development of centralized city plans. This also led to more inclusive plans, and in contrast to many of the NIMBY-style local processes, most of the neighborhoods developed plans with principles of social justice at their core. For example, one of the neighborhoods wanted a library and so voted to increase taxes to raise the city finances needed. More impressive still, they proposed that affordable living units be built on the first story of the library to house families on low incomes. Hence they got beyond the limits of single-use planning and consequent building, instead ensuring a multipurpose building that accommodated the needs of economically marginalized families and that began to counter issues related to gentrification.

The Department of Neighborhoods also managed the city's historic preservation program, a "P-Patch Program" of one hundred community gardens, a large food forest and urban farm, and a leadership-training program. The city celebrated the thirtieth anniversary of the Department of Neighborhoods in 2018.

In 2001, the Municipal League of King County named Jim Diers Public Employee of the Year. He was awarded an honorary doctorate of law from Grinnell College. But while mayors can giveth, mayors can also taketh away. Incoming Mayor Ed Murray had a different view of how to administer the city's dwindling budget, and his back-to-basics policy produced a significant rolling back of the Little City Halls and neighborhood coordinators. "Back to basics" seemed to mean taking power and resource out of neighborhoods and sending it back to city hall.

Cocreating a Way of Living

"Oops! Seattle Mayor mourns death of local official who's very much alive." That was the headline of a CNN blog post detailing the gaffe made by the Seattle mayor's office, which mistakenly reported the demise of Jim Diers after confusing him with another public servant with a similar-sounding name who worked for the city (Karimi and Alsup, 2014).

It's an understandable error. After all, institutions that large can't possibly maintain personal connections, and sometimes that means they simply don't know if we're dead or alive. But isn't that why local government strengthens civil society, and why the principles of subsidiarity are so critical?

Institutions produce services; communities produce care. Communities are the places where others know if we're dead or alive. After decades of disinvestment in communities and community building, however, it's much less likely we'll be cared for and known in the place we call home—yet another reason why community building is so essential.

Many of our local government institutions have become too corporatized and distant from their core business, which, as previously argued, is not the provision of services but the stewardship of local democracy. Their mandatory/statutory functions have meant that many no longer see people as citizens but as customers and ratepayers. Local government has become a business, and accordingly, people have become their clients or customers to one degree or another. Local democracy is not a product to be consumed but a way of living that must be coproduced, with citizens in the lead.

The more you provide services for things that people can do themselves, the more you diminish social capital and democracy. People are transformed from citizens into clients, and the consequences for civic power are devastating. Instead, we must take as a given that people should have as a right the ability to affirm of their place the Citizen Credo shown below.

Citizen Credo

- The necessities are here; they are inexpensive and they are close at hand.

- Services are available, but not overpowering.

- You can contribute, and participate, and truly make a difference around here and beyond.

- Here you can feel accepted; people have empathy.

- Here people work for social justice and inclusion.

- Here the sense of community is strong and our public institutions support us in keeping it so.

- Here everyone can find the resources to have enough to live a good life.

- Here our views and actions have an impact beyond our community.

The Citizen Credo could easily be used as evaluation questions to identify powerful neighborhoods. Do citizens where you live feel this way? Much of the work of enduring community building involves the co-creation of spaces where we can safely stand on the days when our feet are sore and dance on the days when we feel a spring in our step.

In addition to these properties of strong communities, active citizens want the power to produce, as well as the right to determine the outcome of what others produce in their name. The right to produce, or more aptly to make and be fruitful, is at the very heart of our rights as citizens, and it is intimately wedded to freedom of expression (the right to listen) and free association (the right to contribute).

Subject, Customer, or Citizen?

A scientific analysis of Thomas Jefferson's draft of the Declaration of Independence showed the word "subjects" being replaced with the word "citizen" (US Library of Congress, 2010). It proved to be a meaningful edit, since a *subject* owes allegiance (forced or otherwise) to a monarchy, while a *citizen* owes allegiance to fellow citizens. The Declaration of Independence not only marked the beginning of democracy in America, as the door closed for European monarchies claiming millions of immigrants as subjects; it also sought to foreclose on the potential of a monarch ever having sovereignty over the collective inventiveness of the American people. Instead, it declared the country's *citizens* to be sovereign. This act harkened back to the origin of democracy: *demos* means "by the people" and *kratia* means "power." When joined together, the two words make *demokratia*, the Greek for democracy, which meant—at least for some—that the people hold the power, that they are the direct rulers.

Subject

The framers of the US Constitution also opted for representative democracy, narrowly defined by today's standards. Although they excluded significant swathes of the population on the road to a "more perfect union," suffice to say when Jefferson referred to someone as a citizen he viewed them as a primary inventor, along with their fellow citizens, of a better tomorrow, and at the center of democracy.

Client

In the forties, following the New Deal (1942) introduced by Franklin D. Roosevelt, a third word entered the popular lexicon: *client*.

The word "client" in the late fourteenth century meant "one who lives under the patronage of another." Its Latin derivative, *clientem*, meant "follower or retainer." It is also linked to the Latin word *clinare*, "to lean," as in to lean on another for protection. As words go it is steeped in a long history of paternalism and patronizing power relations, literally and etymologically.

While its modern usage typically intends far more positive and equitable relationships, many rightly question the use of the term, as do I. To get beyond the issues of the power imbalance that often exists within the professional-client relationship, and in an effort to be progressive, some helping professions have taken to using *customer* as an alternative.

Their intention is to highlight that the people they serve should have a right to the same quality, standards of service and level of choice as those who have greater purchasing power. While I understand those good intentions, I'm concerned by how often this kindly impulse is driven more by sympathy rather than empathy and therefore lacks authenticity. An authentic customer has real choices; they can, for example, take their money and go to another vendor if they are not happy with the service they are receiving. However, those in receipt of social housing, and other state supports, cannot do that except in very rare circumstances.

There's another limitation to the term "customer," which is that it solely defines the person in terms of what they as an individual purchase and how they relate to the goods and services they *customarily* consume. This is not bad (or good) per se, but it is limiting if what you want is to promote interdependence, economic sovereignty, and a greater sense of citizenship. Referring to people simply by what they personally consume inadvertently demeans, or at least overshadows, their indigenous relationships and what they make, cocreate, and contribute.

Citizen

And so we turn to the term "citizen." For many, the term evokes *Gotong ryong*, an Indonesian term meaning to give to your neighbor with no expectation of return, or *garaiocht*, which emerges from ancient Celtic (Irish) traditions and connotes deep proximity, faithful to shared productivity, bound to culture, and connected into human and environmental encounter.

The meaning of the term "citizen" is far more expansive than voting, which often is no more than an act of handing your power over to another, or holding a passport. There are people who have neither legal documents nor voting franchise, relative to where they reside, yet they do more to build community connection than those who can trace their ancestral roots to the foundation of their nation-state.

Mu: Re-ask the Question

Peter Block (2008) notes that questions bring us together and answers drive us apart. That is generally true. However, some questions also drive us apart, such as "Have you a passport?" or "You're not from around here, are you?"

In Robert Pirsig's landmark book *Zen and the Art of the Motorcycle Maintenance* (1974), which I discuss in more detail in the next chapter, a character invokes the word *mu* from Buddhist practice, which requests that a person asking the question that bruises you un-ask that question and reweave a new one, one with the potential to heal or at least enable us to be better at being human together.

In the final analysis, perhaps the words subject, client, consumer, and citizen are less important than the power to call for *mu*. Can the people you serve say *mu* to your organization and to you? If they can do so with their choices and sense of control intact, then they are certainly not acting as subjects. In fact, I believe—especially if they are also thinking of the well-being of their community—they are living into their citizenship. While they will often consume services, as do we all, if stepping fully into their citizenship they will never love or be enthralled with the things they use, and they will never use up the things they love.

This is the basis on which we shift the current narrative that has been authored by a predatory economy, with its obsession with mass production and addictive consumption, toward the production of mass well-being, with choice and collective power at its core.

The next two chapters return to the old adage "It takes a village to raise a child" to ask: How, as adults, are we doing in creating such places for our children to flourish?

* * *

If we care about participatory democracy, then we will go to where citizens can constructively steward energy in a way that is inclusive and supports people to generate disparate energy into collective democratic power. That place is local—hence democracy is not just an ideal; it has a location, and that location is our community of place. The act of building democracy is therefore an act of homecoming that extends outward to govern the health, wealth, and justice of a nation.

Chapter 13

Building Community and Pathways to Citizenship

Deschooling Society and Practicing the Art of Motorcycle Maintenance

Sometimes questions are more important than answers.

—NANCY WILLARD

I'M AFRAID THAT AT any given time I flit from one book to another from one week to the next, and typically there's little that's common across them. So I was pleasantly surprised when I saw a connection the other day between an article I plonked on a pile on my bedside table alongside two books, both old classics that I'm returning to after many previous readings. The article is about a group called Bikers Against Child Abuse (BACA), and the books were *Deschooling Society* (Illich, 1971) and *Zen and the Art of Motorcycle Maintenance* (Pirsig, 1974).

So what's the connection? Well, they all speak to how we can learn rich lessons within what Illich might call a "convivial space," but also remind us about competencies that as citizens many of us have forgotten we have. In a quote from *Deschooling Society* Ivan Illich offers a clue as to how it happens:

> The current search for new educational funnels must be reversed into the search for their institutional inverse: educational webs which heighten the opportunity for each one to transform each moment of his living into one of learning, sharing, and caring.

Deschooling Society, though written more than four decades ago, holds its appeal and relevance, given the rise of institutionalism and professionalization across civic space. Illich is clear in his call to action: the integrity of

learning across the life course will only be maintained and sustained by growing community alternatives to "established service industry" responses.

Notwithstanding, through my work with schools in Rwanda, I have
come to learn of the power that resides within the respective treasure
chests of local schools. Schools are indeed places with abundant human/
financial/political/physical assets upon which to build better educational,
economic, environmental, and community outcomes. Having said that,
it is also important to recognize that schools are supplementary to the
primary contributions of families, communities, and young people themselves. The challenge for schools is in releasing these assets and ensuring
they mingle, complement, and connect with the assets of the communities
of which they are an integral part.

In Kigali, Rwanda's capital, I am currently mentoring community
builders who are working with schools that have reimagined themselves
into hubs for community building and economic renewal. They are releasing previously untapped community-building potential and stand as
living proof of what is possible when educational institutions ask, How
can we support learning in a way that builds community either side of our
boundary walls?

Schools (their pupils, parents, teachers, and the wider community)
that have come to deeply understand and release the assets they have for
community building, while at the same time coming to understand and
support the assets the community has for learning and teaching, are proving
the transformational potential that such genuine partnerships offer.

As my friend and colleague Jonathan Sher, former Scotland director of
the WAVE Trust, wisely pointed out during our discussion on the themes
within this chapter,

> Illich's words/ideas continue to resonate and appeal, but they
> manifestly have not translated into a deschooled society any-
> where. There are millions of students, and hundreds of thou-
> sands of teachers, who are (and will, for the foreseeable future,
> remain) in schools for a large portion of their waking hours.
>
> The challenge is to make that time far more meaningful for
> students/staff/communities—and those assets far more explic-
> itly and robustly connected to the kind of community develop-
> ment both of us favor.

Wise words indeed! Though I would add that we must figure out how to
face those relational challenges in a way that does not inadvertently demean or displace the capacities and primary contributions of parents and
communities.

A year after *Deschooling Society* was published, an American cultural icon in literature emerged on the scene, but not before setting the Guinness World Record for most rejections of a first book ever—121 rejection letters from publishers. The book's full title was *Zen and the Art of Motorcycle Maintenance: An Inquiry into Values.* The book ultimately sold five million copies worldwide, and despite what the title suggests, it has very little, in factual terms, to do with either Zen Buddhism or motorcycle maintenance.

Zen and the Art of Motorcycle Maintenance

Robert M. Pirsig's book beautifully exemplifies Illich's notion of "educational webs which heighten the opportunity for each one to transform each moment of his living into one of learning, sharing, and caring." It also illustrates the tension between the romantic/idealistic view of the world and the more rational one.

The apparent conflict between the idealistic versus the practical or the intuitive versus the scientific explains the book's title, *Zen and the Art of Motorcycle Maintenance.* Pirsig concludes his philosophically grounded novel by asserting that we need to hold both in creative tension. His call to action is for us to occupy the space between purposefulness and emergence, and to learn to move more gracefully between the two.

For those who haven't read the book, it describes a seventeen-day journey within a journey. The more obvious journey is a father-and-son motorcycle odyssey from Minnesota to northern California, along with two friends who complete the first nine days with them. The second journey is a philosophical one. The book is peppered with philosophical conversations referred to as "Chautauquas," an allusion to the popular, informal adult education/cultural movement across rural America around the turn of the twentieth century. In those explorations, father and son cover the gamut of all things philosophical, from metaphysics to epistemology.

Aside from the wonderful way it illustrates how learning happens outside as well as inside formal educational systems, the book also celebrates the importance of nonprofessional people (citizens) as primary educators, while challenging them (us) to ensure we have enough technical know-how to maintain our "bikes" so that we can sustain our own—and our neighbors'—"journey."

Through the metaphor of motorcycle maintenance, Pirsig makes the basic point that if you want to live a free and care-full life (achieve Zen), then you need to develop at least some of the skills that most of us have farmed out to professionals, like basic motorcycle maintenance. Outsourcing such functions to professionals comes at a high price, he argues: the erosion of our personal and community competencies. The book reminds us that there are many things we once did in civic life that now have become commodities in the marketplace, and we need to cultivate a high level of discernment around the relocation of civic functions to the marketplace, lest we inadvertently hand away our freedoms.

Given the themes that run through both books, raising children who are deeply connected to productive adults within their community strikes me as a germane example of how easily and inadvertently we can relocate civic functions to the marketplace. Our children are for the most part not treated as integral to our neighborhoods. Instead, they have been spirited off to cyberspace, or to the halls and malls of the marketplace.

Peter Block and John McKnight (2011), who often blog on parenting and family as well as broader neighborhood issues on their website and on other platforms, conclude in a piece for the *Huffington Post* that this outsourcing of care functions for our children and our neighbors' children has led to the significant "loss of basic functions belonging to families and neighborhoods." They continue by saying,

> Most have become incompetent in terms of doing the work of families and neighborhoods. The cost of this incompetence is families and neighborhoods that have no real function.
>
> No group persists when it has no reason to be together. Therefore, if families perform no functions we can predict that they will fall apart.
>
> We delude ourselves if we think our high divorce rates are caused by interpersonal problems and disagreements. It's not that people are not getting along; it is that they don't need each other because they have no functions to perform. They are just isolated, unproductive, dependent consumers who happen to live in the same house.

Children need to be needed, as well as needing to have their needs met. They also want to be adultlike. Those combined drives are greater than any one family or state can facilitate unilaterally—hence the oft-repeated assertion that it takes a village to raise a child. It is therefore only when children are connected to productive adults, and are recognized as "at promise" and not just "at risk," that they learn how to contribute and receive relative to their age and stage in life. This is the pathway to adulthood and citizenship, heavily punctuated by play and rituals of celebration. The benchmark of competent neighborhoods, and a functioning democracy, must surely be the extent to which each child can traverse this path.

Having age- and developmentally appropriate and valued roles within their communities and relationships that enable them to grow securely, children can come to feel confident enough to be in the world and to shape it.

Yet many believe that the safety and competence of children is contingent largely, if not solely, on the quality of our educational curriculum and the robust implementation of child protection policies. As one leader of a town council said to me recently, "I love all this community stuff, but a community can't really do a lot about child protection issues, can they?"

To be fair, I'm sure he was actually referring to complex child welfare issues that involve social workers and other professionals. Yet, even then, is it either true or desirable to assert the view, as many do, that communities are incompetent and impotent (they would never be so blunt as to use such language, but the implication is clear) in the face of their young neighbors' abuse or maltreatment? That the protection of our children and our neighbors' children is solely in the hands of outside professional agencies, to whom we have surrendered our own personal and collective agency on such matters, concerns anyone who cares about rekindling democracy and returning power to the people. Acting on the view that communities are incompetent in the face of child protection matters creates the opposite of what it intends: children become less protected, not more. In the United States, for example, crime has decreased every year since the nineties, yet fear has increased as a result of media hype and general fearmongering (Grawert, Friedman, and Cullen, 2017). Crime's intensity may vary from country to country but it is nonetheless a familiar global pattern.

But in response to the question, "Are professionals best placed to deal with some forms of child neglect or abuse?" of course there is a certain point at which the answer is yes. In the same way that certain mechanical issues are beyond the average native abilities of a motorcycle enthusiast and require a skilled mechanic, certain child protection issues require professional stewardship.

But here's the rub. On the one hand, if, as a motorcycle enthusiast, I neglect to maintain my bike, when it does eventually break down, it is true to say I have to call in an expert if I want it to work again. On the other hand, it is also true to say that I have by degrees slowly given away what agency I previously had to fix it, before it got to the point of no return. So too, while it is true to say that some mechanical issues are beyond the competence of the average motorcyclist, preventive maintenance is not. Think about other possessions we prize but do not keep up: the quality of maintenance is often directly linked to our dependence on outside expertise and intervention; this is true even in relation to our own bodies.

Understanding the borderline where my competency as an individual and citizen ends and professional competency begins is critical to sustaining my personal agency and citizen power to negotiate a healthy social contract. It is equally important that I come to completely explore and understand my capacity and that of my neighbors, family, and friends on the civic side of the borderline—to maintain and sustain not just motorcycles but everything we love and care about, including a culture of community where children can grow well and be safe.

Bikers Against Child Abuse

And that brings me to Bikers Against Child Abuse (BACA). This is an association of motorcycle enthusiasts across the world who, in addition to being passionate about motorcycles and the sense of community that that way of life brings, care deeply about keeping children safe. They intentionally form a nonviolent barrier between victims of abuse and alleged and/or convicted abusers and work with the child and supportive family, in close cooperation with professionals, to convince the children that they are and will continue to be surrounded by "scary" looking bikers who are watching out for them. You can appreciate that a group of golfers wearing pink Ralph Lauren sweaters might not create the same theatrical impact! Where possible, these benevolent bikers even try to support abusers to take ownership of their issues and find better ways of resolving them.

BACA members are nonviolent and work in partnership with police. They intentionally commit to protect children where police and social workers cannot, but they do not interfere with or take on the roles of these or any other professionals. They are purposefully acting as citizens to protect young children so that they can grow into their citizenship. This is a powerful act of maintaining and flexing civic muscle while not masquerading as the strong arm of the law. And of course it is highly unusual. It also feels like a very late (though important) intervention. How as citizens can we create the conditions where our current unacceptable high incidences of child maltreatment are prevented in the first place?

Not all of us will take to the open road, as in Pirsig's tale, or be part of a gang of bikers who occupy a schoolyard with Harley-Davidsons on behalf of a seven-year-old boy who is being bullied. Not many of us will even, as Illich proposed, create free-floating book exchanges or civic libraries in local cafés.

But perhaps we can practice the "Art of Community Building and Connection Maintenance." In all the functions and places we inhabit as adults, we can think about what we do and ask ourselves, What could I do, and how could I do it in a way that builds community where I live? By asking this question and acting on the answer we can't help creating opportunities for children to connect in all kinds of productive ways with adults who are near, loving, caring, and safe toward them and those around them, but also accountable to the community.

It is this seemingly "passive" form of child protection that in fact creates the primary prevention layer that is currently all but missing in most of our neighborhoods. Why? Because we are not maintaining our collective capacity to care for one another's children. This is the first and most powerful level of child protection, which requires far greater attention from all quarters in society, starting with us as citizens living in local communities.

Building on the themes of this chapter, the next calls us to shift societal perspectives of certain children labeled as at risk—from seeing them as problems to be fixed to viewing and treating them as youth at promise.

* * *

There are, of course, various forms of child injury that require different community responses:

1. injury from parents, and significant others, in the home;
2. injury from neighbors;
3. injury from institutions; and
4. injury from the environment.

How do we communally respond to each?

Beth E. Molnar and Robert M. George address this question directly in their paper entitled "Neighborhood-Level Social Processes and Substantiated Cases of Child Maltreatment" (Molnar et al., 2016). They note that "child maltreatment is a preventable public health problem." Their research concludes that neighborhoods that had identified, connected, and mobilized their local assets had "lower proportions of neglect, physical abuse, and sexual abuse substantiated cases." More bonded and bridging social capital also "predicted a lower proportion of substance-exposed infants." Their conclusion? "This research indicates that strategies to mobilize neighborhood-level protective factors may decrease child maltreatment more effectively than individual and family-focused efforts alone." Brid Featherstone and Anna Gupta (Featherstone at al., 2018), in critically examining the social work context in the UK, share similar findings in *Protecting Children: A Social Model*. They go further in challenging the level of risk aversion endemic within the social work profession, especially with regard to children services and matters of safeguarding.

So, while we as communities may not be the only responders, we are for the most part the ideal first responders.

Chapter 14

Restoring the Village

From Youth at Risk to Youth at Promise

*Village life gently swirled around them, with the perpetual ebb and flow of people,
scurrying in every direction. The village was a living, organic entity,
with blood flowing through its veins, and with a definite pulse and heartbeat.
It had its own distinct personality and its own dark caustic humour, and was constantly processing and regurgitating information through its winding, meandering streets.*

—Leonardo D'Onofrio

When we assume that police are the first and sole responders to dan-
ger—that they hold a monopoly on keeping us safe, and accordingly, we
completely hand authority for the production of our safety, at the neighborhood level, over to hardworking uniformed officers—we are unintentionally creating a prison for ourselves and our children. Not the kind with
cells and bars, but the invisible kind that looks just like the house and
neighborhood where we live.

Recently police sent flyers to families in a neighborhood in England with a warning: "It is a crime for children to play football and go
on skateboards in the street." It worked. Within twenty-four hours the
street looked like the opening scene from a Spaghetti Western (without,
of course, the rolling tumbleweeds and background music): there was not
one soul on it. The neighborhood's children were literally afraid to play
outside their homes.

To be fair, apologies did issue from the police following a slew of com-
plaints from parents. But for twenty-four hours it must have been heaven
for the few in the neighborhood who don't like skateboarding or ball games
in the streets. What kind of world would we be forced to live in, however, if
the objections of the few resulted in our streets being cleared of children? I

am horrified at the thought of such an eventuality and fearful it is becoming more and more an actuality in neighborhoods around the world. As Mark Twain once said, "I'll take heaven for the climate and hell for the company." It may be hell at times for certain members of our community to listen to the noise of children at play, but there is a far worse hell that follows for communities that do not allow their children to play in public spaces together: the hell of social isolation.

In their apology the police explained they wanted to remind parents of their "legal and social responsibilities" around their children playing games in the streets. This had been a particular feature in the flyer, which also reminded parents that ignoring their legal and social responsibilities might lead to arrest or some other sanction: "Ignore the law and you may be liable to prosecution," the leaflet read.

In Search of Safety

This episode raises quite a few questions—questions not just for police but for us all, including the people who felt the only way they could produce "peace and quiet" for themselves was to lobby the police to threaten to arrest their neighbors.

Here are a few of the more salient questions that come to mind about this view:

1. *Who are the primary producers, investors, and recipients of safety at the neighborhood level?* The answer, I think, is obvious: local residents who live in that neighborhood. Increased police presence does not lead to enhanced safety and security in the same way that a connected community can. Robert Sampson (2013), writing in the *New Scientist*, in an article titled "When Disaster Strikes, It's Survival of the Sociable," affirms this very point: the evidence shows stronger, more connected neighborhoods have significantly less crime. So, completely banishing local children from playing outdoors may reduce noise in the short term but inadvertently increase the conditions for crime to flourish in the longer term.

2. *Even if police could unilaterally produce safety, is it desirable for servants of the state to do so?* The first point to make in response to this question is that the police cannot police the public unilaterally; they police with the support of the public. Even in very extreme circumstances where a state of emergency has been declared for a period of time, they rely heavily on public support and goodwill. The second is that the same principles of institutional counterproductivity in health, as discussed

in chapter 8, play out in institutional policing, which is to say, after a certain scale and intensity, more policing makes us more unsafe.

3. *What if the best measure of a growing and safe democracy is the extent to which our children can play freely with one another in their own neighborhood and associate with their neighbors across the life course?* The foundation stones of all democracies include freedom of expression and free association. These are not just fundamental to democracy; they are fundamental to a free and good life. When we inhibit children's free play on the streets where they live, we also shut down nature's classroom, where the most formative lessons in citizenship are learned. This shutdown sets in train a range of unintended consequences.

For example, children's relationship with the local built and natural environment becomes passive; they are no longer coauthors of it as the climbers of trees, the builders of dens, the chalkers of streets. Certainly in commoditized urban neighborhoods, they are perpetual spectators and faux tourists, because their curiosity has been deactivated. Instead, they spirit through these neighborhoods on foot or in automobiles, encased in an alternative parallel environment created by social media or music piped through earphones. Their feet may hit the pavements but their earphones and smartphones hold their attention. They pass through the neighborhood on their way to somewhere else—to a playdate at a classmate's house or to an adult-led activity, sometimes in their own neighborhoods but most often not. Regularly they are chaperoned out of their communities by a parent, and many spend weekdays with one parent in one community and weekends elsewhere with the other.

The message to children is clear: the spaces beyond the physical boundaries of your homes and where your families have deemed to be "safe" are potentially hostile, unsafe places for a child to be, and it is beyond their power to change that. Consequently all interaction with civic life is structured, supervised, or mediated by a screen. These activities often have financial costs attached, too, and tend to happen outside of the neighborhood where children live and so away from their neighbors.

The irony here is that the widespread assumption that the dislocated online world is benign while the local "onland" world is fundamentally unsafe is a distortion and inversion of the reality. In truth, the online world is far from benign. The predatory potential of online interactions is such that allowing a child to go online unsupervised is equivalent to allowing them go out alone after dark in a busy city. In fact, it's worse; at least in a busy city, there's some chance of passive oversight. Online anonymity not only requires great parental caution and diligent oversight; there also is a more hidden cost to the grand bargain of the digital age, in which consumers have traded their data for free services. We may to our horror one day wake up to the realization that we have assisted our children to become data slaves to the new hidden persuaders, who are using the same tactics used in the fifties but now through new and more pernicious channels. These days the hidden persuaders have raised their sights beyond market share and are in pursuit of our children's mind-share.

The philosopher and revolutionary Jean-Jacques Rousseau once observed, "We walk willingly into our chains." These days we are more inclined to drive or click ourselves and our children into the chains of disconnectedness and separation. Our neighborhoods are becoming more pixelated and elementalized, the ideal breeding grounds for loneliness at every age and stage. In 2018 the British Broadcasting Company reported on the world's largest survey on loneliness to date (Hammond, 2018). Those findings suggest that young people are in fact lonelier than their senior neighbors.

If we continue as we are, our homes and our children's lives will become disconnected islands, and our lives more disjointed than our human nature can tolerate. As a consequence of poor urban design, the ubiquitous presence of cars, our irrational, mainstream media–fueled fear of each other, and our inactivity in turning strangers into friends on the street where we live, we are slowly partaking in ripping the social fabric that for millennia has been intricately woven into a blanket of care, freedom, and safety to be wrapped around children.

Those who are fifty and older know from lived experience that the adage "It takes a village to raise a child" is true. We lived in a time when skipping out of school was infinitely more challenging than it is now. When I was a kid, I had to operate with the omnipresent eyes of Mrs. Newsome, and a hundred others, on me. With that I had a sense of security, and accountability, and my parents had a sense of that too; they trusted those neighbors to share in the raising of me. That was what made our street safe for me and the kids who played with me. Not so for my children. As John Taylor Gatto (2005) says in *Dumbing Us Down*, ". . . without children and old people mixing in daily life, a community has no future and no past, only a continuous present" (p. 21).

Reclaiming Our Streets

The root issues of neighborhood safety have nothing substantively to do with the extent to which unsupervised ball games and skateboarding are played in the street by local children; and they have everything to do with the lack of connectivity between our children and their older neighbors. Making it a crime for children to play in the street is a sure way to decrease public safety and additionally, for good measure, to increase obesity, loneliness, consumerism, and damage to the environment, not to mention crime.

The real solution to youth and community safety lies in community building, not in turning our homes into fortresses or prisons and our streets into no-go zones for children. We need to start an Occupy movement much younger and closer to our doorsteps. This is how democracies get made. So for everyone's sake, let the children reclaim their streets with our support; for goodness' sake, let them play together and let our streets sing once more with their voices and laughter!

Of course, in addition to play, it is essential that young people can associate with productive adults beyond their own immediate family circle. When I read British tabloids, their messaging around young people is unmistakable: young people cause problems . . . have problems . . . *are* problems.

This idea is not peculiar to the UK. It's a global trend, and what's more, we have a long history of running down young people. This deficit-based thinking has led to an endemic labeling of young people. By contrast, a strengths-based view of young people says they are unappreciated problem-solvers and the leaders of today, not tommorow.

All that said, the antidote to thinking about young people as deviant is not instead to think of them as "deserving" of, for example, one-way compensatory services and programs. Defining young people solely by what they receive fails to realize what children and teenagers need most, which is to be needed. And meeting that need is about organizing our communities so that the contributions of young people can be invited and celebrated. Our current way of organizing lifts up consumption to such an extent as to send young people to the margins.

Of course, children need supports and certainly youth work provides essential supports in a person-centered, youth-friendly way. But if we think about youth development only as building a bridge between marginalized young people and the center of institutional youth programs, we will be missing a trick. Besides providing such programs and access to them, youth engagement must also concern itself with building a bridge between young people, productive adults, and the center of their communities—the very same communities, it has to be said, that all too often exile their most "needy" young people to the margins.

Communities and the families that exist within them have a central role to play in raising powerful and connected children, which cannot be replaced by professional intervention, no matter how well funded.

The further a child is from the center of a caring community, the more "at risk" she becomes. By the same token, the closer a child is to the center of a competent community that welcomes both her fallibility and giftedness, the closer she is to her promising present and compelling future.

Bridging to the Center

Today, young people and older people are the most segregated groupings of modern society: segregated by age and supposed dysfunction. Aggregating so-called at risk young people does little in the long run to reduce the risk and sometimes it serves to increase it. The truth is, young people are not "at risk" per se; they are "at promise." They only become "at risk" when the most significant people in their lives fail to recognize that promise.

All of this is no more than nice words unless we can figure out how to build a bridge between young people perceived as deviant by their community and the center of the very communities that perceive them as transgressors. So, how do we move from nice words to restorative practices that heal the wounds between young and old? By starting with three assumptions:

1. There is space and hospitality within every community for the gifts of all young people, regardless of their history or reputation, if we intentionally invite them in and make the connections. These spaces will not be found unless we actively seek them out and animate them.

2. Communities cannot reach their full potential until the gifts of their young citizens are discovered and received.

3. We do not have a "youth problem," we have a "village problem." Every young person, regardless of past transgressions, has strengths that are needed to tackle this village problem and, by so doing, to build inclusive, sustainable communities.

"It takes a village to raise a child" might have been the way of the past, but in the future—if we can learn to embrace the giftedness of our young people—it may be just as true to say it takes a child to raise a village.

Looking at young people as "at promise" instead of "at risk" reframes the challenge before us. It is no longer singularly about stopping harm being "done to" or "done by" young people but about liberating the promise in young people to be productive alongside neighbors of all ages in order to grow a shared and compelling future. When that is our starting point, then accordingly risk reduces.

Consider the Greek proverb "A society grows great when old men plant trees whose shade they know they shall never sit in." It makes sense, really. Who has a greater stake in the future than young people? The raw materials they use are strengths and capacities within themselves, but also within their communities. This is true across the life course, from womb to tomb: we build our futures by using what we have to secure what we need; nothing of worth has ever been built on deviance, strife, or misery, nor indeed, through isolation. Let's start afresh by agreeing that our young people are "at promise," not "at risk," and doing whatever we can to help them realize that promise, actively inviting their contribution in the resurgence of the village. That's a risk worth taking and a legacy worth creating.

* * *

Engaging families, neighbors, and the community as our first line of defense enables us to maintain and sustain our competency to keep our children well and prevent maltreatment in the first place. Then we must also have the discernment to tap into the assets of institutional resources and support to aid us in achieving whatever is beyond local capacity. In this way we can ensure that our public services are not burdened with tasks they are not competent to take on or to act as proxies for, like maintaining and sustaining our freedoms, our community, and adult-to-child relationships.

There are certain things that as citizens we must do—and if we don't do them, they will not get done. The good news is that we have an abundance of gifts with which to work, not least being the gifts and "promise" of our children.

Part Five: **Making It Real**

We are now past the halfway point in our journey together, and I can imagine that more than once you've asked the practical question, What can I do to make these principles visible? The next four chapters address this very question, offering seven practical tips for applying these principles in back-home, real-world contexts.

Chapter 15

Seven Principles of Community Building

Working in the BY Space

A bird doesn't sing because it has an answer,
it sings because it has a song.

—MAYA ANGELOU

"CAN I HELP YOU?" is an often asked question, yet helping can cause unintended harm. That realization places us at a moral crossroads: Do we "help" or do we walk a road less traveled? A foundational premise of this book is the idea that how we have traditionally shown up in the world can be redefined toward a more liberating way of being in relationship with others.

Traditional "helping" tends to come from a place of sympathy, not empathy, and a sense of responsibility as a duty or burden. I believe that the ability to respond empathetically is a gift received from the other, the one to whom you are responding. Throughout, I have suggested—in different ways—three dominant styles of helping: (1) doing things to individuals and/ or their communities (the medical model); (2) doing things for individuals/ communities (the charity model); and (3) doing things with individuals/ communities (codesign and coproduction).

On their own, the first two have caused top-down technocratic, institutional, and service-oriented approaches to dominate since the New Deal and the Marshall Plan. If citizen-centered democracy is to flourish, we must nurture new space for bottom-up, citizen-led action for the things that are done collectively, not just WITH citizens and agencies working together but BY citizens acting as co-creators, mutual makers, and coproducers with their neighbors. This is the lower-right panel in Figure 15.1 (the BY space), a domain that has more to do with curiosity and discovery than helping or healing. Here citizens don't have *a* say, they have the primary say, and they are the prime producers of whatever outputs emerge. In other words, the BY space is where the things that citizens must do as a collective get done.

Figure 15.1

Done TO Communities = Everything done is to us and without us.

Done FOR Communities= Everything done is done for us, without us.

Done WITH Communities = Nothing done for us is done without us.

Done BY Communities = Done by us for us.

The prime assertion of this book up to now is that it is only by committing to the discovery and enhancement of the BY space—what citizens can do themselves, together—that we can make sense of where outside collaboration is warranted. Democracy flourishes not by the growth of top-down services (even ones that are delivered collaboratively) but by the enhancement of freedom for all from the grassroots up.

That assertion begs the question, How can we support appropriate citizen-led growth of the BY space? It is to that question I turn my attention in this and the next three chapters.

Seven Principles of Community Building

There are seven principles of authentic community building that I have found to be recurrent and congruent across an incredibly wide and diverse range of contexts and efforts to promote collective citizen cocreation and cooperation in small local places.

The seven principles are these:

1. Find a trusted local association with sufficient infrastructure to act as a host of the work.

2. Start by making the invisible visible; don't be helpful, be interested.

3. Understand that effective community building goes at the speed of trust.

4. Start with what's strong to address what's wrong and make what's strong stronger.

5. Know that community connectors are critical.

6. Recognize that the optimum population size of a neighborhood is three thousand to five thousand residents.

7. Keep your focus on growing a culture of community, not converting people to asset-based community development (ABCD) or any other approach.

These seven principles are not meant as prescriptions, but simply a good-faith attempt to articulate some of the strategic and practical implications for professionals and their organizations of doing community building in neighborhoods and promoting citizen participation in general.

Principle #1: Find a Local Host

Finding a trusted local association to act as a host for the work is essential. Across Europe, a growing number of public-sector bodies and larger third-sector organizations have become favorably disposed to asset-based community development efforts; some are actively attempting to precipitate such efforts through investment in community animation practices and innovative investment initiatives. That said, if you are in such an organization, it is important to recognize that your organizational size, while an advantage in so many ways to your mission, can be a decided disadvantage when it comes to supporting citizen-led efforts.

As mentioned before, E. F. Schumacher's famous epigram reminds us that when it comes to community building, "Small is beautiful." To that I would add, trust is everything. Hence if you work in a philanthropic organization, or operate in the public sector—indeed, even if you are in a large third-sector organization committed to the principle of doing no harm—growing alliances with much smaller mediating associations locally rooted in neighborhoods is a great way to make a proportionate contribution. Those smaller bodies typically possess hybrid structures that mesh the best of associational life with small but sufficient amounts of institutional capacity.

What to Look For

As potential local hosts for your precipitating efforts, these smaller mediating hybrid associations will display the following characteristics:

1. *Local*: Located/residing within the community where the community-building efforts are to take place.

2. *Broadly concerned*: Committed to the overall welfare of the community at large, not just focused on one theme or target group. Although they may advocate for a particular group or concern, they work with the neighborhood in all its facets: across age, across health, and across safety, economy, environment, and culture. They see like a community and view the neighborhood as the primary unit of change.

3. *Connecting*: Their primary work is in supporting residents, and their associations, to build the capacity to discover and connect local assets.

4. *Power*: They are interested in supporting residents to build and grow collective power from the grassroots up and the sidelines in, and they actively include the stranger at the edge. Their power comes from their associational base in the community, not their contract portfolio or revenue/funding streams.

5. *Hybrid*: They are considered hybrid because they have enough structure to enable them to employ someone or manage a funding/investment arrangement, while also remaining foundationally associational (and so directed and led by local citizens) and fundamentally trusted across the neighborhood.

6. *Prospectors*: They are in a position to discover ever-widening groups of local residents who in turn are committed to weaving their neighborhood together.

7. *Inclusionists*: Thereafter, they can support a team of residents to loosely organize into an initiating group of citizens who themselves are committed to hosting a new conversation at the local level while

paying particular attention to the genuine inclusion of local people who have been pushed to the margins and are vulnerable to not having their gifts seen and received.

8. *Lightning conductors:* Supporting the connection of community through a wide and diverse series of unscripted conversations and informal resident-led initiatives may ruffle a few feathers. This is especially evident among community members who believe that all community business should be channeled through existing formal community structures, such as the residents' association or neighborhood management committee. It is critical that when such tensions arise they are worked through in a constructive and inclusive way. This is an extremely important function of a host association.

Some examples of where you'll find a host at the neighborhood level include locally rooted businesses with the desire to build community; community associations with a welcome for the stranger on the edge; locally based art organizations that believe we are all artists, and the palette is the community; local youth organizations that appreciate it takes a village to raise a child; and faith groups not exclusively caught up with congregational concerns and recruiting new members.

With a hand in the soil and an eye toward the stars, local hosts offer a solid foundation for the growth of citizen-led local endeavors.

Principle #2: Start by Making the Invisible Visible; Don't Be Helpful, Be Interested

The second principle builds on the premise that residents can't know what they need from outside their neighborhoods until they first know what they have locally. Working in accordance with Principle #2 means identifying, connecting, and mobilizing the existing capacities of a place, by supporting citizens to create connectedness and build collective power to be the doers.

A Sea of Potential: Dive In

Every neighborhood is bustling with activity, resources, and capacities, yet these often go unrecognized. Like a river's undercurrent, they're not immediately apparent unless you go swimming. Economically marginalized communities all too often are viewed as backwaters of pathology, with nothing but needs and deficits, where helping professions spend

a considerable amount of time fishing for what's missing rather than sur-
facing the underlying pool of potential.

But what if helpers stopped searching for what was wrong as their
starting point and, instead of being helpful, started being genuinely curious? What if the professional map was set aside in preference to unearthing
hidden treasures in the territory? What if helpers just supported residents in
getting together to make the invisible visible?

For most citizens, this act of discovery is very powerful and revelatory. But discovery of local resources alone changes very little. Having
a list of assets should not be thought of as an action step. A further and
deeper inquiry is needed to understand how the various assets that have
been discovered can be connected more productively. Deepening the connection between individual capacities, the power of associations, the resources of institutions, the potential of the built and natural environment,
the fruitfulness of the neighborly economy and the abundant richness of
local cultures is not a onetime data-gathering exercise. It is an ongoing,
relationship-building process.

This process is beyond the capacity of a Google search, a professional
intervention, or even the work of a lone citizen. Making the invisible visible
is an invitation to create interdependence by asking citizens to act their way
into interdependence from the get-go, by starting a new conversation, which
in turn leads to new discoveries and connections. It takes many citizens,
in deep and meaningful connection with each other, to reveal the hidden
capacity and potential that is in every community, waiting to be discovered,
like a sundial in the shade.

There is no doubting that the intentional act of discovery and connection
across an entire neighborhood (and other small bounded places) is a time-
consuming one. However, if we are committed to sustainable community
development, then a slower, more iterative route such as this one is essential.
Making the invisible visible is a starting point, but it is not yet an action
step per se. It's a foundational step and it is where a community deepens
its appreciation of what capacities it has, ensuring any support from the
outside is relevant to the local context. Without taking the time to build this
interconnectedness and trust across a place, two unintended consequences
can occur, often instigated by well-intentioned outside agencies:

- *Displacement of local invention*: Projects and initiatives, with new resources and expertise (and good intentions), replicate what local people are already doing for themselves and thereby disable and eclipse
  local capacity.

- *Stifling of local invention*: When the working assumption in a given community is that the only way things will get better is when someone from outside comes in to make them better, or that a community can only act when it has permission from outside, it serves to dampen down enthusiasm and creativity. In the same way, professionalization or credentializing of community functions results in a major attrition in citizen-led action. As professionalization increases, citizenship retreats (the hydraulic effect).

Making the invisible visible is not a positive-psychology technique or even a technique in any sense; it is an intentional, collective citizen-led act of building and growing power. Citizens build power as they form mutual trust and connection through action in the same way that La Leche League International has done. In so doing, they come to recognize that much (though not all) of what they need to make change is close at hand. This is not to suggest that a community has everything it needs internally but instead to reaffirm, as I've said many times throughout these pages, that they cannot know what is needed from external actors until they discover what they have internally—and until they realize that what the community has locally is of far greater value than most recognize. Once a community understands what it has within, and in turn what it requires from the outside, they come to confidently occupy a powerful political space from where they can begin to leverage significant change for the future.

How Not to Help

So, if you are from an outside agency seeking to help and you must stick with your organization's theme or mission, you ask questions that make the community's assets visible. For example, if you are interested in health, you certainly could ask residents questions such as these:

1. What does it mean to people living here to be healthy?

2. What is it you do to be healthy in this place, and how can we support you?

3. What would I need to know to be healthy while living here?

Or, if you're interested in safety, you might ask residents, How do you create safety in this place, and how can we support your efforts?

This reframing creates two shifts. First, there is a shift from a more traditional transactional relationship of service provider/client to one of facilitator/citizen. Second, it creates a shift from a single-issue focus/theme or a siloed approach, such as health or safety, which involves working only with target populations or addressing single issues, to a more holistic, place-based approach.

The next chapter considers the question of how we can support local citizens to build a culture of trust from the inside out.

* * *

One of the key assertions of this book is that most of the things people do to be healthy or safe are done by people who are not thinking that what they are doing is healthy or safe. So, the more you can set your agency agendas to one side and simply get to know what the community cares about, the more likely you are to build community while also addressing your organization's concerns. This is why I suggest that instead of being helpful, you try being curious. After all, your agency map is never the territory.

Chapter 16

Working at the Speed of Trust

Serving while Walking Backward

In old days there were angels who came and took men by the hand, and led them away from the city of destruction. We see no white-winged angels now. But yet men are led away from threatening destruction: a hand is put into theirs, which leads them forth gently towards a calm and bright land, so that they look no more backward; and the hand may be a little child's.

—George Eliot

CONVERSATIONS BETWEEN RESIDENTS THAT unveil and productively connect community assets are not meant to be measured, they are meant to be treasured. Trust flows from the experience of being treasured, not measured. It comes from being recognized for your gifts while being accepted with all of your fallibilities. When we treasure someone or something, it is the opposite of miserliness—hence why we do not think of people who treasure someone as parsimonious.

One of my favorite novels is *Silas Marner*, by George Eliot, first published in 1861. Silas, a member of a small Calvinist community in England, is wrongly accused of stealing his faith community's savings. He leaves in shame; his reputation is in tatters and the woman he was about to marry chooses to marry the very man who framed him. On arriving in another, more urbane village, somewhere in the Midlands, he becomes inward and reclusive, obsessing about the gold coins he amasses through his work as a weaver and going deeper into despair. His days are spent counting his gold and hiding it; Silas exhibits all the characteristics of a miser. Eventually it, too, is stolen and he is left bereft.

But then Eppie, a child orphaned through a series of tragic circumstances, comes into his life. He grows to love Eppie and, through her, connects with the village at large, who help him raise her as his own. Eppie, too, grows to love Silas, so much so that when a local well-to-do couple offers her the life of the child of a gentleman and lady, she turns them down. (The gentleman is, in fact, her father, who up to then has hidden the fact.) Silas and Eppie treasure each other. They share a trust and love that is abundant. The more they give away, the more they have.

The Reality of Trust

Eliot's novel may be read as the three related life stories of Silas Marner, and these stories are instructive for building the trust that true community requires. In the first, Silas lives in a community where trust is weak. His best friend is the man who sets him up and his congregation damns him on flimsy grounds. The lady he is to marry rejects him, and so he is used and rejected by the very people he loves and trusts.

In his second life story, to cope with having been betrayed and let down by those he loved in his first experience of community, he moves to a new village, where nobody knows him or his story. He falls in love with something that can't reject him, namely his gold, but it cannot love him back. He lives through a cycle of ever-deepening dissatisfaction. As a miser, pursuing satisfaction through materialism—to avoid the necessary risks associated with interdependence, with community life and relationships with friends and family—was a futile endeavor. His first life story, which casts him as an open, affable, and trusting character, is exchanged for a new story—an individualistic, consumeristic life of quiet dissatisfaction.

Silas's first two life stories, when combined, are an allegory and indeed a composite of the stories of everyone and anyone who has been raised in a shame-based community, overly defined by the labels of others and not recognized for their gifts, skills, and passions. It is also a parable, of a sort, that speaks to the challenges of transitioning from the parochial and cloistered worlds of small, inward-looking communities to industrialized, anonymous, metropolitan environments.

Fleeing from the judgments of nosey neighbors and harsh shaming environments to the larger city of secret spaces and private places, where the primacy of the individual is beyond question, comes with many trade-offs. Still, if you have experienced rejection from your village, as did Silas, then the call of the "Big Smoke" is an alluring one.

What is essential to note here is that neither of the first two stories offers a definitive description of reality. They are, instead, just versions of reality, fictions if you like, merely stories. All stories to one degree or another are heavily laced with fiction, but all versions of reality are themselves stories.

Neither of Silas's first two stories speaks of the experiences you expect to encounter in a trusting community. Like Silas, throughout our lives we are the subjects of multiple stories. In some we are "cause" (agents) and in others we are "effect" (victims). In Silas's first story, he is cast as both a member of his community and a victim of his community's poor judgment. In the second story he becomes radically individualistic, with no sense of belonging to the community, having foreclosed on his previous desires to be rooted in a place and deeply connected to the people who reside there.

From this hyper-individualized position, he becomes obsessed with his private property, most particularly his gold. Like character of Gollum in J. R. R. Tolkien's *Lord of the Rings*, who refers to "the ring" as his "precious," Silas is consumed by the gold that he has amassed through honest effort, in much the same way that extreme consumerism can result in consumers being psychologically consumed by the products they acquire and the money they use to acquire it.

Like Gollum in his relationship to the ring and Silas in his relationship to the gold, the consumer, too, can become addicted to the goods and services that the marketplace offers. Addiction nearly always results when we expect goods and services, which are necessarily limited and unsatisfying, to take the place of relationships and community. The more desperate we are that "the ring" take the place of a lost love or "the gold" take the place of the respect and role one yearns for within a community of peers, the more addicted and dependent we become. The more addicted we become to that which can never love us or respect us, the more depressed and isolated we find ourselves, and so the deeper we fall into addiction.

Fortunately for Silas, a stranger from the edge of the community he has fled to arrives unannounced into his miserly existence. She finds him because he, too, is at the edge. She arrives in the guise of a little girl called Eppie, whose opiate-addicted mother has died in the snow. Eppie is the daughter of a well-to-do gentleman of the village, who hides her existence and the fact that he is married to her mother, a woman of supposed low standing from a neighboring village.

The death of Eppie's mother is most convenient for her father, who is now free of his shame of having married someone below his social standing. The arrival of this little girl on Silas's doorstep is the beginning of his third life story and ultimately his liberation. Eppie loves Silas as unconditionally as he loves her.

Throughout Silas's three stories, there is an invisible determinant at play, and that is trust. Silas gives trust freely in his first life's iteration but does not enjoy an adequate return. In his second chapter he withholds trust and hides his assets for fear they will be stolen, and yet that is precisely what happens. His risk aversion makes what he fears more likely to become a reality. Accordingly, his distrust of people deepens.

Silas's third life story teaches us that trust is environmental and cultural, not just personal or even interpersonal. The third version of his story is not just about his relationship with Eppie but also about how it takes a village to help him raise this child. In turn, Eppie becomes the child that animates the village and transforms it into a place with a community culture. Eppie, the stranger at the edge, becomes the light that Leonard Cohen writes about in his song "Anthem," Silas is the crack that lets the light come in, and the wider community comes around them to keep the flame alive. In a sense they are both the hearth of the fireplace and the metaphorical bell that Cohen sings about.

Community Building Principle #3: Effective Community Building Goes at the Speed of Trust

Every human community is made up of people with similar multiple stories to those of Silas Marner's, but community building struggles in the context of closed inward communities, with defined in-groups and out-groups, as much as it does in contexts that are hyper-individualized and consumerist. Hence, for a culture of community to hatch there must be some precipitants, actions or conditions that open up the heart of the place, making the invisible visible and creating a welcome for the outsider. Occasions such as flooding or other natural disasters offer powerful glimpses of community potential, but such upsurges of restorative efforts should not be confused with the birth of a culture of community and inclusion.

Giving life and long-term investment to welcoming and powerful communities calls for a willingness to create permeability in our personal and associational lives and to move beyond monocultures. As with Silas, that takes time. The golden thread that runs through all three stories is how Silas slowly learns a critical life lesson: you can only connect with the experiences in life that truly matter when you willingly travel at the speed of trust. Thought of this way, we can see that the three stories weave together to form a passage through which Silas journeys and learns critical lessons for community building everywhere, including ways to

- build reciprocal relationships;
- connect with supportive associations;
- build life-giving relationships with and within his local economy, and to re-embed the economy into the local community;

- take risks and create a space at the edge of his "almost-closed" world to actively welcome the stranger (Eppie) into his midst, and to celebrate her difference and the diversity she created;

- say to other members of the community, "If I am to raise this child, I need you; I cannot do this without you. It takes a village";

- recover from his addiction to goods and gold by discovering the power of community connection;

- become rooted and invested in the ecosystem—in the environmental and cultural sense of the term—of the place where he and Eppie live; and

- go beyond the victim narrative, with all its helpless/hopeless talk, and retributive pursuits of faux justice, to a restorative sense of self and others.

In short, Silas moves from the victim and consumer narrative to the citizen and contributor narrative. Accordingly, he becomes defined not by what he allegedly has stolen, or what is stolen from him, nor indeed what he amasses or consumes in material terms, but by what he contributes to the well-being of his new community, and to a person closest to its edge.

Liberating a community culture to call these characteristics forth from local citizens takes decades, not years. It goes at a generational speed, not the speed of a funding or an election cycle. Those who think that they can measure the growth of community culture with key performance indicators (KPIs) are as misguided as Silas was when counting his gold in the vain hope that more counting, more measurement would result in a freer life.

We can only hope that those obsessed with measurement and auditing may see that Eppie is on her way, trudging through the snow to remind them that if they are focused on efficiency, measurement, and scale while receiving salaries for building community, they have lost their focus and purpose. Her footsteps toward a citizen-led culture should be treasured, not measured. *Silas Marner* teaches that as trust deepens, a culture of belonging takes root.

The following chapter invites a shift of starting points in community building, from what's wrong to what's strong and from leaders to connectors.

* * *

Community will never be built faster than the speed of trust and will never be stronger than the person who experiences the least sense of belonging. For me that begs the question, Can we create the "Eppie effect" in our neighborhoods? I believe we can, and we will deal with that in a lot more detail in the next couple of chapters.

Chapter 17

Practicing the Art of Connectorship

Starting with What's Strong

> *Did you win? he asks.*
> *It wasn't a match, I say. It was a lesson.*
>
> —CLAUDIA RANKINE

AN ASSET-BASED PERSPECTIVE WORKS from the belief that enduring change only happens from the bottom up; it comes about when local people discover they have invaluable capacities and can create and build power by coming together to enact and embody the common good.

This form of change happens from the inside out. The sequence of such enduring change occurs in this way:

1. The identification, connection, and mobilization of assets that are local and in community control. It means putting authority for the invention and production of solutions in the hands of local people, not outside experts.

2. The process then progresses to focus on resources that are local but outside of community control. Bringing these resources under democratic community influence is made increasingly more possible by starting at point #1 above.

3. Ultimately powerful, inclusive communities can confidently turn their attention toward assets that are outside of community control and proximity when and if they need to. This will not always be easy and hardly ever conflict free. This process enables communities that are often defined as problematic and needy to build civic muscle and the collective authority as citizens to produce their own solutions using

local resources where appropriate, and then to draw in external support as needed.

This sequence, which has been well rehearsed through earlier chapters of this book, ensures that when outside solutions come they match up with the abundance of community, not its scarcity. This takes us to the fourth principle of authentic community building: start with what's strong to address what's wrong.

Community Building Principle #4: Start with What's Strong to Address What's Wrong

A scarcity mindset would have us start—and all too often remain—at the third stage of the sequence described above, with a focus solely on the external. The scarcity perspective would have us believe that the most valuable resources exist outside of our communities, in institutions. This is a half-baked truth, and even if it were completely true, attempting to liberate those external institutional resources without first liberating local capacities nearly always results in top-down, bureaucratic solutions that simply do not work. That is why it is so essential to start with what is strong, not with what is wrong.

Still, the dominant narrative is deficit-oriented and would have us start with what is wrong. This deficit process is questionable and unhelpful at ten separate levels:

1. It maps the territory negatively and then assumes the map is the territory, creating a self-fulfilling prophecy.

2. It fails to get to the root of the problem because it mistakes the symptoms for the cause. It further compounds the problem by confusing human necessities, like the need for a listening ear, with service categories, like professional counseling.

3. It creates a dangerous dichotomy in thinking about people living in economic isolation, where the only options are perverse: economically marginalized people are either (*a*) deviant and in need of surveillance or sanction, or (*b*) deserving of services and programs. Either way they are powerless to produce valid solutions, without first supplicating to outside interventions.

4. It suggests that the best solutions come from outside experts, in a top-down way.

5. It suggests the given problem is persistent, pernicious, permanent, and pervasive. It's part of the "culture" now.

6. Resources largely flow toward funded programs, not to economically marginalized families and communities.

7. People receiving services come to be defined by their deficiencies, not their gifts, skills, and passions, and come to be defined outside of their communities not as friends and neighbors but as clients and needy, isolated service users.

8. Active citizenship retreats in the face of ever-growing professionalism.

9. People come to assume that their associational, economic, cultural, and ecological assets are irrelevant, and eventually come to ignore them completely.

10. Communities internalize the deficit map and come to see themselves as the sum of the problems others have previously defined them by. They collectively come to believe that the only way things will improve is when external agencies come in to make them better.

Starting with what's strong should not blind us to what's wrong. In some of the communities we serve around the world, people are dying prematurely—sometimes twenty years before people who live in neighborhoods only a mile away. Their deaths are not the result of a deficit in their "positive mental attitude," or proof that they need another therapeutic program; they are the consequence of social and economic injustice and inequity. To ignore such realities is quite simply dangerous and feeds directly into the hands of the neoliberal agenda which is in the throes of a very strong comeback in America, the UK, and Brazil, to name just a few global hotspots.

ABCD is not about leapfrogging over what's wrong; starting with what's strong does not mean ignoring people's problems or concerns or skirting around social justice and political issues.

Here is where the nuance comes in, and in a world of sound bites, where you have fifteen seconds to get your message across, nuance is not always welcome. Nevertheless, the choice before communities and practitioners is not a binary one, where the glass is either half full or half empty. It's not about what we ignore and what we acknowledge but about where we choose to start. The logic flows like this: "I know the glass is both half full and half empty, but if I'm going to address the half-empty part, where am I best starting?"

Here the question gets reframed and we beat the binary trap. In this formulation, it's about sequence: We choose to start our efforts toward a solution with a focus on the half-full part of the glass, not as an act of willful blindness toward the half-empty part, but because we have truly looked at the whole glass situation and truly named and claimed the holistic challenge before us.

In this conception of ABCD, there are no parodies, no shortcuts, no tricks. It's about citizens creating an alternative by starting with what they have in their control to get what they want and offering an invitation for outside resources when it is helpful and when they are ready.

This begs another question: Why choose this sequence over the alternative of starting with an external focus?

How to See the Whole Glass

Mindful of the ten reasons why the deficit approach is undesirable, we know that reversing the sequence, starting with a focus on the half-empty part of the glass, results in a willful blindness toward the half-full part of the glass and dependency on external, top-down solutions. ABCD is, therefore, an act of willfully seeing the whole glass, and beyond.

There are three essential pieces in the process of starting with what is strong:

1. Learning conversations that draw out what people care about enough to take action on, as distinct from their opinions about what others should do for them. The key question is, "Are you a citizen, or do you just live here?" In these conversations, people are "heard into expression" around their dreams (what they want to move toward), concerns (what they want to move away from), gifts and talents, political impulses, knowledge, and who and what they'd like to connect to.

2. Once we get a clear picture—through hundreds of one-to-one learning conversations—of the dreams and concerns, we can connect people to each other at an individual and associational level to share their dreams and concerns in small groups of local kitchen-table conversations and move toward shared action.

3. These groups look at their dreams and concerns through the lens of ABCD and ask, "How can we use what's strong to address what's wrong, but also make what's strong, stronger?" As these small groups gather momentum and agency, they are then supported to connect, to figure out what they can do collectively that they cannot do alone.

In this way individual energies get connected, amplified, and multiplied through the building of new associations. Ultimately, over time, an association of associations begins to take shape, using their shared agency to contribute to their community's well-being.

This action is deeply political and not at all aligned to positive psychology. These efforts should be referenced under the Politics, not the Psychology, section of the library. What is distinct from classic Alinsky-style community organizing, which has made a virtue of staying focused on the problem and pointing communities toward external solutions, is that ABCD calls our attention to the internal resources we have as a fresh starting point. This dramatically changes the power orientation. Power is no longer thought of as a finite resource and power struggles as a zero-sum game. Instead, power is considered to be infinite; it grows with every new connection, every new relationship.

Strong communities are those where the skills and talents of residents are known, recognized, and connected. But they are also places where citizens can define their own problems, their own solutions to those problems, and the action they wish to take to make those solutions visible. Quite simply, our lives are full of ups and downs; there is no recipe for infinite happiness, except perhaps to recognize that happiness, like unhappiness, is fleeting. We do, however, experience joy, particularly, as evidence confirms, when leaning into our relationships with others and in contributing to the well-being of our communities.

What I'm suggesting here is that we do not ignore structural inequity, but neither do we ignore our collective capacities and gifts to deal with it—and we try to have fun along the way! To do this, local connectors are a key part of the process.

Community Building Principle #5:
The Vital Role of Connectors

When two assets that are not joined become productively connected, change happens; in fact, this is the smallest unit of change. The function of a local connector is to bring these resources together. Connectors are residents who, unbeknownst to others (and often unbeknownst to themselves), regularly function as the invisible glue of community life. They are not spies for the government or volunteers to be recruited for agency programs; they are good neighbors and friends. Often, calling them "connectors" really turns them off. Another notable feature of how they show up is that, generally, they hate meetings and formalities. If they are in the room, or at the table, it will not be in a formal sense; they'll be in the middle of the crowd, handing out cake, or at the edges, inviting people in. When they are at the center of community action they tend to be occupied in creating a welcome for the people whom most others see as strangers.

Some leaders can be excellent connectors, but in my experience connectors do not tend to relate well to the term "leader." In fact, they tend to react to it in much the same way that someone who's uncomfortable wearing a collar and tie reacts to having to put one on for an interview. "Leader" is a term that feels stuffy and uncomfortable when connectors try it on; descriptions like "pal," "friend," "neighbor," and even—as we'll see in the story to follow—"unsung hero" fit better than "leader." In truth, though, any label is problematic because, in the connector's mind, what they do is not anything special. They came into the world "made this way," and this is how they live and move and have their being.

This conception of what connectors do and how it plays out in practice in a neighborhood context highlights the limits of outside agencies starting their engagements with a neighborhood by inviting "leaders" to a meeting. To do so is to largely miss the connectors, who for the most part are already naturally doing the very thing that creates health, well-being, safety, and prosperity—they won't see much point in going to meetings to talk about it, when they can use that time to just do it. The challenge, then, is not to provide capacity building to leaders but to afford due respect and appreciation to connectors, and then support them at the speed of trust to get more organized with their neighbors if they so choose.

A Story: Hodge Hill, Birmingham, UK

When Rev. Al Barrett, a Church of England priest, arrived in Hodge Hill in Birmingham with his wife and two young children, they came not just to minister to the local congregation of Firs and Bromford but also to take up residence. They moved into their new house on the Hodge Hill Estate, and now, several years on, they continue to live and minister as near neighbors and not as salaried strangers. I suspect that, as they turned the keys in the front door of their new home all those years ago, they opened up the potential that is only available to those outsiders who are prepared to recognize that even though they may never be completely accepted as insiders, they can, through practice, trust, and radical presence, hope to be embraced as "alongsiders"—which is to say, trusted companions who live alongside those they serve as neighbors. Al is an alongsider, and he is fortunate that the Church of England enables him and his family to play that role, economically as well as spiritually.

In the early days of arriving in Hodge Hill, he and a small number of his parishioners/neighbors intentionally began to seek out what they called "unsung heroes." They regularly went to the places and spaces on the estate where people bump into each other or gather formally and informally. By going to these places and regularly showing up as neighbors, they began to learn with their community, not as researchers studying a community, and to build genuine trust. By paying attention and by asking questions, they surfaced many community-building stories that had within them the breadcrumbs that led to ninety-three connectors in a population of nearly five thousand residents. They then sat with and spoke to each of those "unsung heroes," who in effect function as connectors among their neighbors, and shared with them the stories their neighbors had shared about them, stories about the connections their efforts had enabled and the importance of their contributions.

Al and his faith circle also threw a party for their unsung hero neighbors to celebrate all they had done and continue to do to weave their community together. When they invited the unsung heroes to the party they asked them to bring a neighbor along with them, broadening the circle of participation even further. In seeking to discover connectors and weavers in this way, Al and his small congregation actively resisted the temptation to seek out "believers" or convert "nonbelievers." Instead of trying to get local people to be interested in what they prescribed as a good life, Al and members of his congregation set their institutional agendas aside in order to become more genuinely interested in how people grow community in Hodge Hill and how they as neighbors themselves could contribute to the well-being of the whole community. Their theological perspective is that they are not bringing God to the neighborhood but instead are joining God in the neighborhood. They are not combating original sin, they are celebrating original blessing.

From the outset, their great insight was to understand that the people who could help them see most deeply behind the negative narrative that had grown up around the estate were the unsung heroes. We have seen the same phenomenon play out in urban, suburban, and rural communities around the world, with people of faith and people of none. Throughout my travels in neighborhoods worldwide, I have come to appreciate that there are residents in every community of place that embody the functions of a connector.

How Community Connectors Work

A community connector is a local resident who has come to be defined, both by themselves and others, more by what they contribute to the well-being of their community than by what they receive from the marketplace. They are good at discovering what their neighbors care about enough to act upon, and they know how to connect them with other residents and local resources. They are not single-issue people, although they have their pet projects and personal passions; they are more driven by the desire to create a culture of community, what they most likely would refer to as "community spirit."

Connectors are not superheroes, nor should we expect them to be. Still, there is huge power in connectors joining together; indeed, when a group of connectors who reflect the broad diversity of a neighborhood band together, they can move mountains. Here is an overview of the combined gifts, skills, knowledge, and passions that you might expect to find in an association of connectors; they are:

- *Gift centered:*They believe everyone has a gift, skill, or passion that is essential to building community spirit. As far as they are concerned, there is no one's gift that is surplus to requirement.

- *Well connected*: Their relationships are deep and wide and diverse. Their relationships are mostly reciprocal, and are not exclusively reliant on the connector. Connectors will have scores of connections to neighbors in their neighborhood.

- *Trusted*: They are trusted because they build relationships at the speed of trust.

- *Comfortable reaching out*: They believe they are welcome. In a hyper-individualistic, consumerist society, it's striking how insecure people often feel about reaching out to neighbors they have not been introduced to or to whom they can't introduce themselves formally. Informal, unscripted conversations come naturally to connectors; they feel welcome to reach out to their neighbors and to help them connect with each other.

- *Hosts*: They are naturals at the art of hosting. And when at parties organized by others, they arrive early to help, stay late, and hang around the edges, helping people who are not sure they are welcome to find a way in.

- *Welcomers*: They are bridgers to the stranger at the edge. They are skilled at brokering people who are at the edge into associational life. Connectors will actively stake their social capital on the virtue of welcoming the stranger and their gifts into the fold of a club or group they personally know already. In this way, they are the practical architects of social inclusion, and while they rarely talk about it in such terms, they make it visible by the way they live their lives.

- *In the background*: Connectors delight in stepping back. They tend to feel powerful, having a sense of contribution in the world, when people who were disconnected become connected and form reciprocal relationships. That sense of contribution grows as those connections deepen and the associations spread.

  They experience a certain glee in hearing how two neighbors who hadn't known each other got connected and then went on to do something together and with others. In other words, connectors are comfortable with people getting on and connecting behind their backs; they don't need to claim kudos for having created the conditions that made that new relationship possible.

This list of characteristics does not seek to describe any single connector; instead, it is an overview of what you might expect to encounter among a wider group of connectors in a neighborhood context. Be on the lookout. Authentic community building depends on the power of your local connectors, and often it takes one to know one.

The following chapter concludes this section of the book on the practical application of asset-based community development approaches in a community context by considering the issue of scale and the importance of maintaining a cultural orientation.

* * *

The glee connectors experience when people act together is grounded in joy at the idea that a culture of community is taking hold. There is no apparent need to objectify or control their relationships with or between neighbors; therefore, they grow their power by giving it away. Connectors are naturally possessed by what the humanistic psychologist Carl Rogers referred to as *unconditional positive regard* and they have the added advantage of not coming to fix, cure, or rescue. They came into the world ready to start with what's strong and have continued unencumbered. The necessity of starting with what is strong, not wrong, cannot be left to connectors alone; organizational leaders, colleagues, friends, family, and neigbors all have a critical role to play in creating this shift from scarcity thinking to abundance.

Chapter 18

Thinking Small

Animating Community at the Human Scale

Notice the small things. The rewards are inversely proportional.

—LIZ VASSEY

IN HIS ESSAY "CONTEMPT for Small Places," Wendell Berry—the world's foremost authority on the question of thresholds before which we can be in deep relatedness with each other and nature—reflects that:

> The health of the oceans depends on the health of rivers; the health of rivers depends on the health of small streams; the health of small streams depends on the health of their watersheds. The health of the water is exactly the same as the health of the land; the health of small places is exactly the same as the health of large places . . .
>
> We cannot immunize the continents and the oceans against our contempt for small places and small streams. Small destructions add up, and finally they are understood collectively as large destructions.

Berry's insight is that small places are interconnected not just to the elements of that place but to the world. Even though we tend to think of community in terms of small places—the neighborhood, the congregation, the association—the word "community" has a vast array of definitions, so much so that it has come to mean whatever any given person says it means. When there's no agreed-upon meaning, definitions become arbitrary. Still, the lack of a standard definition does not mean the word "community" is meaningless. Quite the contrary; in fact, it is so brimming with meaning that each of us must make sense of what it means to us. It is easier to make meaning of the term "community" when we think of it as a verb instead of a noun. A noun identifies a class of people, places, and things—hence most people would think of a community in these terms. Yet when we think of community as something we do—as an experience we act into, so much so that when we describe such experiences we use a grammar that leads us to speak in terms of "doing community together," rather than simply speaking of community as a static thing or set of people—a wider vista comes into view.

What if instead of asking, "What is community?" we asked, "Where is community alive for you?" No doubt answers would still vary widely and remain largely subjective, but certainly many of the answers would have a postal code; the stage on which they play out would be a physical place: a town, a block, a neighborhood, a subdivision, a village. This meaning doesn't preclude other contexts within which community finds expression, or the fact that community can be located in different places for different people at different times and life stages; it simply makes clear the relevance and value of place in rooting the experience of community for many people.

Learning about small places in urban and rural contexts provides us with a fascinating view on the world. You get to see so many interactions between citizens, their associations, local economies, and cultural life, all of which in turn are in relationship with the built environment and the local ecology, and so many of those relationships in turn reach beyond the boundaries of local places to the wider world, through online and on-land connections. Still, the place to start for the most part is quite small and hyper-local.

Community Building Principle #6: The Optimum Population Size of a Neighborhood Is 3000–5000 Residents

The benefit of working with people in small local communities—aside from the cultural, economic, and ecological potential they offer—is found in the size itself. If your primary interest is in supporting people to act powerfully together in a way that's good for them, their neighbors (especially those who have been relegated to the position of "the stranger"), and the planet, it is an ideal scale.

There are many reasons that working at a small scale holds such promise; for example:

1. Most people will mobilize around the things they care about and feel they can influence. People are more likely to act together on issues that are close to their own doorsteps and that affect them and their neighbors.

2. The small place, even when contested, offers a common focal point.

3. The hyper-local scale makes identifying, connecting, and mobilizing local assets more achievable than, for example, a city-wide scale.

4. The small local place ups the potential for relationships with near neighbors to form, at the bus stop and other bumping places and gathering spaces.

5. The neighborhood or small town can become the shared unit of change—it is "everybody's baby"—so that agencies and communities can work together on a common concern and get clear about who does what best. This helps agencies get out of their silos by agreeing on the neighborhood as a primary unit of change.

Small Is Beautiful and Essential

Small local places are not the same as political or administrative boundaries; they are typically defined in a million informal ways by the people who live there. Consider the typical answers to questions such as these:

- Where are you from?
- Where do you reside?
- What lends to the livability of this place?
- At what scale would you feel confident you could make a contribution to the well-being of your neighbors?

The answers for the most part are small, local, and personal. That scale can vary but my experience is that there is a threshold or a tipping point between three thousand and five thousand people, and once you get beyond five thousand it really starts to get much more challenging to support residents to build community from the inside out. Size matters.

Wendell Berry (2005) puts the small-is-beautiful narrative into a more global, modern context when he says,

> "Every man for himself" is a doctrine for a feeding frenzy or for a panic in a burning nightclub, appropriate for sharks or hogs or perhaps a cascade of lemmings. A society wishing to endure must speak the language of care-taking, faith-keeping, kindness, neighborliness, and peace. That language is another precious resource that cannot be "privatized."

That quote is a great reminder that if we are going to save our planet from impending ecocide, then a vital starting point is in collective action at the neighborhood level. And that is the point of the final community-building principle.

Community Building Principle #7: The Focus Is on Growing a Culture of Community, Not Converting People to Asset-based Community Development (ABCD)

For me, the central value of approaches like ABCD is that their founders and stewards do not pretend that they offer a panacea. Furthermore, they refuse to allow such approaches to be characterized as models. Instead, they continually invite us to ask of each other and our neighbors, "What's best for this place and this place in particular?"

Throughout John McKnight's and Jody Kretzmann's careers, spanning the last six decades, their primary focus has remained on the emergence of hospitable communities, not on the growth of ABCD. I suspect that, somewhat ironically, that is why ABCD has spread so far and wide across the globe. The ability to strike a balance between the structures needed to maintain an identity and a real presence in the world, and the informality needed to build trusting relationships that enable us to be truly present to local people and practitioners, will remain a central challenge for the future of ABCD efforts. If John and Jody's example is to be followed and the ethics and ethos of the ABCD approach are to be maintained, we will need to have the confidence to affirm the virtue of the ABCD approach while simultaneously having the humility to emphasize the greater importance of growing a culture of community wherever we are. Principle # 7 asserts the importance of not prescribing ABCD as the cure for modern social or political ills but instead using it as a lens and a set of practices through and by which to open our eyes to what's present and what's possible in local neighborhoods.

Most would agree that movements like the slow food movement are living expressions of ABCD, though I hazard to guess that the majority of people within such movements have never heard of it. Still, this should not be a cause for concern for those who are ABCD enthusiasts since our shared objective is not to convert people to ABCD but to support them to reseed and enlarge associational life and free space for civic action.

From Neighborhood to Community

ABCD is not a model; it is a description of how a neighborhood becomes a community. It is essentially a description of how people generally come together to grow power and be in right relationships with each other, their culture, ecology, and local economies.

It is a means toward such deep community because it provides us with a positive description of how others have previously engaged in building their own communities and how savvy practitioners have supported them.

Nevertheless, ABCD should not be thought of as an end in itself. Caution is in order because in a consumer society, obsessed with programs and models, outcomes and targets, it is easy to inadvertently turn approaches like asset-based community development into sacred cows to be worshiped in their own right. My experience is that, in the long run, this is to be guarded against, since to do so is to risk alienating local folk who have worked hard to build their community long before ABCD came on the scene.

ABCD is a means to an alternative future, not an end in itself. Collectively producing an alternative future requires collective commitment to create the conditions for a culture of community to flourish; the efforts of a heroic few will never be sufficient. Hence, that commitment is not the same as the aggregation of a multitude of individuals who make a personal commitment to be kind toward each other. Creating a culture of community is not therefore the net result of what numerous individuals do for each other through random acts of kindness (although they help), but through the capacity of the collective to call kindness forth as "our way" around here.

Here is an example of what I mean: last November, when I was in the Austin area of Chicago, I overheard a local resident say to a kid who had wolf-whistled at a lady across the street, "We don't treat women that way 'round here. Real men don't intimidate women. This ain't a jungle. You're a good kid, don't do that. She's someone's mama, and you'd beat on someone if they did that to yours."

And that was that. The gentleman who spoke to the kid had a powerful public voice and a real physical presence. The kid heard him but wasn't afraid of him. This man called forth respect from this young person on behalf of the community. It was not a random act of kindness; it was an intentional lesson from an elder to a youngster about the ways of the village. This elder was not threatening toward the kid; he didn't use his physicality, nor was he insinuating that he'd report the boy to the authorities. Instead, what this community elder did was invoke the local culture as the authority, because he understood the meaning of the adage "It takes a village to raise a child."

In a hyper-individualistic society, it's hard to find many similar cultural expressions to match this one, though they are there if we search hard enough, but the results of their absence are evident everywhere: gang violence, endemic loneliness, atomized communities, neglect of local ecological systems, economic disinvestment, falling property prices.

The story about the wolf-whistling kid is a subplot of the story of the Westside Health Authority, a community-driven effort by residents to make every block in Austin, Chicago, a village to take back authority for their health and raising their children. This effort is the opposite of what happens in a shame-based culture where children are punished and repressed.

Shame-based cultures demand conformity; if you don't conform you're ostra-cized, made an outlaw (outside the protection of the community).

The Westside Health Authority welcomes the stranger at the edge of their community; it encourages diversity, decency, and difference but also affirms the need for a culture that says, "Let's join your uniqueness into our local way so that you can enrich it and it can enrich you." The enrichment process means change is endless, but because it is cocreated, it evolves into a deeper, more inclusive culture while maintaining its core, so that everyone of every age group can feel an affinity toward "it" and feel related to "it," since they are "it." They can proudly affirm, "We made this, and we remake it every day. Come join us, we need your gifts."

In times past, shame cultures had the power to label certain members and push them to the edge. Isolated from their kin and communities, those who were marginalized were forced to find new affinity groups, often among others who like them were rejected. In this way, certain closed and cloistered communities have become architects of their own destruction; by rejecting difference they commenced a war of attrition against their way of life. Com-munities can only flourish when they learn to create a culture of welcome at the edge of their established customs, traditions, norms, and mores and establish explicit practices, rituals of inclusion, and a place of hospitality for the stranger—for example, the Quaker tradition of keeping an empty chair for the stranger at the family dinner table during their Sunday meal.

That culture of welcome must accept both the fallibilities and the gifts of the stranger. Equally important is the willingness of existing com-munities to accept each other's fallibilities. It's through the door of human fallibility that possibility enters; it's through the door of capacities and cul-tural, ecological, and other shareable assets that possibility finds actionable expression and becomes a gift to others—but only when the gift is received. Hence the great possibility the world offers us is in the exchange of gifts and not in personal development or behavioral change. Those exchanges can only flourish and prevail in a culture of community.

Small is beautiful and optimal from the point of view of reseeding as-sociational life, but can such small-scale, soft-power, hyperlocal approaches speak to the broader structural issues that press down on economically ex-ploited communities? It is to that question we now turn.

* * *

In the final analysis, the community-building processes described over the previous four chapters are a restorative and generative act, which could as easily be described by many other terms. The approach also expresses an anticolonial stance, since while colonialism destroys local culture, community building seeks to honor it. The process of supporting the restoration of local culture starts with an invitation to residents to appreciate their existing culture as they journey toward cocreating a more current and inclusive expression. The message must be "growing a culture of community matters," not "please convert to the ABCD way." The method should never be the message, nor should it ever do anything to eclipse the message. We want to cheer on community weavers, not convert more ABCD believers.

Part Six: Connecting Community and State

The effective state recognizes that civil society does not in fact expand commensurate with the number of citizens' needs addressed by the state, but to the extent that people's assets are connected and expressed in free space.

Chapter 19

Widening Our Sphere of Influence

Enacting Democracy with a Whisper

> *There is no such thing as a single-issue struggle*
> *because we do not live single-issue lives.*
>
> —AUDRE LORDE

WHAT HAPPENS WHEN CITIZENS, families, and commuities stop performing community functions as a consequence of being colonized by top-down institutional ways? The answer, I believe, is that community culture collapses. It is said in psychological circles that a mother is never happier than her most unhappy child. If that is true, it must also be true that a village is never happier than its most unhappy resident. A village without a community culture is a sick place. One can never be well in a sick village. So, at the root of many of our social maladies is the "village problem." The remedy for this is (largely though not exclusively) collective civic action embedded within a citizen-centered democracy—the application of civic muscle in the stewardship of abundant communities.

However, in the same way that a muscle atrophies from lack of use, so too do the health-, wealth-, and wisdom-producing capacities of a community—when their collective influence is not brought to bear on the thirteen irreplaceable cultural functions of community and civic life introduced in chapter 1. At its extreme, muscle atrophy can bring about heart failure. In the same way, cultural atrophy can bring about a sort of social heart failure. The symptoms include economic, environmental, and political malaise, enveloped within which are the roots of gang activity, drug trafficking, failing schools, loneliness, and a myriad of other health, socioeconomic, and political issues. Put more plainly, the root cause of most of our social problems is social fragmentation.

These problems become further compounded when professional help-ers mistake the symptoms for the cause and use the existence of such symp-toms to validate their interventions and the growth of their systems. With that in mind, isn't it odd that every institutional needs analysis concludes that what the people who are being analyzed need are the services of those who are analyzing them?

This helps explain why so many citizens who are uncredentialed by vested institutional authority believe that the only way things will get bet-ter is if an outside expert comes in to make them so. No one is immune to the allure of this modern-day bewitching, so it is not surprising—given that our assets lie hidden behind such colonial ideologies as consumerism, managerialism, and globalization—that so many people see the solutions to life's challenges as being wholly external to them and their communi-ties. This is why so many of us find it so hard to believe that our econo-mies, ecologies, and even our health and well-being are within our own sphere of influence.

We doubt our nonprofessionalized selves and our unaccredited neigh-bors; we doubt our potential power, and we shudder at the prospect that we might be the "cause" of democracy, not the "effect." Our service economies apply the ointment to that doubt, with the perversely reassuring professional words "Don't worry, you'll get better if you accept that I know better." From fiscal banks to food banks we are clients—needy, passive recipients.

Our rights are defined exclusively by what we receive, with little men-tion of what we have a right to produce and cocreate. This clientelistic mindset is grounded in an ideology that views economically marginalized and labeled people as non-producing and frames justice solely in terms of the service and programmatic idiom, in place of income, choice, control, and community.

The Politics of Small Things

The scarcity ideology at the heart of the economic global system—which in turn drives our service economies—goes unnoticed for the most part, as do its consequences. After all, as French philosopher Louis Althusser notes, "Ideology can perform its function only if it is not recognized as ideology; if it is recognized as the way things have to be" (1966).

Yet there have been moments in history—if only for a moment in his-tory—when the institutional world and its service/programmatic idiom has been constricted and consequently recoiled out of civic space long enough to show just how sophisticated the "demos" can be. Consider the civil rights movement in the United States at key stages throughout the sixties; the

Solidarity movement in Poland in the eighties; the citizen response movements in Christchurch, New Zealand, following the earthquake in 2011; the emergence of the Solidarity Campaign in Greece. Indeed, with regard to Greece, after seven years of obscene austerity measures, the July 2015 referendum put it up to the Troika as never before but also illustrated in undeniable terms the sophisticated capacity of citizens to engage in deliberative democracy, if not also the limits of the established political systems to hear them, despite all their promises to do so.

These are, of course, just some of the many examples of "the politics of small things" at play (Goldfarb, 2007). Less well known, but no less important, are the countless imperceptible moments of civic action and mutuality that see people step over such ideologies into self-determination through civic deliberation.

Moments like this occurred in Bristol, UK, where Lucy Reeves initiated Window Wanderland, a project that connected thousands of people across the city. Or consider the civic work that is underway in Hackney, London, where local residents are intentionally acting as civic doulas in the changing life of their streets. Or Damian Carter's journey in getting to know forty-five hundred of his neighbors by their first names and their key passion for where they live.[1] Thousands of similar experiences occur every day around the globe.

All of these undertakings belie the assumption that change happens with a big bang and is swiftly signed into law across the cabinet table. In truth, as Goldfarb notes in *The Politics of Small Things*, more often than not it happens in whispers, across a million kitchen tables, where people feel free to deliberate, disagree, and still break bread together.

In a world that has become schooled in the value of professionalization and massification, these are significant moments in time, when people act as if they can be the primary shapers of their world and prove themselves right in the act of doing so. These are moments when the prevailing map goes up in smoke and the territory starkly reveals the truth, or at least as valid a version of the truth as any other. If anything of enduring worth is to rise up from these ashes (and assets!), it will be as a result of our collective efforts at the local level. That is precisely what happened in the US, Poland, and hundreds of other jurisdictions around the world, if only for a moment in history and her story.

1. You can learn more about Lucy Reeves and the Window Wanderland by visiting this website: http://www.windowwanderland.com/. Learn more about Hackney's "civic doulas" in this BBC documentary: http://www.bbc.co.uk/programmes/po2vyxqc. Damian Carter describes his work in this video: https://www.youtube.com/watch?v=oOMD8PnSi8E.

Outsourcing to Serviceland

Franz Kafka, the Czech writer and public intellectual, cautions that "every revolution evaporates and leaves behind only the slime of a new bureaucracy" (Janouch and Rees, 1971). Our industrial systems, even those that emerge following a popular revolt, for the most part assume that socioeconomic problems and societal breakdown in families and communities, especially in economically marginalized neighborhoods, are the net result of a deficiency of one kind or another within such people and their "sub-culture." This in turn "proves" the need for more technocratic services, either to police them or to rescue them, or so the popular argument goes.

In actuality, societal breakdown is not the result of deficiencies within the human condition. Rather, it is the result of the incessant attempts by elites to outmaneuver (manage) the limits of our human and ecological reality through unfettered corporate expansionism, managerialism, aggressive technological developments, and the commodification of human care. That way, we can engage in unlimited growth and wealth creation and consume more stuff. The price is personal and collective dissatisfaction, loss of economic sovereignty, and the degradation of our ecologies and indigenous cultures. When people lose the sense of their indigenous capacity (the thirteen functions of community-powered change), they become cannon fodder for the disembedded marketplace. What was once done by communities is now outsourced to Serviceland.

Contrary to what we may have been schooled to believe, rediscovering our basic familial and civic functions is therefore more pressing than addressing our basic needs, since, ironically, performing our basic civic functions provides us with the purpose through which we can find the resilience to address our basic needs, which in fact are human necessities. And where our assets are insufficient to the task of addressing our neccessities, we can ensure that when we leverage in outside assistance we do not pay for it with our dignity, indigenous culture, and collective capacities.

I fully appreciate that the implication of all of the above runs contrary to the general view that things improve when our institutional systems and their leaders get their act together. Nevertheless, if we wait for our systems to reform and our leaders to redeem themselves before we act, then nothing will change. We are our best hope for the future, but only if we can learn to act powerfully together and become its fruitful producers.

Flipping the Switch

The brilliant social and political thinker Hannah Arendt, in exploring the relationship between power and violence, believed contrary to Mao Zedong that power does not come "out of the barrel of a gun" (1972). For her, power and violence are distinct; indeed, violence erupts in the absence of real power. Power for Arendt emerges as a consequence of communities of consenting citizens acting in concert: power is consent in concert. In modern lingo, we might say that what she was describing were nonhierarchical networks, flat organic systems, operating according to the rules of the commons, hence functioning as social movements. In any case, they stand in contrast to institutional structures that are for the most part encased within a hierarchical exoskeleton, where the few control the many in the name of standardized production of goods and services.

Our systems are not designed to produce health, well-being, safety, prosperity, and so on, certainly not unilaterally, and certainly not to produce the quotients that communities are best placed to provide. Put simply, in every indigenous community there are irreplaceable health-, safety-, and prosperity-producing capacities that are at least as sophisticated, if not more so, than any institutional proxy. Think breast milk versus formula milk, as previously discussed; think functioning twelve-step Alcoholics Anonymous (AA) groups versus pharmacological interventions; think Toastmasters versus professional coaching in public speaking.

Here's the rub: the institutional world has a switch that can go from "advance" to "retreat." Most institutions, whether for profit or not for profit, governmental or nongovernmental, are stuck in the "advance" mode. When they see a supposed need they don't ask, "Can this be addressed at the local level?" and "How might we support such a process?" They simply advance to address the need. They then compound the situation because while in advance mode they seek not to find viable solutions to the problem they are addressing, but rather to advance their own growth and progress.

This is the way most institutions sustain the very problems they believe they are solving.

The overall solution, however, is not to flip the switch to "retreat" mode, as that would just trigger a whole set of different moral dilemmas. Rather, the challenge is to figure out how the system can loosen up and switch between modes to allow for proportionate responses to given situations. The only way this can work is if citizens have the power to govern in a participatory and not just a representative sense; in other words, it requires us to create a citizen-centered democracy.

There will be times when in a citizen-centered democracy the demos will want big government, be that to face down the Troika in Greece or the banks in Iceland. And there will be times when we want government to be more facilitative, to lead by stepping back. And so, a citizen-centered democracy cannot therefore be built on Big Society, or Big Government, any more than it can be built on small society, or small government. It must be built on proportionality between community and the state, in right relationship to the given situation, and that can only happen when it is citizen led.

Social movements—indeed, any community-led change—while often surprising are not without their touchstones. An obvious one is that social movements have "swing." *Swing* is a jazz term that denotes a kind of spontaneity the likes of which you'd experience during a jam session between musicians. Orchestras don't swing; the fact that they are led from the front, orchestrated top down, and organized into different sections (woodwinds, brass, percussion, strings) militates against their having swing. Swing is what happens at three o'clock in the morning, when five enthusiasts without sheet music join their musical gifts in an impromptu session that creates something timeless yet fresh and new. Democracy needs more swing, not more orchestration. With that in mind, it is worth listening for the rumors as to where the next democratic jam is likely to pop up and joining in.

The next chapter considers the delicate interface between creating the conditions for pop-up democracy and the virtues of some things being a little more intentional in organizing to build civic power.

* * *

All of this reminds me of a story I heard in South Africa about Carl Jung, the neo-Freudian psychoanalyst. (I've subsequently tried to find a reference but have failed, so I can't attest to its veracity.) The story goes that Jung was traveling in South Africa, where he met a Zulu elder. Not surprisingly, Jung began a discussion about dreams and was pleased to find the elder very engaged. Jung remarked that in his experience there are typically two categories of dreams: the more banal ones are concerned with day-to-day living; and then there are those that relate to visions, dreams of the future, of higher meaning, and so forth. Jung chanced to say that he thought perhaps people in the West are more caught up with the first type, and that perhaps people of Africa were more inclined toward the latter sort of dreaming.

To his surprise the Zulu elder said, "Yes, I have those kinds of banal dreams regularly, just as you do, and yes, we once also had great dreams of meaning and purpose, dreams where we were the producers of our own future. But now, sadly, the district commissioner has them for us."

Chapter 20

The Tools for Social Change

Growing an Association of Associations

You received gifts from me; they were accepted.
But you don't understand how to think about the dead.
The smell of winter apples, of hoarfrost, and of linen.
There are nothing but gifts on this poor, poor Earth.

—Czesław Miłosz

Sustainable social change emerges through a web of seemingly dis-connected whispers, which in fact are imperceptibly connected in countless complex ways. It is these whispers that are the enactment of democracy. Connections, networks, associations, and social movements—those that actively include those who are at the edge of their networks and endure over time—are decidedly different in purpose and function from hierarchal systems in how they distribute power and bring about change.

So, in a topsy-turvy world like ours, where institutions dominate over networks, how can we possibly enact a citizen-centered democracy? Well, to start, we need to become much clearer about the tools for social change we have at our disposal and what it is these tools can and cannot do. To paraphrase Ivan Illich, all progress is contingent on understanding institutional limits (1971).

Curiously, across the right-left political spectrum, there are two points of agreement, both of which constitute fundamental bottlenecks for the growth of citizen-centered democracy:

- The right and left share the belief that a good life is primarily con-tingent on individuals receiving the right amount of services. They simply disagree on the amount, who should deliver, and who should pick up the tab.

- As noted previously, the right and the left are as one in the belief that economically marginalized people cannot self-determine their own futures. They simply disagree on the reason why and what corrective or palliative interventions are required to improve matters. One considers "poverty" to be the consequence of laziness, while the other thinks it's the failure to effectively rescue vulnerable/needy people.

So, when it comes to the provision of services, programs, and interventions, there is utter unanimity across the political spectrum. After all, who would dare to argue against the equation that more professionally run, better services—as long as they are run cost effectively—equal a better, more just society for all? To make such an argument would be tantamount to heresy and would certainly earn you the ire of the liberal left, who would cast you as a neoliberal. Even the right would raise an eyebrow, wondering whether you were an anarchist or some other such odd creature.

Notwithstanding, I've argued throughout this book that the ubiquitous assumption that services can unilaterally make for better lives is scientifically flawed. In his paper "Regenerating Community: The Recovery of a Space for Citizens," John McKnight recounts the early efforts of the Center for Urban Affairs to understand how urban communities generally get healthier and better. He and his colleagues came to understand that starting with a focus on institutional reform was unscientific, since the determinants of health are primarily social, not institutional. He recalls the moment of insight when the faculty of the Center for Urban Affairs realized they had been caught in the "institutional assumption." They were first challenged around this assumption by Dr. Robert Mendelsohn, the medical heretic profiled in chapter 9:

> He joined our seminar and quickly learned of our commitment to health through institutional reform of medical systems and hospitals. He reacted with amazement at our institutional focus and said it was unscientific. The great preponderance of the scientific evidence, he explained, indicated that the critical determinants of health were not medical systems or access to them. Therefore, he said, our primary focus on medical system reform was a misguided effort if we were concerned about the health of neighborhood residents. Indeed, he said, we were caught in the "institutional assumption"—the idea that health was produced by hospitals, doctors, and medical systems.

We quickly checked the epidemiological literature and found near unanimity among health researchers supporting Dr. Mendelsohn's claim. It was clear from this research that the four primary determinants of health were individual behavior, social relationships, the physical environment, and economic status. Access to medical systems was not even in the scientific list of primary health determinants. Nor did medical systems have much potential to affect basic health determinants. So we would have to do our analyses and research outside of medical systems if we were to join in serious efforts to change individual behavior, social relationships, and the physical and economic environments that determined health.

This faculty experience led some of us to adopt a new intellectual focus, and that group became the Community Studies Program. We agreed that we should *not* begin with the "institutional assumption" that held that hospitals produced health, schools produced wisdom, legal systems created justice, social service systems produced social well-being, etc. Instead, we decided to initially focus on the positive conditions of a good life: health, wisdom, justice, community, knowledge, and economic well-being. We decided to examine the scientific evidence regarding the critical determinants of each of *these* conditions.

Once we began this new exploration of the determinants of well-being, we found that the health example was a "generalizable" model. There was clear evidence that school is not the primary source of wisdom or knowledge; social service systems are not major factors in community social well-being; and clearly, criminal justice systems and lawyers are not the primary determinants of safety or justice. In each area, the evidence pointed us in other directions as we focused on the basic determinants of community well-being.

Our inquiry then began anew, and we gathered evidence regarding the primary determinants of well-being in urban neighborhoods. (McKnight, 2003)

This is not an ideological stance; it's a scientific one. Attempting to address health, social care, and so forth within the grasp of the "institutional assumption" is doomed to have little to no effect on the things that primarily determine better outcomes in people's lives, such as income, choice, control, and community connections.

As Jerome Miller so ably demonstrated in the "Massachusetts experiment" (chapter 10), institutional reform will only ensure that "the institution" does a better job of providing services and programs, as well as framing policies and legislation that govern these outputs—since the function of institutions is limited to the production of standardized goods and services. Institutions do not care. People do. And care and human connection is the root solution to most of our health and social care challenges.

The Heart of the Democratic Challenge

Yet the notion that institutions can unilaterally produce and provide care, wisdom, justice, health, and well-being is all-pervasive in academia and policymaking, among practitioners and indeed among citizens in general. This notion is the net result of a democracy that is institutionally or technocratically centered. In this paradigm, democracy is therefore defined in terms of consumer rights, not active citizenship. Sadly, the right to vote, the right to a service, and so on, while centrally important, are hollow victories on their own.

In a democracy, as well as having consumer rights, we also require the rights of citizenship to sit alongside our rights to services and ameliorative interventions. The essential freedom at the heart of all these rights is the right of a citizen to be a producer of the future and to participate in all aspects of civic and relevant commercial life. A consumer casts a vote as an act of delegating their civic work to another. A citizen exercises their democratic franchise so that institutional functions can be created to support citizen-led invention and also to create protections for those whose gifts would be otherwise overlooked or oppressed. They vote for a life of free expression and free association for all. Services are in the mix, but they are not the primary goal; rather, they are there in reserve when needed. After security, the primary goals of citizenship are income, choice, inclusion, and community. And all of these must be grounded in principles of social justice.

The main assertion of this section is that in a citizen-centered democracy there are two tools available with which to create change. One is civic inventiveness; the other is institutional capacity. Both have their place and also their limitations. The genuine radical never allows the misguided assumptions of their chosen ideologies to blind them to the root of any given problem. Hence, in their hunt for hope and deeper democracy, they don't settle simply for the reform of institutional systems. Instead, they seek the power to redefine institutional functions and the relocation of authority from institutional systems to citizens and their associations. Why? Because they understand that at the heart of the democratic challenge is the reduction of institutionalization in favor of increasing interdependency in community life.

In an institutional-centric democracy we can only ever hope to secure the power to codesign policies, services, and programs—and even then, at best, we can only aspire to be satisfied consumers. In this version of democracy, when people have insufficient income, choice, control, and community, they become service users by default. In contrast, within a citizen-centered democracy that is not de facto caught in the grasp of the "institutional assumption," the primary pursuit is not consumer satisfaction (though that is an important goal) but a dignified income, one that is sufficient to weather the frigid and unforgiving winds of the predatory economy. Democracy then is the place where citizenship prevails despite an economy that has become dislocated from society, not because of it.

All this describes the molecular structure of citizen-centered democracy and offers a contrast with the molecular nature of the government-centric versions that are currently universally supported by the establishment. What it does not do is articulate the atomic elements of the citizen-centered version. So, let's drill down yet further: What are the atomic elements of a deeper version of democracy?

Well, if the evidence tells us that the primary determinants of well-being, justice, prosperity, and wisdom are contingent on our community assets and not our consumer-based capacities to access services, then the logical place to start is in the world of local noncontractual connections, not the institutional one.

The Power of Place

Places where people can associate close to their own doorsteps offer significant untapped potential for interdependent connections that are of consequence in the areas of health, well-being, justice, prosperity, and wisdom. Not just interpersonally but also associationally; not just based on single-item issues but around a diversity of concerns and possibilities; not just around affinity or age but across the life course and across a wide spectrum of political and local opinion. We find all those ingredients both nascent and active in communities of place—what I have described throughout this book as neighborhoods.

We rarely see the power of place, and rarer still is the opportunity to compare that power with the competency of institutions to address social justice issues. But a classic example of what can happen when people collectively take action to include those who traditionally have been marginalized is to be found in ethnographer Nora Groce's study of Martha's Vineyard, *Everyone Here Spoke Sign Language: Hereditary Deafness on Martha's Vineyard* (1985).

At the time of her writing, the rate of deafness in the United States was 1 in 2,730, or 0.04 percent of the population. Groce estimated that at the end of the nineteenth century 1 in 155 people living on Martha's Vineyard were born deaf (0.7 percent), more than twenty times the national average. High rates of hereditary deafness on the island had been evident for more than two centuries, and many of the inhabitants had come originally from the Weald, on the borders of Kent and Sussex in the UK, but no direct link between these two facts has been established.

Groce noted that for a sustained period all members of the community were bilingual and that the town of Chilmark had managed to dissolve the traditional social barriers that many deaf people experience. She tells us that not only did the deaf people in the Vineyard adapt but that the hearing people adapted to life with deaf people. Consequently, people in this small community were not categorized by whether or not they could hear but instead by the person they were and what they could contribute. In effect everyone was heard and could express themselves equally and associate freely.

By comparing her findings to the experiences of deaf people across the United States, Groce demonstrated that deafness is not a disability but a different way of communicating. On Martha's Vineyard, deaf people lived their lives just as easily and as fully as everyone else in town because for an extended period of time everybody on the island spoke sign language. They were defined neither as people with disabilities nor as disabled people, but as fellow citizens. Groce's work introduced an empirical case study to a discussion that had previously been mired in ideological rhetoric and established that disability is primarily "defined by the community in which it appears" (Groce, 1985).

Across all major health and well-being indicators, deaf people did as well or better than their hearing neighbors on the island. The findings of the study also demonstrate the stark contrast in health and well-being outcomes for deaf people across mainland America and those resident on Martha's Vineyard.

Were these folks neoliberals? Were they letting agencies off the hook for the provision of services to deaf people? Or did they understand that part of their function in life was to foster a culture of inclusive community?

Beyond globalism and massification, the absence of a coherent political narrative that transcends partisanship and places citizens at the center of democracy is the single biggest threat to our futures and the planet. It is clear, following what happened in Greece in July 2015, that political and intellectual elites cannot or will not—you decide—do this for us. We must therefore reflect on how we can mobilize the base at the grassroots level.

How can we start a positive, constructive whisper campaign that spreads the audacious message that in a democracy, citizens are at the center as the primary inventors and producers of the future? While we may consume services in a democracy, as distinct from a marketplace, we own the shop. We are the golfers; politicians and those paid to serve us are the caddies. That the opposite is currently the case is not a result of the right-left schism. It is the consequence of an ever-growing divide between hometown people and the governments that are elected to serve them. Elitism and technocracy have all too often replaced civic professionalism and servanthood. It is a stain on the democratic ideal for which both ideologies must be equally held to account.

Communities are all at once both profoundly resilient and fragile. When the agencies that are meant to serve them pull out and refuse to fulfill their mandate or mission they do untold harm. But, equally, when they provide top-down bureaucratic services that diminish or demean community capacity they do as much harm, if not more. Sometimes helping hurts as much as abandonment. The role of government and its agents—indeed, the role of all helping agencies—is one of service, not to be confused with service provision. Being of service in a democracy involves supporting community-driven invention, not replacing it.

For example, when we enter communities as outsiders, we should do so by invitation and without an overbearing agenda. As a "helper," when you enter a community with a defined development agenda like "health," then your methodology clearly is not citizen-driven or asset-based. However, when you enter a community with a commitment to support local residents to make the invisible visible, you discover a significant untapped reservoir of human and associational potential just waiting to be identified, connected, and mobilized by the residents of that place (Figure 20.1). After all, in doing most of what people do to maintain their health, like walking, joining clubs, and so forth, they are not doing it while thinking, "I'm doing this for the good of my health."

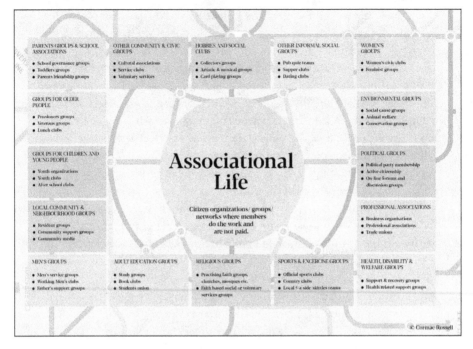

Figure 20.1. A portrait of associational life

Figure 20.1 presents the diverse categories of associations that I have encountered in community life around the world. Creating a portrait of the community you live or serve in using this framework will help you establish a baseline against which you can see the extent to which associational life is deepening and broadening as a result of your community-building efforts.

When developed by residents, this picture of associational life depicts in graphic detail the atomic elements of molecular democracy, as well as many, though not all, of the ingredients needed to grow a good (healthy, well, prosperous, safe, and wise) life. This picture also offers to local residents ordinates and songlines that will guide their journey from being clients to being citizens.

All of these ideas flourish well at the kitchen table and neighborhood scale, but these contexts are not impervious to economic and political pressures. The next chapter considers how technocracy, consumerism, and globalization impact on our civic impulses to group up powerfully with our neighbors and what we can do together, regardless of such pressures.

* * *

Recently I went for a walk on the Bath Road in Cheltenham with a number of what I refer to as civic professionals—that is to say, paid people who have figured out how to support citizen-led invention. Some of us broke off and went onto Suffolk Road, where we discovered a militaria shop. Drawn in by the elaborate menagerie of military antiques in the shop's front window, we soon struck up a conversation with the owner. He told us that most of his trade was done online; he filled us in a little on what he had on display, and then our conversation took an interesting turn. When we told him about what we did, he shared with us that he hosts a group of retired military men, who meet in his shop once a week to reminisce and provide each other with mutual support. It's a completely informal get-together but it is nonetheless of profound consequence to these men.

It's a simple enough example, but emblematic of what does not appear on our current map of health-producing and social care–producing assets. This shopkeeper's health-producing capacity is invisible to most policymakers, practitioners, and even fellow citizens. Instead, our traditional map sees only the label over his shop and the invisible labels hanging over these men's heads.

When we do not see the relevance of what this militaria shop has to offer to health and well-being, we offer these men a service or a program. The truth is we can never know what these men need until we first know what their community has.

Chapter 21

Enacting Democracy

Behind the Veils of Technocracy, Consumerism,
and Globalization

Democracy is not just an election, it is our daily life.

—Tsai Ing-wen

Currently, populist theories of social and economic change in the Global North suggest that crises in the domains of democracy, health, economics, and our ecological systems are matters exclusively for legislative and institutional reform. The prevailing assumption is that these are the big-ticket political items of the day, which can only be resolved at scale by technocrats. This belief draws our focus away from small, local, relational efforts that rely on tacit knowledge and local assets and directs it toward international trade agreements, biotechnology, and global networks. In so doing, it relocates the authority for shaping democracy into the hands of institutional elites and away from regular people.

That said, clearly, at the edge of every culture, alternative scripts to the dominant narrative are written. In an era of massification, these fringe narratives, while seemingly marginal and inconsequential, are hugely significant (Goldfarb, 2006). The work of civic leaders intent on restoring the commons suggests that much has been going on behind the obscuring veils of technocracy, consumerism, and globalization, which illustrates the power, innovation, and sheer cunning of regular citizens who are uncredentialed by vested institutional authority. We just can't see it very clearly right now.

Technocracy and Managerialism

One veil blocking our view of what regular people accomplish around the globe is technocracy. It was Harry Boyte who noted in *The Citizen Solution* (2008) that the rising dominance of experts—in other words, technocracy—is hollowing out civic agency throughout American society. This observation, in my view, holds equally true across all industrialized countries.

Boyte argues that professionals have all but lost their connections to neighborhoods, and they are now far more likely to identify with fellow professionals in their respective field than with their neighbors and the people they serve. It was not always this way.

Closely related to technocracy is managerialism; both have had a toxic effect on democracy. Elton Mayo, a professor at Harvard Business School, popularized managerialism in the twenties and thirties, believing that corporate managers within well-functioning organizations could restore a sense of societal coherence lost during the First World War as a consequence of mass immigration and increasing industrialization.

Managerialism is now ubiquitous across all industrialized countries. Since the twenties, managerialism has consistently taken the view that effective management is a science that should follow a standard set of rubrics, applicable across all organizations. Accordingly, a new class of professionals has emerged whose primary, if not only, expertise is "management." This standardization of how institutions are managed, through the science of managerialism, has meant that the structural exoskeletons of government institutions and large not for profits have become almost indistinguishable from those of for-profit corporations. Some of the institutions intended to be stewards of the public good have become the human services side of the marketplace.

Consumerism

Consumerism is similar to technocracy in that it offers a deal that separates the individual from the group or community for a private transaction. In doing so, it negates the problem-solving role and inventiveness of neighbors and inflates expertise, clientelism, and dependency.

Old Testament scholar Walter Brueggemann suggests that consumerism operates to the principle "There is not enough, let's get everything," a belief in scarcity introduced by Pharaoh. It is an extractive force, since it says, "To meet the requirements to own what I'm selling, you must excise something from yourself and your community; then transfer it to a distant corporation or institution." And it relies primarily on indebtedness; hence the myth of scarcity is perpetuated with the intent of drawing us into debt with people to whom we are not related.

Consumerism alongside professionalization (Leiss, 2014) transforms citizens into clients. When thought of this way, it becomes clear that the phenomenon is not exclusive to capitalist societies. The erosion of citizenship in favor of supine dependence is prevalent throughout most, if not all, economic and political systems, including communism and socialism. If you doubt this, count the number of "clients" in former Soviet-bloc countries that were incarcerated in some of the largest institutions the world has ever seen. Clearly, consumerism is not just about shopping but extends to include all activities that transform citizens into clients. In practice, capitalists, socialists, and communists are all institutionalists who share a common belief that communities are no more than ugly ducklings in need of help of one kind of another, and that help comes in the form of professional services and expertise.

Consumerism is, of course, a many-headed Hydra, and individualism is the most dangerous of them all. The allure of the "modern world" is toward an individualistic, cosmopolitan way of life, one that favors the bright lights and the big city over the smalltown, parochial way of living. The consequences of not actively resisting this narcotic-like entrapment are devastating to both people and the planet.

In *The Vanishing Neighbor* (2014) Marc Dunkelman writes about the changes in the social architecture of American neighborhoods. He notes that adults today relate differently than did their grandparents, tending toward a few intimate relationships (the inner rings) and a wide expanse of more distant surface relationships (the outer ring). The casualties are the relationships in between: the middle ring.

These middle-ring, "in-between" relationships are characterized by conviviality, friendship without intimacy, and what the ancient Greeks called *philia*, or what today we might refer to as civic connection or association. Dunkelman attributes the erosion of the middle ring to a range of factors, including technology, greater mobility, and a growing disconnect with institutions that once mediated the space between civic life and bureaucratic structures. "We've been empowered in nearly every aspect of our lives to move past many of the burdens that once prevented us from pursuing our personal interests and concerns," he writes. In the seemingly endless pursuit of our "true self" we have sought to fill the hollowness of the middle ring and so have (albeit unwittingly) further eroded our associational lives. The practices of growing associational life and ecological stewardship are not transactional in the market sense, but relational in the local and interpersonal sense.

Of course, consumerism in a globalized world takes on many more complex personas than would be the case where economic sovereignty is secure. The question is, How many nation-states can confidently boast that they have economic sovereignty over the bond markets? Portugal, Ireland, and Greece experienced the full might of the so-called European Troika (a decision group formed by the European Commission [EC], the European Central Bank [ECB], and the International Monetary Fund [IMF]) and, like so many other nations, have had to admit that economic sovereignty is mostly the stuff of political rhetoric.

Economic Globalization

According to Thomas Friedman (2005) globalization has evolved over three phases across recent human history: phase one (1492–1800) was the globalization of countries; phase two (1800–2000) was the globalization of companies; and phase three denotes our current version of reality (2000 to now), the globalization of people.

The promise of globalization is that human ingenuity at scale, through technology, will make the world a better place for everyone. Advocates of economic globalization consider proportionality and attention to local culture to be distractions and delaying tactics to the advancement of a single global market. And so, as an ideology, globalization exhorts us to remember that playing small and thinking local will not get us to a single global economy.

Stewart Wallis, a well-respected economist, in his paper "A Great Transition" (2011), reviews the last thirty or more years since the eighties when Thatcherite and Reaganite policies supercharged globalization. His commentary is an absolute indictment of economic globalization, in which he notes that our ecological, geopolitical, and economic world is hanging on by a thread. Contending that expansionism has triggered a crisis of planetary proportions, he points the finger of blame directly at economics: "Our economy is unsustainable, unfair, unstable, and is making us unhappy," he writes.

On a planet with millions of species, humans are not the only species that is suffering (Goldenberg, 2011). Humans are consuming the planet's resources and then dumping the waste of their frenetic consumption at such a rate that, without change, the outcome will be nothing short of ecocide. According to Wallis, in the last thirty years consumption rates have increased by 30 percent and are now well in excess of planetary boundaries. To further compound the matter, this burden and the pyrrhic gains of globalization are not shared equally across the planet; the Global South is picking up the ecological tab for the excesses of the Global North.

Wallis and others like him rightly point out that if everybody made the same lifestyle choices that Americans make we would need five planets to sustain the demand. The UK is not far behind; by Wallis's standards, three planets would be required. This reality demands a reframing of how we define social justice and equality.

The consequences of so seriously overrunning our planetary boundaries are already evident. Fifteen out of twenty-five major ecosystems are in decline or in serious decline. It is clear from more recent commentaries from the likes of Naomi Klein (2014), and the hugely compelling research emerging from the Stockholm Resilience Centre, that confining our concerns to discussions on climate change alone is naïve. The environmental consequences are of a planetary scale and affect nearly every aspect of our lives and the ecosystems of which we are part and through which we live.

Yet the systematic deregulation of corporate activity, unrestricted free trade, and the privatization of enterprise have all but neutered the powers of sovereign states to protect their workers, the health of their populations, their ecology, and their indigenous cultures.

Globalization as we know it today was hailed as an attempt, following World War II, to prevent another world war by creating a new centralized global economic system to accelerate worldwide economic development. This, in turn, we were assured, would trigger technological and consumer revolutions at scale, ensuring enough for all. In actuality, the reverse has happened. The great divergence between the wealthiest and most economically marginalized countries, and between individuals within these countries, has accelerated in the last thirty years to a point unprecedented in human history. Wealth distribution is now profoundly out of kilter with any generally acceptable measure of fairness. Ninety-nine percent of the world's population to one degree or another have become "debt slaves" or, to soften the term, indebted to the wealthiest one percent.

The Chemistry of Democracy

What can we do to use what's strong to advance the cause of citizen-centered democracy? Our mistake over the last hundred years or so has been to try to effect change at the molecular level, either by working solely on a structural plane or through personal growth. If, however, communities are the atomic elements of molecular democracy, then we need to start working more at the atomic level.

Of course, atoms here are a metaphor for the various elements of community. The problem in only working with particular atoms, or the parts of those atoms that interest us—protons (citizens), neutrons (associations), and electrons (associations of associations)—is that in doing so we fail to effect any real growth in citizen-centered democracy, since this domain is neither individualistic nor institutional but civic and therefore collective. Deep democratic change happens when we attend not to the atoms alone but to how the atoms get connected up to form a useful molecular relationship or productive enterprise.

In everyday life H-O-H or H2O looks, tastes, and feels like water, but when we zoom in we see its molecular structure. We see how two hydrogen atoms and one oxygen atom have connected, with covalent bonds, to form a water molecule. Our current democratic malaise may be likened to a society where people have become obsessed with the molecular structures (its form) as opposed to its functions. Molecules in nature take the form they do to be productive, not so that they can assume a particular preordained structure. Nature is adaptive, nonideological, and immensely practical.

In government-centric democracies the atomic elements of our democracies, our communities, get stuck together in very prescribed and imperial ways, somewhat like today's Lego blocks. Not so in a connected, citizen-centered democracy, where connections are mostly nonmechanical, nonlinear, and emergent. Of course, even in this context, eventually over time structures form to enable certain functions to take place. But most importantly they form to enable us to perform our functions as citizens, for the people, by the people, of the people.

You may remember when Legos were first sold, without instructions. You got your box of blocks and you invented. Sometimes you did so with friends, other times alone. But you were the creator. Beyond the limits of what you could do with the various building blocks, nothing was preset. Then came the Lego templates, the forty-four-page instruction leaflets that told you what to make and how to make it. They were followed by the Lego movies and characters, which told you how to think and feel about those characters. These days you cannot buy a simple bucket of blocks.

We have an eight-year-old son, called Isaac. He is the most inventive person I know, and consequently he is wisely disinterested in those glossy brochures and instruction manuals. Instead, he wants to connect and create the things he cares about. And this is, I think, precisely the way we will navigate ourselves out of this current set of crises as a planet. As Myles Horton and Paulo Friere (1990) counsel, we must "make the road by walking" it. In other words, it is not a paint-by-numbers or cookie-cutter solution that we are pursuing, but solutions that are particular to our context, and ours alone.

Sadly, our democracies have become like today's prescriptive Lego boxes, where we can have any kind of democracy we like as long as it is one of those on the shelf, with instructions on how to do it right (or left). If we are to progress beyond this stifling lack of real choice, we need to become like Isaac and invent our own way. Institutions need to lead by stepping back from civic space so as to enable that to happen or at least do no harm to citizen-led invention. But how?

Connecting the Blocks

Community building is all about discovering, connecting, and mobilizing the building blocks that exist in every community—street by street, neighborhood by neighborhood—not so that we can re-create a preordained version of democracy but so that we can enact democracy.

In each of our neighborhoods, towns, and villages there is a great reservoir of waking and sleeping assets, most of which are invisible. In the same way that, with the right lens, we may see the water molecules that form when hydrogen atoms bond with oxygen, with a new lens we may discover what's actually there in our democratic domains. And that means we need to jettison the old lens that has served to obscure our democratic assets. Part of this discovery process means zooming out of certain other things. It is hard to see our neighbor's gifts when we have one eye on a shop window and another on a screen.

When Isaac builds things, he has a ritual of keeping them for a while and then reusing those parts to build something else. It's a wonderful model of fluid emergent invention, a model I admire and try to learn from. I believe that if we are to create a citizen-centered democracy we need to see our institutions like cars: when they stop functioning, we should salvage the working parts and use them alongside other assets to replace the original form with a better-functioning model. Many of our institutions function like vintage cars. I understand the sentimentality but doubt that they are any longer fit for their intended purpose.

Citizen-centered models of democracy will not be so predictable, secure, or governable as a car or molecule or Lego structure. They will be nonlinear, interdependent but disaggregated, flat, and disruptive, and that means they will at first be overlooked—and when they become more powerful, they will be resisted by the establishment. Still, it is possible to speculate on how a more citizen-centered democracy might emerge:

1. *By supporting community building at the neighborhood level*: Everybody cares about something in civic life enough to act on it; we simply do not yet know what that is for most people.

2. *By organizing our institutional structures to serve, not stifle, citizen-led invention*: Let the genie out of the bottle! Our institutions could be treasure chests for community-led change. Indeed, some currently are.

3. *By challenging the "institutional assumption"*: Decrease institutionalization and increase interconnectivity in community life. Ensure people have sufficient income, control, and community to make real choices toward a good life.

4. *By becoming internally focused and proliferating outwards*: There are external forces that will do us over as communities, but to take them on as communities we must first connect powerfully to organize our internal resources. In doing so we will discover that our internal resources can keep parasites at bay, but they can also help us to flourish locally as stewards of each other's well-being and the well-being of our wider ecologies, to grow abundant communities from the inside out.

5. *By recognizing that the Third Sector/not-for-profit realm is not a surrogate for community*: In the same way that we describe a group of birds as a flock, we describe a group of citizens as a community. We would not call a group of bird enthusiasts a flock, nor should we call a group of charities or not-for-profit institutions community representatives.

In the preface of this book I shared some of the groundless "certainties" that I operated under as a wounding and wounded helper. In the next chapter I want to expose ten of the most common certainties held by many policymakers that urgently need to challenged and replaced.

* * *

The transition from an institution-centric democracy to a citizen-centered one is analogous to the restorative transition that a forest must make after a forest fire or the ways land recovers after decades of monocropping. Communities too have their ways, built into their very design, of recovering democracy. But many have forgotten those ways.

On that recovery journey there will be those who sow seeds, those who plant flowers, and those who nurture the climate where indigenous growth flourishes from the inside out. A climatologist! A climatologist! My kingdom for a climatologist!

Chapter 22

Rekindling Democracy

The Wide View

Tomorrow belongs to those who can hear it coming.

—DAVID BOWIE

UP UNTIL NOW, IN the context of recent modern history (circa 1933 to today), the BY spaces have been subordinate to the TO/FOR and WITH spaces; communities have been known for the sum of their problems and needs, not for their abundance of hospitality, gift-giving capacity, and associational life. The citizens that occupy the BY spaces have not been viewed as the primary inventors of a preferred future for all and for the planet. In part, the reason is that consumer society obscures the small, local, everyday exchanges that so delicately, so imperceptibly knit us and our well-being together. The popular culture renders that which is most abundant invisible.

In equal measure, political policies have inverted the democracy of small things in four ways. First, the role of citizens is now defined as what happens after policymakers, politicians, and professionals have completed their expert functions. I have argued for the opposite: the roles and functions of public servants should be defined as what happens after citizens complete their indispensable work. Ensuring state supports then becomes an extension of civic capacity instead of a replacement for it, as they often currently are.

Second, modern societies since the New Deal have defined helping as relief, rehabilitation and, in recent years, advocacy—and even then, almost exclusively within the parameters of programs and services. In so doing, services have become the sea in which we swim. Third, the units of change up to now have been limited to two: individual behavior/lifestyle change and institutional expansion. This view fails to recognize a third, more essential unit—the neighborhood or village—as the primary unit of change. Fourth, regardless of whether they are left- or right-leaning, in ideological terms policies are in accord with the belief that people who are economically marginalized or negatively labeled cannot be trusted to self-determine their futures or navigate life's vicissitudes. And in this regard they are fundamentally misguided.

The right supports business interests through privatization of services, while the left advocates for the human services side of the economy as deserving pole position in helping the "needy." These are in fact economic, not political debates, which mostly fail to relocate money and authority into the hands of the people who are being supported. Instead, the lion's share of resources goes toward maintaining the institutional infrastructure and salaries of those providing the help. This is to say that, in economic terms, the helping institutions need people's needs, often more than people need their services. This debate reduces human beings to bundles of eternally defined deficits, willfully refusing to recognize them as citizens with invaluable contributions to be liberated in rekindling democracy. I invite helpers to ask themselves this question: if those I am helping had my salary, how much of that salary would they use to purchase the service I am providing?

Ten Questionable Certainties

The chapters of this book are attempts to share the wisdom of a wide array of wayfinders whom I was fortunate enough to encounter on my journey from the overconfident, underexperienced professional to the curious, itinerant listener, storyteller, and court jester. These wayfinders are the persistent questioners of societal certainties, and they have taught me and so many others some of the songlines and cardinal points to follow in this endless inquiry toward a satisfying, sufficient life. They offer citizens, practitioners, and policymakers invaluable coordinates in moving toward a preferred future.

Here are the top ten certainties that have been questioned throughout these pages.

Questionable Certainty #1:
We Are Evolving from Primitive to Civilized.

The term "primitive" carries extremely negative connotations, while the term "civilized" tends to be seen wholly positively, often as the high-water mark of human potential. "Primitive" means the primordial or original ones or stateless people governed solely by customs and kinship, while "civilized" refers to those who live their lives within states and governed by laws. After expansive phases of Western colonization those terms dichotomized, as exemplified in the words of the English philosopher Thomas Hobbes, who, in his political treatise *Leviathan* (1651), described the lot of humans before state formation, the introduction of the rule of law, and the influence of formal education as "solitary, poor, nasty, brutish, and short."

History is generally understood as an evolutionary advancement from the backwardness of Stone Age humans to the sophistication of the moderns. As mentioned in chapter 7, the anthropologist Marshall Sahlins (1974) challenges this view, arguing that Stone Age communities were, in fact, the "original affluent society" in that they had more than sufficient means to meet their modest needs. So-called primitive societies should not be understood as failed attempts at being civilized; rather, they should be understood for their incredible adaptive abilities to learn how best to prevail, in any given place and time, through the cocreation of a cultural way of being. Based on how fruitfully primitives lived, civilized societies have much to learn from them about the importance of nurturing community culture in preference to individualism and economic advancement.

Questionable Certainty #2:
Our Good Life Will Be Protected by Consumer Rights
and the Invisible Hand of the Free Market.

The free market is a chimera. For centuries, states have taken an active hand in enabling commercial interests to advance, often at the expense of citizens' well-being and local ecologies—from the enclosure of the commons in the seventeenth century to current patent and copyright laws, which often commodify and privatize cultural assets. Moreover, the notion that our good life is to be found in the consumption of goods and services flies in the face of studies in the fields of longevity, health and well-being, and even prosperity. As American philosopher Eric Hoffer (1951) once commented, "You can never get enough of what you don't really want." It generally seems that people don't really want unlimited personal power and big bank accounts at the expense of personal relationships and deep belonging, but the so-called free market, like a meat grinder, has a way of pulling us out of community life and into the industrialized world of the Empire. From the curse of hidden persuaders like Edward Bernays to the gigantism of Globalism, we have been socialized to consume goods and services to such an extent that we are rapidly overshooting the limits of our planetary boundaries, and that which we are consuming is starting to consume us.

Questionable Certainty #3:
The More Data and Science We Bring to Understanding What's Wrong, the Closer We'll Be to Solving the World's Most Intractable Problems.

Facts and figures are important, but when it comes to sense-making around complex socioeconomic challenges, thick data matters more than thin or Big Data. Data that is simply factual (thin or Big Data) speaks to the when, who, and what and is less important than thick data with context, which speaks to the where and why. But contextual data is not always enough; often we are called to make decisions that require good collective judgments, especially where the road ahead is unpredictable. There are times when we must take risks and make judgments, having the courage to create new possibilities together as we go. In fact, throughout history, dialects, cuisine, childrearing, rituals of worship, learning, and the passing on of traditions—what we cumulatively refer to as culture—all have emerged as deeply rooted expressions of small communities' willingness to walk collectively and courageously toward a shared future with little logic behind them. Their hunt for hope drew them forward. Their belief in each other, their ecologies, and their traditions sustained them. And their stories and songlines ensured their ways prevailed long after their lifetimes ended. They spoke the mother's tongue.

Questionable Certainty #4: We Must Get Better at Delivery.

"Deliver on time, at scale, in efficient, measurable, and cost-effective ways" has become a modern credo of consumer society and has infiltrated the mindset of leaders in the public and not-for-profit sectors. Those who deliver services to us and for us tend to be endowed with high levels of institutional prowess, financial backing, expertise, credentials, and political support. These endowments combine to place them in pole position as the most competent to efficiently deliver the supposed "best solutions" to modern problems. Yet, before the institutions of a given society can be effective at delivering required goods and services, citizens at the receiving end of those services must know what they truly need, and citizens can only know what they require from external delivery agents when they know what they can do with the resources they have locally. This truth highlights the need to place discovery ahead of delivery. We must know what is there and connect it, before diagnosing what is missing and prescribing top-down solutions. Put another way, society gets stronger when citizens are fruitful together for each other, when they ensure that when services are delivered nothing is done for them, without them. When services are delivered to them or for them, they can ensure they retain authorizing powers over what outside professionals do and how they do it (see Figure 22.1).

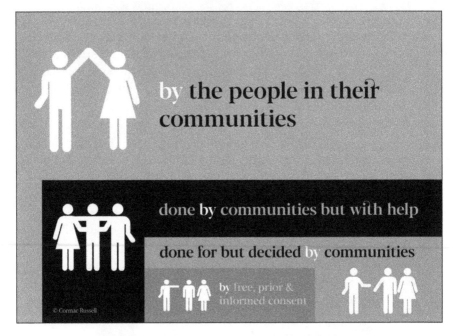

**Figure 22.1. Proportionality between TO/FOR/WITH/BY
when Democracy works as it should**

Questionable Certainty #5: Neoliberal Economies Are Here to Stay.

Many legislators believe the more networked and expansive (globalized) economies become, the closer we'll all be to ensuring that wealth trickles down to include everyone. If this fable of growth and progress toward equality continues to hold sway, it will consume us and the planet, in short order. As noted in chapter 7, Oxford University economist Kate Raworth (2017) argues that our economies are not closed market systems engaged in a reinforcing produce/consume ping-pong between households and industry. Our economies function within and are interdependent on our cultural and associational lives and the environment. When we draw on the planet's resources and turn them into pollution and waste, we all at once destroy our environment and our economy. Peter Block's (2016) model of what he calls the neighborly economy is both a compelling and accessible way of ensuring that those who are most economically marginalized can be connected to the resources of the commons. Neoliberal economies are enveloped within a fable that will succumb to a better story; our challenge is to cocreate that better narrative.

Questionable Certainty #6: Competition Is a Defining Feature of Who We Are as Human Beings.

Dominion over the earth and each other is the global ethic: if we don't get on board with this, we'll be left behind. Look no further than the Bible (Gen 1:26): "Then God said, 'Let us make mankind in our image, in our likeness, so that they may rule over the fish in the sea and the birds in the sky, over the livestock and all the wild animals, and over all the creatures that move along the ground.'" This otherworldly, top-down, anthropocentric narrative runs deep within the modern psyche. Yinon M. Bar-On and colleagues (2018) assert that humans constitute a mere 0.01 percent of all life but have destroyed 83 percent of wild mammals. The influence of humans has been so profoundly negative in recent history that scientists have noted that the Holocene is being eclipsed by a new epoch called the Anthropocene, where human influence will be the dominant and perhaps terminal influence on planetary well-being.

The American educator Alfie Kohn, in his book *Competition Is Ruining Us! There Is a Better Way* (1994), notes the unspoken rule we are subject to from our earliest school days is "For me to win, you must lose." Still, competing with the planet, and everything on it, is not a defining feature of who we are as human beings. The neurobiologist and primatologist Robert Sapolsky (2001) provides fascinating evidence from his study of savannah baboons of East Africa—which have the highest rate of aggression of any variety of primate—and notes what we humans can learn from them. His findings challenge the idea that aggression is innate; rather, he proves that it is inculcated, and most importantly that we can change the culture toward a more empathic, cooperative, community-oriented way of being.

Questionable Certainty #7: Bigger Is Better.

In 1973 E. F. Schumacher convincingly argued the opposite in *Small Is Beautiful*. Still, obsession with scale and bigness prevails. There is nevertheless reason for hope, as well as evidence that small is both preferable and possible. The sticking point is whether it can be profitable. Interestingly, the answer is yes. The Gallup (2010) and Knight Foundation study "Soul of Community" of forty-six thousand Americans in twenty-six cities demonstrates that a key determinant of local economic prosperity is connection, and that requires proximity, or smallness. It invites us to make small the new big and validates that the principles of subsidiarity are not just defensible on social and ethical grounds but also on the basis of enhanced economic outcomes.

Questionable Certainty #8: Reforming Our Systems Is the Answer.

It is not. Better to focus on why we do what we do. Concentrating on why we seek change is rooted in enhancing freedom, not improving or increasing services; although services may be a very valuable route into change, they are never an end in themselves or the only route available. Rekindling democracy, then, is about nurturing interdependence among neighbors, not creating more dependence among citizens in services delivered by salaried strangers. Jerome Miller (1991) makes this case in most persuasive terms. In the seventies, tasked with running Massachusetts' juvenile reformatories, he shifted the emphasis from merely reforming systems and enhancing the quality of their programs to re-functioning the communities the young boys came from and determining whether they experienced an enhanced quality of life.

Questionable Certainty #9: Technological Advances Will Save Us.

Technology can augment and act as an extension of community capacity, but it can also eclipse and replace our indigenous vernacular resources. The challenge, then, is to ensure that proportionality prevails between nontechnological community assets and technological resources that enable the human community to be more fruitful and ecologically sound.

Questionable Certainty #10:
Technocracy (Rule by the Elites) Is Better than Democracy
(Which Is but "Mob Rule," the Tyranny of the Masses).

The notion of the philosopher king introduced by Plato is perhaps the most famous expression of this thesis; it is possible without much effort to track the progeny of this school of thought from the Greeks through the Middle Ages into the Enlightenment and on to current thinking around behavioral economics. The primary thrust of this book has been to refute this old saw and to assert that the reverse is true; to achieve such a community-centered expression of power, rather than a government-centric one, we must more deeply understand *community* and *democracy* and how the two are *intertwined*, seeing them not as static nouns but putting them in context with action verbs.

Communities are the nurseries within which, from babes in arms right into adulthood, we learn how to be citizens and grow democracy. So, while it is true to say that it takes a village to raise a child, it also takes an aggregation of villages to create a democracy. We must therefore move beyond talking about what *community* means to "doing" community together in meaningful ways and, while doing so, come to self-consciously understand that those collective actions are a central part of the work that citizens do in a democracy, for a democracy. That work calls us to engage collectively—conversation by conversation, neighbor to neighbor, place to place—and then aggregate and proliferate the inventiveness and care that emerges, moving toward mass localism and deeper democracy as we go.

In the next chapter, the finale, I offer a summary of what has gone before and, I hope, a compelling invitation toward practical action.

Conclusion

Serving in Civic Space

Death is not the greatest loss in life.
The greatest loss is what dies inside us while we live.

—NORMAN COUSINS

SHORTLY BEFORE COMPLETING THIS book, the stark reality of COVID-19 became clear: borders were being shut down, and flights grounded, but at the same time the canals in Venice have never been cleaner, and people are serenading their neighbors from their balconies. It feels as though the world is in pursuit of answers to a question yet to be figured out.

Perhaps, as the all-consuming influences of the marketplace recede for a time and the world self-organizes community by community, we can work together to amplify a more hopeful and sustainable story for us and our planet—a better story, of the rise of abundantly caring, connected, and creative communities that are also learning to walk more lightly on the planet. Perhaps then the question we are all seeking is not so much how do we survive this pandemic, as how do we sustain the community building that this pandemic precipitated? Pandemics end and the professionals who had to shelter in their own home communities return to serve in citizen space once more. Let us hope that, as they do, they remain both mindful of the incredible reservoir of assets that COVID-19 revealed and inspired to support the civic inventiveness still existing in every neighborhood, just waiting for the right precipitant and context. After all, if the coronavirus pandemic can reveal, connect, and mobilize so much kindness and social capital, then surely professionals can act as positive catalysts toward the rekindling of citizen-led democracy.

* * *

A CITIZEN IS NOT someone crouched over kindling waiting for someone else to light their fire. This book is a guide for professionals interested in working with citizens so that they can rekindle democracy. Within a wide array of domains, including health, justice, education, community development and social protection, there is a dominant assumption that more institutional intervention equates with better outcomes for more people, more often. This is what I have referred to as the "TO" and "FOR" approaches to helping and change-making more generally. Aside from being undemocratic, this assumption is simply groundless. It is a patriarchal drama but it does not need to be our reality.

The preceding pages offer a counternarrative, affirming another view and a concrete alternative approach grounded in the context of our daily lives and local environments, which in essence notes that for people who have been socialized to view themselves primarily as consumers of human services, there is a hydraulic-like relationship between institutionalization and interdependence at the center of a natural community. The journey from being predominantly defined (and defining oneself) as a client of an institution toward being an active citizen leading a life of your own choosing, one who may or may not use services, is fraught with all kinds of unstated asymmetries in terms of power. For ethical practitioners, the primary concern therefore is to ensure a relocation of assumed authority from the institutional world to the life-world/citizen space.

This journey from an often exclusive and exclusionary dependence on salaried strangers to interdependence in the heart of a community of near neighbors is a power struggle. That struggle is advanced when we start with communities first, not in an effort to demean the role of institutions, but rather to actively decenter the secondary functions of their services and programs, while simultaneously recentering the primary functions that communities play in cocreating well-being, justice, learning, and care for each other, our ecologies, deep democracies, and shared prosperity.

The power struggle is against an inversion that has taken place where today the role of the citizen is typically defined as that which happens after the important work of the professional is completed. By that way of thinking, police produce safety, doctors health, judges justice, development agencies development, and so on. This is back to front. In a democracy, the functions of professionals and their institutions should be defined as that which happens after the important collective and individual functions of citizens are enacted, with a view to ensuring institutional functions act as an extension of, not a replacement for, collective citizen creativity.

Recall that the term "democracy" is derived from two Greek words: *demos*, meaning "the people," and *kratia*, meaning "power." The redressing of this inversion of the democratic imperative stresses that "the people," not external experts, have the primary powers and functions to collectively cocreate well-being. It is what citizens and ethical practitioners are moving toward each time they seek to promote citizen-to-citizen participation as the preferred starting point in addressing socioeconomic and political challenges. It requires they believe that citizens working together, while respecting differences of opinions and diversity, are the rightful primary inventors of our best futures.

From nursery rhymes to cargo cults, I have commended a range of prohibitions against institutional overreach (TO and FOR modalities of change), inviting current examples and powerful guiding voices to help us see beyond such institutional monopolies toward the powerful functions of communities as our new and better story and our starting point for the future. I have argued that human services have in many cases become the human face of the marketplace, albeit with the exact same exoskeleton and similar institutional-centric imperatives as profit-seeking corporations. This, along with globalization and consumerism, has created a heady concoction of persuasive influences that have drawn people away from an interdependence on each other and nature toward a strong dependence on programs and services.

I have gone further to assert that that dependence cuts both ways, thus forming a codependence where institutions need people's needs often more than people require their institutional services. This is why I so seriously doubt the veracity of most needs assessments, since invariably they seem to conclude that what people need are the services of those that have analyzed them. In truth, the only thing that needs analysis is needs analysis. Indeed, it is hard to overlook how regularly human necessities have been transmuted into needs that ought to be addressed by credentialed people. In other words, human needs and necessities are often confused with service categories. So the necessity of having a good friend who offers a listening ear becomes the need for a shrink; the necessity of social connections and activity in general becomes the need for a social prescription; the desire to lead a stress-free life becomes the need for antianxiety and antidepressant medications; and the necessity of good health becomes the need for more health care and medicine. This is nothing short of the monetization of human necessities, an illustration of how the curse of Edward Bernays has crept into public services and the not-for-profit sector. The antidote to professionalization and commodification of human necessities is democracy. We must actively seek the renegotiation of the social contract, starting from the BY space, then progressing to the WITH, and from there authorizing what is done FOR us and TO us from a place of power and free, prior, and informed consent.

In pursuit of this more proportionate, citizen-led democracy, the songlines of this book have brought us away from boardroom tables and back to kitchen tables, from formula milk to mothers' milk, from screen time to street play. They move us from organized greed at the expense of the many and our ecosystems to gift economies that include all and promote cooperation with all species and ecologies. We have journeyed from the political hue and cry for more hospital beds toward the more foundational necessity of nurturing more hospitable communities, with institutional beds in reserve when needed. We have contested reductionary views of physical and mental health as medical and personal problems, arguing instead for a more expansive view, in recognition of the fact that health is primarily a social and political concern. We've traveled from the distant canyonlike ideals of globalization to the hills and hollows of our home places, where "small" must necessarily become the new big and embedded neighborhood economies must replace the alienating economies of the global market. Across the life course, and beyond labeled conditions, we have sought to bring all the aspects of human communities that have been fragmented and pathologized, from the Industrial Revolution till now, back into communion with each other, their ecologies, and their cultures.

As our journey draws to a close, before finishing this book, it is fitting to linger awhile at life's final milestone: death and dying. By way of so doing, allow me to share a final story from my home country about one man's end of life journey and how his community responded:

> On Saturday, April 1, 1978, in the village of Brosna, County Kerry, Ireland, the burial of a local man punctuated an otherwise normal day. Tradition had it in those days that friends and relations of the deceased dug the grave. Among them on this day was Con Carey. In the early hours of the following morning, Con Carey himself was found dead, and as it was a Sunday morning, he was buried in a rather rushed fashion on Monday, April 3rd. The parish priest made the arrangements, as Con had no family to speak of.
>
> Con Carey's friends took the view that he had not been properly interred. Local custom of the time would have demanded a proper wake be held for mourners to keep watch or vigil over "their dead" until they were buried, and to "say a proper good-bye." Talk soon turned to action, and the day after Con's burial, eleven men and one woman—all

friends—travelled to the neighboring parish of Mountcollins where Con had been buried.

In a profound act of respect, they set about digging up Con's grave, removing him from the coffin, washing his body, laying him out properly and praying over him. These actions earned them the name the Twelve Apostles and the deep and enduring respect of their neighbors, all of whom would have known what had happened, given that the body was dug up in plain view during daylight hours. An investigation quickly followed, with the file sent to the Director of Public Prosecutions. The village folk kept quiet and so none of the Twelve Apostles were ever publicly identified. John B. Keane, the famous Irish playwright and poet, immortalized this true story in "The Ballad of Con Carey" (1978).

Just to set some context, in the Irish countryside, in 1978, twelve people traveling three miles from one rural village to another during daylight hours would have been pretty conspicuous. People would have known what they were up to; gossip would have been rife. Digging up a dead body buried six feet deep in a graveyard that was likely beside the church is even more conspicuous. But even if everyone had missed seeing the procession to the graveside, they could not have overlooked the exhumation, the washing of the body and the ritual prayers, followed by Con's reburial. Indeed, there's a strong likelihood that some or all of the vernacular liturgy was observed by the local Gardai (police) and the parish priest. Yet neither took action, nor did they speak against the Twelve Apostles. Most likely for different reasons, the local constabulary was probably in support of the action taken, while the priest, who I'm guessing felt ashamed, most likely decided discretion was the better part of valor.

There were and still are very serious taboos against disturbing a grave. Certainly in rural Ireland in 1978, the thought that, after a parish priest had officiated over someone's burial, unordained people would undo and redo a formal "blessed" burial would have been tantamount to sacrilege. Yet in this instance it wasn't. Why? Because although the details are scant and contradictory in places, what is consistent in the various versions of the story is that Con, who was a bachelor and popular among his neighbors, died of a heart attack on his way home from his local pub. He collapsed into a sand mound at the side of the road and lay there through the night. That night it rained heavily, and when he was found the following morning he was in a very disheveled state.

His body was subsequently placed in a wooden box, a plastic bag was placed around the Wellington boots he was wearing when he died and his face was still stained with mud and sand. He was laid out for a time in this state at the door of the community center, in a box with no lining. Soon after, he was buried. It was these circumstances that led to the events that followed, resulting in Con being buried twice. The first time the institutional way; the second, the community way.

The final adjudicators of the appropriateness of Con's last rite of passage were his community, and they decided that the job had been poorly done by the priest. So without so much as "by your leave," they bypassed state and canon law and followed the natural law of the commons to give their friend the send-off he deserved. He might have had no family to speak for him, but he had his community. The villagers of Brosna were reminding their local priest that there is a way, our way, to bury our dead, and if you rush it or displace our role within it, while we will respect the sacramental role you have played, we will redo the community piece ourselves.

Con's reburial was a profound and hugely courageous act of love for a friend and neighbor. I like to imagine the Twelve Apostles were buoyed up by the confidence that comes with understanding the way that things and people fit together, so as to give shape and form to each other. They knew that Con and they were interdependent, and to not bury him the right way was to throw the entire cosmos out of sync. The harmony of their lives, their seasons, the growth of their land, and their future living and dying depended on that fateful and courageous deed on April 4, 1978. The Twelve Apostles, in an act of institutional irreverence, committed the ultimate act of the Beloved Community for which every man, woman, and child in their village and the neighboring village of Mountcollins was prepared to remain silent. In so doing, they spoke with one voice about the power of community and who is really in charge in life and in death when a culture of strong community prevails. That day they brought death back from the institutional world into the nest of community life.

And so accordingly death brought a community to life, and consequently Con Carey could rest in peace.

Beyond Stewardship

Some may say the priest failed in his stewardship duties; others may argue he acted in good faith to help a parishioner with no family and scant resources. I think, whether due to oversight or blindsided by dogma, he failed to see that Con had a family of neighbors who loved him and that they were rightly the first responders. The priest engaged in overreach and drew functions to himself that belonged to the community; he got the hydraulics wrong. In this instance, the community took those functions back, an all too rare occurrence.

But the priest nevertheless was out of step; he had gotten the sequence by which dying is done in Brosna wrong. The role of the priest is what happens as an extension of the community's role, not a replacement for it.

Perhaps that is the difficultly with the concept of stewardship: it still places a certain minority of supposed elites in charge of the majority and of nature; it simply cautions them to lead in a different way from traditional autocratic or paternalistic modes that do TO or FOR and to move toward doing things WITH people. The core message of this book is that while stewardship is better than colonization, it will not be sufficient in attaining the promise of deep democracy. There is a stage before stewardship that those who wish to promote citizenship participation must support. It is the stage that Robert Mendelsohn, Vendana Shiva, Jerry Miller, Marian Tompson, and others featured throughout this book understood and deeply valued. It was the civic space that the Mayor of Amqui was cheering on when he asked concerned citizens, "Do you know anyone who could help with that?"

Reaching this space is about serving while walking backward, with the courage to commit heresy on occasion. As with a coal miner stepping backward in the depths of a mine, while their helmet and torch shed light on the space they step back from, professionals who work effectively in citizen space step back to illuminate and cheer on abundance, never to abandon the place they come from. The proscriptions around the Jewish Sabbath are instructive here: broadly, they prevent the faithful from creating or destroying anything; instead they are encouraged to bring their focus toward celebrating everything for what it is. The message regarding the natural and metaphysical world is "Leave it alone, trust it, enjoy it."

Stewardship without such built-in restraints is wide open to the potential of the steward's stewing in their own goodness and becoming arrogant and godlike. The truth is simple: neither you nor I know enough to run the show. Hence stewardship without the sabbatical ethic will not work, and will likely do harm.

Promoting citizen participation also takes courage. As the economist Albert Hirschman (1970) would counsel, it comes down to the choice between "exit, voice, or loyalty." Do we leave? Or stay and exercise our authentic voices? Or stay but remain loyal to the objectives of the institutional world? The power of authentic voice, especially when well organized and joined with that of others, should never be underestimated.

The salutary tale of Con Carey channels the prohibitions and the practices that a professional working ethically and elegantly in citizen space will want to embrace as they exercise voice. It is, I hope, a suitable epitaph for this book, which in essence is no more than a call to remember that development can create its own sort of scarcity, medicine can produce its own kind of sickness, and justice can perversely yield more crime. In sum, if communities are to be placed back in the driver's seat, as democracy promises, then professionals working in citizen space must be clear about what they are not going to do.

Figure C.1 lists some of the key things effective practitioners would place proscriptions around and what they would endeavor to promote.

Prohibit	Promote
Harm to social capital and FESWAW	Community impact assessments
Institutional overreach	Serving while walking backward
Institutional content preceding citizen contact	Citizen-to-citizen participation
Needs analysis: starting with what's wrong	Asset inventories: starting with what's strong
Monetizing human necessities	Discover, connect, mobilize and where appropriate capitalize human capacity
Professionalizing community functions	Honoring, cheering on, and supporting community capacity. Using powerful questions to promote citizen participation
Elementization	See the neighborhood as the primary unit of change
Counterfeit progressiveness/ innovations	Authentic, appropriate intermediate innovations. Having the courage to serve while walking backward
Bigger is better/scaling/ standardization	Small, localized, specific

Figure C.1. Prohibitions and practices

I have had the privilege of seeing a lot of professional practitioners wrestle with the dilemmas that asset-based community development presents, "serving while walking backward" being chief among them. Figure C.2 is a simple spectrum of the change that I have seen the most courageous of them undertake. I've rarely, if ever, seen all of these things happen in one place, but I remain open to that possibility.

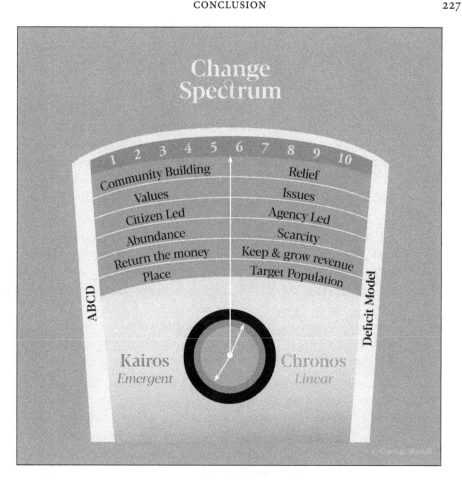

Figure C.2. Change spectrum

There is no particular hierarchy in the way I designed this graphic, but taking them in the order in which they appear, left to right and top to bottom, each of the suggested shifts provides a reasonable synthesis of the book:

1. *Community building, not relief:* Relief can be defined as financial or practical assistance given to those in special need or difficulty. It's the outside-in kind of help, where things are done TO or FOR people. Community building, in contrast, enables people to do things in association WITH each other. It is done BY the people themselves.

2. *Heavy on values, light on the issues:* The way we frame issues like homelessness, for example, can set us down a road of direct service provision before we've fully understood what it is the people we are serving

really want. What if, for example, people who are homeless value autonomy more than shelter? Fixating on issues instead of respecting the values of those we serve and getting clear about our own practice values has been the birthplace of many a white elephant.

3. *Relocating authority from institutional to citizen space*: This shift simply asks who's in the driver's seat of social change. The answer far too often is that the institutions are. How can we relocate that authority, so that communities and citizens are the primary architects of an alternative future, where they are the golfers and the paid practitioners are the caddies?

4. *From scarcity to abundance*: The scarcity mindset starts with an exclusive focus on what's missing or broken, and having identified that, we quickly move into fixing mode at the lowest cost possible. It further drives us into a wholesale as opposed to a retail model of human services, where we aggregate people with the same conditions together, for efficiency, instead of working with people in their local context. The scarcity mindset also leads to top-down, silo-based approaches. Abundance thinking starts with a recognition that people come to know what external resources they need by first discovering, connecting, and mobilizing the abundance they have within and around them.

5. *Return the resource that has been appropriated*: I often ask human service practitioners to honestly answer this question: "If the people you serve had the same level of income as the helpers have, would they use that income to purchase the services currently being offered to them?" To date, not one person I've asked around the world has said yes. How can we ensure people have choice and control in shaping their own lives when this is the case? A significant part of the answer is ensuring we do not disable choice and control by hoarding resources to do what we believe to be right. Instead, let's repatriate the power and resources to their rightful place: to the people who themselves have to live with and through those choices.

6. *Moving from reactionary silos to place-based service*: It is typical of most public-sector and third-sector organizations to work out of silos. We have the youth sector, the eldercare agencies, those that work in the field of disabilities, and so on. But this approach has led to ghettoization and inadvertently to the further erosion of communities of place. Thinking about the village or place-bounded community as the primary unit of change provides a much-needed antidote to the dominant target population model, as it enables connections to be made across population groupings, their economy, cultures, and ecology. Additionally, it also

enables various services to step beyond their administrative boundaries on to the common ground of the neighborhood, where they can form genuine humble relationships with local residents.

The Greek words at the bottom of the spectrum, *chronos* and *kairos*, were inspired by my friend and ABCD Institute faculty member Al Etmanski (2015). In his blog he reminds us,

> *Despite the urgency, lasting change takes much longer than we appreciate.*
>
> *Darn.*
>
> *One way to counteract our impatience is to shift from "chronos" to "kairos" time. Chronos time is sequential time, measured by the clock and which seems to be speeding up. Kairos time bends and stretches; sometimes it even seems to stand still. Chronos is measured by the clock, which many of us try to beat. Kairos unfolds like the seasons, following a natural rhythm and waiting for the right moment.*

Most of our change-making efforts are afforded a gestation period of three to five years (the average funding or election cycle), and they are expected to be hatched as fully mature and ready to change the world. If we're truly honest with ourselves we know that social and political change does not unfold in a linear, chronological way; it is emergent, messy, and goes as fast as the speed of trust.

Getting Practical, Getting Going

Returning to the story in the opening pages of Carin and Lotte's endeavor to turn an old school into a community center by connecting the talents of their neighbors, like every other unsung hero in this book they followed several straightforward practices:

1. *Discovering*: Discovering resident connectors who naturally weave their community together through neighbor-to-neighbor and associational relationship building. Convening a table of connectors, as distinct from leaders, that represent the diversity of an entire neighborhood can be a powerful means of building community throughout that neighborhood.

2. *Welcoming*: Actively welcoming neighbors, and those who are pushed to the margins, through inclusive learning conversations and listening campaigns. Learning conversations and listening campaigns surface

what people care about enough act to upon with their neighbors. Some communities find it helpful to have a community organizer (called community builders or community animators in Europe) to support these processes. It is important to remember that if a paid practitioner is supporting a community this is a backseat role. Local citizens must remain in the lead. Community organizers can be helpful when it comes to figuring out tactics for deep inclusion and addressing issues of conflict and power imbalance alongside a range of other essential functions. They can help build the ship, but they must never become the ship's captain.

3. *Portrait making*: As people discover what they care about enough to take collective action on, creating dynamic portraits of the local resources that they can use is a helpful way of making assets visible to everyone. No one person can hold a full picture of all the resources that a community has, so creating a shared and evolving portrait (what some call an asset map) is a powerful method of enabling citizens to discover what resources they already have and to figure out how best to connect unconnected resources.

4. *Sharing*: Intentionally doing things together, from breaking bread to tending a community garden, brings us into a radical presence with our neighbors. Sometimes we also create "shareable moments," times when we intentionally create the conditions for neighbors to become friends. Such shareable moments can include skills exchanges, seed swaps, and repair cafes. They create a community on-ramp for people who may be unsure about how to get into community life. The more these moments enable gift exchange, hospitality, and association, the more likely they will become part of a community's way.

5. *Celebrating*: Celebrating neighborliness and community life—through food, fun, song, and dance—is one of the best and most natural ways to honor our past achievements and dream up new community possibilities.

6. *Visioning*: Creating a collective vision that both sets down the priorities and reveals the opportunities for the shared future of a community is a powerful community-building method that ensures the community will own the process and will be the primary producers of it and the actions that flow from it.

The communities that will be at the center of our global futures will use local resources and some or all of the six methods just described to perform many essential community-building functions.

These are the foundational functions on which community is generated and democracy is rekindled; the resources and methods needed to perform these functions are not to be found on Wall Street. Instead, they reside in the neighborly connections we make, on the streets where we live, and in the quality of civic participation and gifting we engage in with our neighbors. Our job as citizens is to do together what we cannot do apart and what institutions and technology can never do appropriately for us: care for our shared freedoms and responsibilities and, in so doing, get better at being human together. Our job as professionals working in citizen space is, when at work, to support those efforts and, when at home, to engage with similar gusto in our own community efforts.

Humpty Dumpty sat on a wall,

Humpty Dumpty had a great fall.

But all of his neighbors were ready to catch,

They built him a nest, where he safely did hatch.

I know there are many heretics and wayfinders within the institutional world who have taken time to read through these pages and are very eager to co-conspire with citizens to rekindle community. I know you stand ready to scale the empathy wall that has emerged of late in many industrialized countries and, once over that wall, to restore the commons and citizen-centered democracy. Why?

Because you know that—from sperm to worm, from womb to tomb, from birth to earth, and from the first cry to the last sigh—we are human, fallible, finite, and fabulous. Gloriously interdependent with all that was and is to be, from stardust to the salty tears of a lover's grieving remembrance, we are our brothers', sisters', and planet's keepers.

Onwards!

Afterword

REKINDLING DEMOCRACY IS A book that needed to be written. At a time when the words "community," "neighborhood," and increasingly "place" are thrown around with casual abandon, a book that brings focus and a rigorous conceptual framework to these words is hugely welcome. But this book is more than simply a necessary corrective to loose and careless thinking. It is a manifesto for a different sort of society and a more relational, more human way of doing business. Cormac illuminates a debate that is too often characterized by assertion, rather than evidence and experience. Drawing on personal experience that is both deep and broad, Cormac maps out the opportunities facing communities and offers a careful and compelling understanding of the shortcomings of some of the institutions and systems created to respond to "social need."

The way in which Cormac enters into the current debate about the social policy challenge is welcome. There is a debate which—at the risk of parody—is frequently characterized by one corner shouting about austerity and the undoubted need for greater public expenditure, while the opposing corner applauds community self-organization. In this thoughtful contribution to the debate Cormac avoids both positions. He makes it clear that while state intervention, and crucially contribution, is always needed, there are ways in which it can be done in the service of community, just as there are so clearly ways in which it only serves to weaken and destroy the power of communities. The subtle understanding of the different perspectives is an important part of the credibility of this book.

The assets found in communities are frequently eroded by institutions *that only seek to extract*. This publication weaves together a narrative about mutual dependence, a much more community-based future, and at the same time a clear understanding of the challenges and pitfalls facing all those who advocate in this way. It offers a route map for our increasingly uncertain future, and one that is based in deep knowledge, practical experience, and a profound commitment to the common good.

Julia Unwin, DBE, FAcSS

Former chief executive of the Joseph Rowntree Foundation and
Joseph Rowntree Housing Trust Chair of Civil Society Futures,
The Independent Inquiry, 2018

Acknowledgments

WE ARE NOT SELF-RELIANT, we are other-reliant, and the writing of this book has truly reaffirmed this invaluable life lesson. *Rekindling Democracy* is the culmination of several decades of collaboration with countless way-finders from across the world. Special thanks go to the more than seventy fellow travelers who were generous enough to review the later drafts of this book. Too numerous to mention individually here, I list them on the online promotional platform for the book, where I also include their re-views and reflections. To each one I extend my huge gratitude for their contributions to my thinking and my admiration for their respective community-building efforts.

Key to the success of this publication has been the unyielding sup-port that I have received from my wife, Colleen, and our children. Without Colleen's belief in me and the goals of this book, it simply would not have come to fruition. Her regular invitation to step out of my head and back onto solid ground, along with her genuine love and positive outlook—ably assisted by my five sons—have caused my words and thoughts to become more rooted in the realm of the handmade and the homemade. I write for them and because of them.

Special thanks go to Leslie Stephen, whose expert companionship in editing the numerous drafts of this book have shortened the road, making it a most enjoyable learning experience. Her support at critical junctures struck a very rare editorial balance between, on the one hand, offering inci-sive advice that was critical to the overall shape of the final manuscript and, on the other hand, refraining from saying or doing anything that would diminish my "voice" or constrict my message. Leslie, I could not have done this without you.

I feel incredibly fortunate to count John McKnight as one of my closest friends and collaborators. His work in developing the Asset-Based

Community Development (ABCD) approach has provided the world with something of a Rosetta stone for deciphering the irreplaceable functions, resources, and methods used by citizens to collectively build powerful and productive communities from the inside out. His review of the closing drafts of this book provided critical reorientation in some sections and gave vital encouragement in others to trust my own instincts and stick with my line of inquiry or assertions. John, I am incredibly grateful to you for your continued generosity and interest in my work and my efforts to continue to frame the essential elements of ABCD. But most of all, I am grateful for your friendship. I am also honored that your words grace the Foreword of this publication.

Tom Dewar is another dear friend and mentor on my ABCD adventure and in life in general; after John McKnight he has taught me most about the potency of community-driven change and continually reminds me, lest I forget, that institutions are never benign. Tom, for your friendship, sense of fun, and unwavering commitment to the core principles of citizenship and ABCD, thank you.

Special thanks also go to Julia Unwin CBE, who in her capacity as the former CEO of the Joseph Rowntree Foundation has been a long-term supporter of authentic ABCD efforts in the United Kingdom. She has very kindly provided a fitting Afterword to the book. In recent years she has provided invaluable stewardship in co-creating the future of civil society within the UK; I am deeply humbled by her support of and enthusiasm for the message within *Rekindling Democracy*.

I also wish to acknowledge the following people: thanks to Jim Diers for his many years of friendship and his important comments related to social justice and the role of government in neighborhood development. Dr. Howard Rosin (DePaul University), Helima Khan (Nesta UK), Tony Bovaird, John Nicholson, and Clay Forsberg all deserve particular thanks for their extremely thorough book reviews, which shed clear light on the need to focus more on the role of professionals working in citizen space. I am grateful to Paul Born (codirector, Tamarack Institute) for his kind review and keen interest in developing further dialogue around the core themes within the book. Reverend Mike Mather has been a great friend and fellow traveler on the ABCD journey, and few have done more to so deeply root ABCD within their practice and the neighborhood where they live and serve than he. Mike, I have learned so much from your work and the way you show up in the world; many thanks for all you do. Thanks also to Dr. Thomas Hayes for his scholarly review but more importantly for his encouragement to "speak my truth." And to Al Etmanski, who, as well as being a close friend, has warmly encouraged me and offered sage counsel at critical times, which on more than one occasion has prevented me from falling on my face.

Finally, I wish to acknowledge my colleagues at Nurture Development, the social enterprise I am honored to lead; a special word of thanks goes to my colleague Chris Chinnock, who has been a constant companion and co-conspirator in recent years in developing the practical tools and supports to better enable professionals working in citizen space.

All those acknowledged above, along with the thousands of residents that they and I serve, who are at the vanguard of the rekindling of democracy, are the people that this book salutes. They are my inspiration, and my greatest hope for our shared futures.

Cormac Russell
August 2019

About the Author

CORMAC RUSSELL IS MANAGING Director of Nurture Development and a faculty member of the Asset-Based Community Development (ABCD) Institute at DePaul University, Chicago.

Over the last twenty years Russell has worked in more than thirty countries around the world. He has trained communities, agencies, NGOs and governments in ABCD and other strengths-based approaches in Kenya, Rwanda, South Sudan, South Africa, the United Kingdom, Ireland, Sweden, the Netherlands, Canada and Australia.

He is passionate about the proliferation of community-driven change and citizen-centered democracy and has supported hundreds of communities to make ABCD visible through what he calls ABCD Neighborhood Learning Sites. His motto, paraphrasing Benjamin Franklin, is: "When it comes to community building, well done is better than well said."

In January 2011, Russell was appointed to the Expert Reference Group on Community Organising and Communities First by Nick Hurd MP, Minister for Civil Society in the UK, which he served on for the term of the Group.

Community-Building Work Locations

The list below includes some of the places where Russell is working or has worked:

Ayrshire & Arran Learning Site

Gloucestershire Learning Site

Aberdeen

Ghent (Belgium)

Scotland

Norrköping and Linköping (Sweden)

Melbourne (Australia)

Singapore

Central Rumbek (South Sudan)

Articles

"Making the Case for an Asset-Based Community Development (ABCD) Approach to Probation: From Reformation to Transformation." *Irish Probation Journal* 7 (2010) 119–32.

"Communities in Control: Developing Assets." Published by the Carnegie UK Trust. Availabe at https://www.academia.edu/37616739/Communities-in-Control-Developing-Assets.pdf.

"From Needs to Assets: Charting a Sustainable Development Path in Sub-Saharan African Countries." Coauthored by Ted Smeaton. Available at the website of the Asset-Based Community Development Institute: https://resources.depaul.edu/abcd-institute/publications

"Pulling Back from the Edge: An Asset-Based Approach to Ageing." *Working with Older People* 15 (2011) 96–105.

"A Strength-Based Approach to Ageing Well: The Housing Dimension." Coauthored by Lawrence Miller for the Housing Learning & Improvement Network, July 2012. Available at https://www.housinglin.org.uk/Topics/type/A-strength-based-approach-to-ageing-well-the-housing-dimension/

Books

Asset-Based Community Development: Looking Back to Look Forward. Kindle ed., 2017.

Video Clips

"Cormac Russell Explains Asset-Based Community Development" (2011). https://www.youtube.com/watch?v=y6EkaMpAgdE.

"Sustainable Community Development: From What's Wrong to What's Strong." TEDxExeter (2016). https://www.youtube.com/watch?v=a5xR4QB1ADw.

About Nurture Development

NURTURE DEVELOPMENT FACILITATES MEANINGFUL conversations between citizens within communities, and between communities and the agencies that serve them, all with the aim of moving from top-down service delivery to supporting bottom-up, citizen-led action, and supporting agencies to effectively come alongside communities.

The Dublin, Ireland–based firm offers a menu of support options that include training, consulting, evaluation, and mentoring and that can be tailored to suit the specific context. The firm's involvement can start with a keynote address, a two-day training event, or a long-term ongoing relationship; its menu of supports can be accessed individually, sequentially, or as part of an individually tailored, coherent package that goes beyond training and support toward real transformation.

See the Nurture Development website at https://www.nurturedevelopment.org/.

Notes and Sources

Introduction

Desjardins, Lynne. "Loneliness Is a 'Significant Issue' in Canada, Says Doctor." January 19, 2018, Radio Canada International, http://www.rcinet.ca/en/2018/01/19/health-risk-alone-lonely-canadians/.

Edwards, Todd M., et al. See, e.g., "The Treatment of Patients with Medically Unexplained Symptoms in Primary Care: A Review of the Literature." *Mental Health in Family Medicine* 7 (2010) 209–21.

Fredrickson, Barbara L. *Love 2.0: Finding Happiness and Health in Moments of Connection.* Reprint ed. New York: Plume, 2013.

Holt-Lunstad, Julianne, et al. "Loneliness and Social Isolation as Risk Factors for Mortality: A Meta-analytic Review." *Perspectives on Psychological Science* 10 (2015) 227–37. See also "Loneliness Might Be a Bigger Health Risk than Smoking or Obesity," *Forbes*, January 18, 2017, https://www.forbes.com/sites/quora/2017/01/18/loneliness-might-be-a-bigger-health-risk-than-smoking-or-obesity/#1c86273125d1.

Huber, Machteld. "How Should We Define Health?" *British Medical Journal* 343 (2011) 235–37.

UK Prime Minister's Office. "PM Commits to Government-wide Drive to Tackle Loneliness." Press release, January 17, 2018, https://www.gov.uk/government/news/pm-commits-to-government-wide-drive-to-tackle-loneliness.

Vernooij-Dassen, Myrra, and Yun-Hee Jeon. "Social Health and Dementia: The Power of Human Capabilities." *International Psychogeriatrics* 28 (2016) 701–3.

Walburg, Jan, et al., eds. *Performance Management in Health Care: Improving Patient Outcomes; an Integrated Approach.* New York: Routledge, 2006.

Waldinger, Robert. See, e.g., Wadlinger's 2016 TED talk "What Makes a Good Life? Lessons from the Longest Study on Happiness." https://www.youtube.com/watch?time_continue=1&v=8KkKuTCFvzI.

Chapter 1: "Discoverables," Not Deliverables: The World of Asset-Based Community Development

Block, Peter. *Community: The Structure of Belonging*. 2nd ed. Oakland: Berrett-Koehler, 2018.

Brooks, David. "The Neighborhood Is the Unit of Change." *New York Times*, October 18, 2018, https://www.nytimes.com/2018/10/18/opinion/neighborhood-social-infrastructure-community.html.

Ganz, Marshall. "What Is Public Narrative: Self, Us and Now (Public Narrative Worksheet)." Working Paper, Kennedy School of Government, Harvard University, 2009, http://nrs.harvard.edu/urn-3:HUL.InstRepos:30760283.

McKnight, John. "Community Capacities and Community Necessities." Speech presented at the From Clients to Citizens Forum, Coady International Institute, St. Francis Xavier University, Antigonish, Nova Scotia, 2009, https://resources.depaul.edu/abcd-institute/publications/publications-by-topic/

Monbiot, George. "This Is How People Can Truly Take Back Control: From the Bottom Up." *The Guardian*, February 8, 2016, https://www.theguardian.com/commentisfree/2017/feb/08/take-back-control-bottom-up-communities.

Sampson, Robert J., Jeffrey D. Morenoff, and Felton Earls. "Beyond Social Capital: Spatial Dynamics of Collective Efficacy for Children." *American Sociological Review* 64 (1999) 633–60.

Chapter 2: Black Swans, White Swans and Ugly Ducklings: Why Top-Down Approaches (Mostly) Don't Work

Keller, Richard C. *Fatal Isolation: The Devastating Paris Heat Wave of 2003*. Chicago: University of Chicago Press, 2015.

Klinenberg, Eric. *Heat Wave: A Social Autopsy of Disaster in Chicago*. 2nd ed. Chicago: University of Chicago Press, 2015.

Kretzmann, John P., and John McKnight. *Building Communities from the Inside Out: A Path toward Finding and Mobilizing a Community's Assets*. Evanston, IL: Center for Urban Affairs and Policy Research, 1993.

Taleb, Nassim Nicholas. *The Black Swan: The Impact of the Highly Improbable*. New York: Random House, 2007.

Williams, M. J. "Black Swan." In *New Zealand Birds Online*, edited by C. M. Miskelly, http://www.nzbirdsonline.org.nz/species/black-swan.

"World Bank Open Data." Data.worldbank.org, http://data.worldbank.org/ [accessed December 13, 2017]

Chapter 3: The Bernays Curse: Countering the Seven Tactics of Hidden Persuaders

Bernays, Edward L. *Biography of an Idea: Memoirs of Public Relations Counsel Edward L. Bernays*. New York: Simon & Schuster, 1965.

Bernays, Edward L. *Crystallizing Public Opinion*. 1923. Reprint, N.p.: Indo-European Publishing, 2019.

Bernays, Edward L. *Propaganda*. 1928. Reprint, Brooklyn: Ig Publishing, 2004.

Curtis, Adam. *The Century of the Self*. BBC documentary, 2002.

Freire, Paulo. *Pedagogy of the Oppressed*. New York: Herder & Herder, 1970.

Graeber, David. *Debt: The First 5000 Years*. Brooklyn: Melville House, 2011.

Hennezel, Marie de. *The Warmth of the Heart Prevents Your Body from Rusting: Ageing without Growing Old*. Translated by Sue Dyson. New York: Pan, 2012.

"Hoover Economic Report Sees Prosperity Ahead for Nation." *The Evening News*, May 15, 1929, 6, https://news.google.com/newspapers?nid=1977&dat=19290515&id=7lIiAAAAIBAJ&sjid=Q6QFAAAAIBAJ&pg=950,4421314&hl=en.

Kohn, Alfie. *No Contest: The Case against Competition*. Boston: Houghton Mifflin, 1986.

McKnight, John L. *Mask of Love: Professional Care in the Service Economy*. London: Marion Boyars, 1984.

Packard, Vance. *The Hidden Persuaders*. New York: David McKay, 1957.

Polanyi, Karl. *The Great Transformation: The Political and Economic Origins of Our Time*. 2nd ed. Boston: Beacon, 2001. Originally published 1944.

Chapter 4: Paradise Lost: Cargo Cults and Austerity

Attenborough, David (producer). *The People of Paradise*. BBC television series, 1960.

Baudrillard, Jean. *The Consumer Society: Myths and Structures*. London: Sage, 1998.

Beveridge, William. "Social Insurance and Allied Services." British government report, 1942. British Library Archives, London. See https://en.wikipedia.org/wiki/Beveridge_Report.

Graeber, David. *Debt: The First 5000 Years*. Brooklyn: Melville House, 2011.

James, Oliver B. *Affluenza: How to Be Successful and Stay Sane*. London: Vermilion, 2007.

Nurture Development. "Universal Unconditional Basic Income (Part 1 of 2)." August 17, 2018, https://www.nurturedevelopment.org/blog/abcd-approach/universal-unconditional-basic-income-part-1-of-2/.

Sahlins, Marshall. *Stone Age Economics*. London: Routledge Classics, 2017. Originally published 1974.

Chapter 5: Too Small to Fail: Lessons from E. F. Schumacher, Stan Hallett, and Marian Tompson

Illich, Ivan. *Tools for Conviviality*. London: Marion Boyars, 2001. Originally published 1973.

Kohr, Leopold. *The Breakdown of Nations*. London: Routledge & Kegan Paul, 1957.

McKnight, John, and Peter Block. *The Abundant Community: Awakening the Power of Families and Neighborhoods*. San Francisco: Berrett-Koehler, 2010.

Russell, Cormac. *Asset-Based Community Development: Looking Back to Look Forward*. Kindle ed., 2017.

Schumacher, E. F. *Small Is Beautiful: Economics as if People Mattered*. London: Blond & Briggs, 1973.

Stein, Gertrude. *Everybody's Autobiography*. New York: Random House, 1937.

Chapter 6: In Critique of Development: Choosing Sufficiency over Greed

Apffel-Marglin, Frédérique. *Wives of the God-King: The Rituals of the Devadasis of Puri.* Oxford: Oxford University Press, 1985.

Collier, Paul. *The Bottom Billion: Why the Poorest Countries Are Failing and What Can Be Done about It.* New York: Oxford University Press, 2007.

Easterly, William. *The Tyranny of Experts: Economists, Dictators, and the Forgotten Rights of the Poor.* New York: Basic Books, 2013.

Miles, Angela R. *Integrative Feminisms: Building Global Visions, 1960s–1990s.* London: Routledge, 1996.

Moyo, Dambisa. *Dead Aid: Why Aid Is Not Working and How There Is a Better Way for Africa.* New York: Farrar, Straus & Giroux, 2009.

Patel, Raj. *Stuffed and Starved: The Hidden Battle for the World Food System.* Rev. ed. Brooklyn: Melville House, 2012.

Sachs, Jeffrey. *The Price of Civilization: Reawakening American Virtue and Prosperity.* New York: Random House, 2011.

Shiva, Vandana. *Staying Alive: Women, Ecology and Development.* London: Zed, 1989.

Shiva, Vandana. *The Violence of the Green Revolution: Third World Agriculture, Ecology, and Politics.* London: Zed, 1991.

Vaughan, Genevieve, ed. *Women and the Gift Economy: A Radically Different Worldview Is Possible.* Toronto: Inanna Publications and Education, 2007.

Chapter 7: Economic Imperatives: Departing the Marketplace and Rekindling Local Economies

Berry, Wendell. "People Who Own the World Outright for Profit Have to Be Stopped." 2012 Earth Day Speech, https://www.youtube.com/watch?v=ushcvD2yDFI. See also https://thinkprogress.org/wendell-berrys-earth-day-speech-people-who-own-the-world-outright-for-profit-will-have-to-be-stopped-5bb42709abd1/.

Block, Peter. "Building Economically Viable Neighborhoods." Post for Zingerman's Speaker Series 2016, http://www.zingermanscommunity.com/2016/08/peter-block-creating-a-compassionate-econcomy/. See also "The Economics of Neighborliness: A Requirement for an Abundant Community," May 25, 2011, https://www.abundantcommunity.com/home/posts/peter_block/parms/1/post/20110525_the_economics_of_neighborliness.html and "Neighborly Economics: A Way Towards the Exchange of Gifts," n.d., https://www.restorecommons.com/neighborly-economics-a-way-towards-the-exchange-of-gifts/.

Duda, John. "The Italian Region Where Co-ops Produce a Third of Its GDP." *YES! Magazine*, July 5, 2016, https://www.yesmagazine.org/new-economy/the-italian-place-where-co-ops-drive-the-economy-and-most-people-are-members-20160705.

Graeber, David. *Bullshit Jobs: A Theory.* New York: Simon & Schuster, 2018.

Hum, Derek, and Wayne Simpson. "Income Maintenance, Work Effort, and the Canadian Mincome Experiment." A study prepared for the Economic Council of Canada, 1991. https://doi.org/10.5203/FK2/JWVHEJ.

Illich, Ivan. *The Right to Useful Unemployment and Its Professional Enemies.* London: Marion Boyars, 1978.

Nebraska Community Foundation. "2016 Annual Report." http://www.nebcommfound. org/news-events/newsletters-annual-reports/read/2015-annual-report/.

Nebraska Community Foundation. "Fact Sheet Nebraska Community Foundation 2011 Transfer of Wealth Study." http://www.nebcommfound.org/media/docs/ Fact_Sheet_for_Media.pdf.

Polanyi, Karl. *The Great Transformation: The Political and Economic Origins of Our Time.* 2nd ed. Boston: Beacon, 2001. Originally published 1944.

Raworth, Kate. *Doughnut Economics: 7 Ways to Think Like a 21st-Century Economist.* White River Junction, VT: Chelsea Green, 2017.

Sahlins, Marshall. *Stone Age Economics.* London: Routledge Classics, 2017. Originally published 1974.

Schumacher, E. F. *Small Is Beautiful: Economics as if People Mattered.* London: Blond & Briggs, 1973.

Chapter 8: Pulling Back from the Edge: Growing Old in the West

Denning, Stephen. *The Springboard: How Storytelling Ignites Action in Knowledge-Era Organizations.* KMCI ed. London: Routledge, 2011.

Foot, Jane, with Trevor Hopkins. "A Glass Half-Full: How an Asset Approach Can Improve Community Health and Well-Being." Report to the Improvement and Development Agency (I&DEA) of the UK Local Government Association, 2009, http://www.janefoot.co.uk/downloads/files/Glass%20half%20full.pdf.

Fueyo, A., and N. Perez. "Help Thy Neighbour." *Costa Blanca News,* February 24, 2011.

Guha, S. "The Dordogne: These May Not Be Englishmen's Castles, but It Feels Like Home." *The Independent,* October 24, 2010.

Harrop, Emily, et al. "Resilience, Coping and Salutogenic Approaches to Maintaining and Generating Health: A Review." Cardiff Institute of Society, Health and Ethics at Cardiff University, 2007.

Illich, Ivan. *The Right to Useful Unemployment and Its Professional Enemies.* Reissue ed. London: Marion Boyars, 1978.

Jones, D. "New Charity Offers to Help Costa Brits." *Costa Blanca News,* May 27, 2011.

Kett, S. "Brits Abroad 'Should Be Entitled to Benefits.'" *Costa Blanca News,* July 2, 2011.

Lichfield, John. "Sarkozy's Plan to Tax Holiday Homes Alarms 'les Rosbifs.'" *The Independent,* June 14, 2011.

Marques, G. A. "Don't Sell Too Cheaply." *Costa Blanca News,* May 6, 2011.

McKnight, John, and Peter Block. *The Abundant Community: Awakening the Power of Families and Neighborhoods.* San Francisco: Berrett-Koehler, 2010.

Sampson, Robert J. *Great American City: Chicago and the Enduring Neighborhood Effect.* Chicago: University of Chicago Press, 2012.

Uglow, Jenny. *The Lunar Men: Five Friends Whose Curiosity Changed the World.* New York: Farrar, Straus and Giroux, 2002.

Chapter 9: It Takes a Village:
In Search of Medical Heretics

Block, Peter. *Community: The Structure of Belonging*. 2nd ed. Oakland: Berrett-Koehler, 2018.

Diagnostic and Statistical Manual of Mental Disorders: DSM-5. Washington, DC: American Psychiatric Publishing, 2013.

Gawande, Atul. "The Art of Well-Being." Reith Lectures, 2014, http://www.bbc.co.uk/programmes/articles/6F2X8TpsxrJpnsq82hggHW/dr-atul-gawande-2014-reith-lectures. See also Atul Gawande, *Being Mortal: Medicine and What Matters in the End*. New York: Henry Holt, 2014.

Godrej, Dinyar. "A Healthy Mind in a Healthy Society." *New Internationalist*, May 1, 2012, https://newint.org/features/2012/05/01/mental-health-society/.

Illich, Ivan. *Limits to Medicine: Medical Nemesis; The Expropriation of Health*. London: Marian Boyars, 1976.

Illich, Ivan. *Tools for Conviviality*. London: Marian Boyars, 1973.

McGarvey, Darren. *Poverty Safari: Understanding the Anger of Britain's Underclass*. Edinburgh: Luath, 2017.

Mendelsohn, Robert S., et al. *Dissent in Medicine: Nine Doctors Speak Out*. Chicago: Contemporary Books, 1985. See also Robert S. Mendelsohn, *Confessions of a Medical Heretic*. Chicago: Contemporary Books, 1979.

Marmot, Michael, et al. "Fair Society Healthy Lives (The Marmot Review)." Institute of Health Equity (UK) report, February 2010, http://www.instituteofhealthequity.org/resources-reports/fair-society-healthy-lives-the-marmot-review.

Russell, Cormac. *Asset-Based Community Development: Looking Back to Look Forward*. Kindle ed., 2017.

Sahlins, Marshall. "The Original Affluent Society." Excerpt from *Stone Age Economics*, http://appropriate-economics.org/materials/Sahlins.pdf. See Marshall Sahlins, *Stone Age Economics*. London: Routledge Classics, 2017. Originally published 1974.

Social Marketing Gateway. "Asset-Based Community Devlopment in Ayrshire." https://www.socialmarketinggateway.co.uk/case-studies/?cs-name=asset-based-community-development-in-ayrshire.

Williams, Rachel. "Why Social Prescriptions Are Just What the Doctor Ordered." *The Guardian*, November 5, 2013, https://www.theguardian.com/society/2013/nov/05/social-prescribing-fishing-group-doctor-ordered.

Yan, Jun. "Percentage of Americans Taking Antidepressants Climbs." American Psychiatric Association, *Psychiatric News*, September 15, 2017, https://doi.org/10.1176/appi.pn.2017.pp9b2.

Young, Andy. "Good Mental Health Is Rooted in Social Cohesion, Not the Individual." *Nursing Times*, January 18, 2010, https://www.nursingtimes.net/nursing-practice/clinical-zones/mental-health/good-mental-health-is-rooted-in-social-cohesion-not-the-individual/5010486.article.

Chapter 10: Rekindling Well-Being from the Inside Out: Learning from Institutional Radicals

Miller, Jerome G. *Last One Over the Wall: The Massachusetts Experiment in Closing Reform Schools.* Columbus: Ohio State University Press, 1991.

Russell, Cormac. *Asset-Based Community Development: Looking Back to Look Forward.* Kindle ed., 2017.

Social Marketing Gateway. "Building Community: An Evaluation of Asset-Based Community Development (ABCD) in Ayrshire—Final Report to NHS Ayrshire and Arran." May 2018, https://www.nurturedevelopment.org/wp-content/uploads/2018/08/ABCD_Final_Report_May2018.pdf

Chapter 11: Generating Change and Innovation: The Leadership Question

Institute for Local Self-Reliance. *Building Local Power* (podcast). https://ilsr.org/building-local-power/.

Newby, Kris. "Stanford Bioengineer Develops a 50-Cent Paper Microscope." Stanford Medicine, March 10, 2014, http://scopeblog.stanford.edu/2014/03/10/stanford-bioengineer-develops-a-50-cent-paper-microscope/.

Pahl, Greg. *Power from the People: How to Organize, Finance, and Launch Local Energy Projects.* White River Junction, VT: Chelsea Green, 2012.

Pink, Daniel H. *A Whole New Mind: Why Right-Brainers Will Rule the Future.* New York: Riverhead, 2005.

Prakash, Manu. "A 50-Cent Microscope That Folds Like Origami." TED Global Conference, June 2012, https://www.ted.com/talks/manu_prakash_a_50_cent_microscope_that_folds_like_origami?language=en.

Chapter 12: Growing Collective Power: Power from the People, Power to the People

Barber, Benjamin. "Why Mayors Should Rule the World." TED Global Conference, June 2013, https://www.ted.com/talks/benjamin_barber_why_mayors_should_rule_the_world, 2013.

Block, Peter. *Community: The Structure of Belonging.* San Francisco: Berrett-Koehler, 2008.

Bunt, Laura, and Michael Harris. "Mass Localism: A Way to Help Small Communities Solve Big Social Challenges." Analysis and Policy Observatory discussion paper, March 17, 2010, https://www.nesta.org.uk/report/mass-localism/.

Jacobs, Jane. *The Death and Life of Great American Cities.* 50th anniv. ed. New York: Modern Library, 2011. Originally published 1961.

Karimi, Faith, and Dave Alsup. "Oops! Seattle Mayor Mourns Death of Local Official Who's Very Much Alive." *CNN*, February 28, 2014, http://edition.cnn.com/2014/02/28/us/seattle-man-not-dead/

Knight Foundation, in partnership with Gallup. "Soul of the Community." 2010, https://knightfoundation.org/sotc/. See also "Soul of the Community 2010 Overall Findings," 2010, https://knightfoundation.org/sotc/overall-findings/.

Mollison, Bill, and David Holmgren. *Permaculture One: A Perennial Agriculture for Human Settlements*. N.p.: International Tree Crop Institute USA, 1981.

Pirsig, Robert M. *Zen and the Art of Motorcycle Maintenance: An Inquiry into Values*. New York: William Morrow, 1974.

Skidmore, Paul, and John Craig. *Start with People: How Community Organisations Put Citizens in the Driving Seat*. London: Demos Magdalen House, 2005. Available at https://www.demos.co.uk/files/startwithpeople.pdf.

US Library of Congress. "Subject to Change." August 2010, https://www.loc.gov/wiseguide/aug10/subject.html.

Chapter 13: Building Community and Pathways to Citizenship: Deschooling Society and Practicing the Art of Motorcycle Maintenance

Block, Peter, and John McKnight. "Why Families Fall Apart." *Huffington Post*, November 1, 2011, https://www.huffingtonpost.com/peter-block/why-families-fall-apart_b_945235.html.

Featherstone, Brid, et al. *Protecting Children: A Social Model*. Bristol, UK: Policy Press, 2018.

Grawert, Ames, Matthew Friedman, and James Cullen. "Crime Trends: 1990–2016." Brennan Center for Justice, April 2017, https://www.brennancenter.org/publication/crime-trends1990-2016.

Illich, Ivan. *Deschooling Society*. New York: Harper & Row, 1971.

Molnar, Beth E., et al. "Neighborhood-Level Social Processes and Substantiated Cases of Child Maltreatment." *Child Abuse & Neglect* 51 (2016) 41–53.

Pirsig, Robert M. *Zen and the Art of Motorcycle Maintenance: An Inquiry into Values*. New York: William Morrow, 1974.

Chapter 14: Restoring the Village: From Youth at Risk to Youth at Promise

Gatto, John Taylor. *Dumbing Us Down: The Hidden Curriculum of Compulsory Schooling*. Gabriola Island, BC: New Society, 2005. Originally published 1992.

Hammond, Claudia. "The Anatomy of Loneliness." BBC Radio, 2018, https://www.bbc.co.uk/programmes/articles/2yzhfv4DvqVp5nZyxBD8G23/who-feels-lonely-the-results-of-the-world-s-largest-loneliness-study.

Sampson, Robert J. "When Disaster Strikes, It's Survival of the Sociable." *New Scientist*, May 8, 2013, https://www.newscientist.com/article/mg21829160-400-when-disaster-strikes-its-survival-of-the-sociable/.

Chapter 16: Working at the Speed of Trust: Serving while Walking Backward

Cohen, Leonard. "Anthem." Released on the album *The Future* (1992). See, e.g., Charlotte Runcie, "There Is a Crack in Everything / That's How the Light Gets In: The Best Leonard Cohen Lyrics." *The Telegraph*, November 11, 2016, https://www. telegraph.co.uk/music/artists/the-best-leonard-cohen-lyrics/.

Chapter 18: Thinking Small: Animating Community at the Human Scale

Berry, Wendell. "Contempt for Small Places." In *The Way of Ignorance and Other Essays*. Washington, DC: Shoemaker & Hoard, 2005.
Westside Health Authority. http://healthauthority.org/.

Chapter 19: Widening Our Sphere of Influence: Enacting Democracy with a Whisper

Althusser, Louis. "Three Notes on the Theory of Discourses." In *The Humanist Controversy and Other Writings (1966–67)*, edited by François Matheron, 33–84, selected 47–53. London: Verso, 1966.
Arendt, Hannah. *Crises of the Republic*. New York: Harcourt Brace, 1972.
Goldfarb, Jeffrey C. *The Politics of Small Things: The Power of the Powerless in Dark Times*. Chicago: University of Chicago Press, 2006.
Janouch, Gustav, and Goronwy Rees. *Conversations with Kafka*. Rev. and enlarged ed. New York: New Directions, 1971.
McKnight, John, and Peter Block. *The Abundant Community: Awakening the Power of Families and Neighborhoods*. San Francisco: Berrett-Koehler, 2012.

Chapter 20: The Tools for Social Change: Growing an Association of Associations

Groce, Nora Ellen. *Everyone Here Spoke Sign Language: Hereditary Deafness on Martha's Vineyard*. Cambridge: Harvard University Press, 1985. See also Cormac Russell, "Fantasy Island: Is Disability Just a Construct?" *Nurture Development* (blog), August 2014, http://www.nurturedevelopment.org/blog/fantasy-island-is-disability-just-a-construct/.
Illich, Ivan. *Deschooling Society*. New York: Harper & Row, 1971.
McKnight, John. "Regenerating Community: The Recovery of a Space for Citizens." Institute for Policy Research at Northwestern University, Distinguished Public Policy Lecture Series, May 29, 2003, https://resources.depaul.edu/abcd-institute/publications/publications-by-topic/Documents/regenerating.pdf.
Miłosz, Czesław. *Selected Poems*. New York: HarperCollins, 1996.

Chapter 21: Enacting Democracy: Behind the Veils of Technocracy, Consumerism, and Globalization

Boyte, Harry Chatten. *The Citizen Solution: How You Can Make a Difference.* Saint Paul, MN: Minnesota Historical Society, 2008.

Dunkelman, Marc J. *The Vanishing Neighbor: The Transformation of American Community.* New York: Norton, 2014.

Friedman, Thomas L. "It's a Flat World, After All." *New York Times Magazine,* April 3, 2005, https://www.nytimes.com/2005/04/03/magazine/its-a-flat-world-after-all.html.

Goldenberg, Suzanne. "Planet Earth Is Home to 8.7 Million Species, Scientists Estimate." *The Guardian,* August 23, 2011, https://www.theguardian.com/environment/2011/aug/23/species-earth-estimate-scientists.

Goldfarb, Jeffrey C. *The Politics of Small Things: The Power of the Powerless in Dark Times.* Chicago: University of Chicago Press, 2006.

Horton, Myles, and Paulo Freire. *We Make the Road by Walking: Conversations on Education and Social Change.* Philadelphia: Temple University Press, 1990.

Klein, Naomi. *This Changes Everything: Capitalism vs. the Climate.* New York: Simon & Schuster, 2014.

Leiss, William. *The Limits to Satisfaction: An Essay on the Problem of Needs and Commodities.* Toronto: University of Toronto Press, 1976.

Wallis, Stewart. "A Great Transition." Speech given at Responsibility in Economics and Business Conference, University of Antwerp, Belgium, September 2011, https://centerforneweconomics.org/publications/a-great-transition/.

Chapter 22: Rekindling Democracy: The Wide View

Bar-On, Yinon, Rob Phillips, and Ron Milo. "The Biomass Distribution on Earth." *Proceedings of the National Academy of Sciences of the United States* 115 (2018) 6506–11.

Block, Peter. "Building Economically Viable Neighborhoods." Post for Zingerman's Speaker Series 2016, http://www.zingermanscommunity.com/2016/08/peter-block-creating-a-compassionate-econcomy/. See also "The Economics of Neighborliness: A Requirement for an Abundant Community," May 25, 2011, https://www.abundantcommunity.com/home/posts/peter_block/parms/1/post/20110525_the_economics_of_neighborliness.html; and "Neighborly Economics: A Way Towards the Exchange of Gifts," n.d., https://www.restorecommons.com/neighborly-economics-a-way-towards-the-exchange-of-gifts/.

Hobbes, Thomas. *Leviathan.* 4th ed. London: Penguin Classics, 1982. Originally published 1651.

Hoffer, Eric. *The True Believer: Thoughts on the Nature of Mass Movements.* New York: Harper, 1951.

Knight Foundation, in partnershp with Gallup. "Soul of the Community," 2010, https://knightfoundation.org/sotc/.

Kohn, Alfie. *Competition Is Ruining Us! There Is a Better Way.* British Deming Association Seventh Annual Conference, April 1994.

Miller, Jerome G. *Last One over the Wall: The Massachusetts Experiment in Closing Reform Schools.* Columbus: Ohio State University Press, 1991.

Raworth, Kate. *Doughnut Economics: 7 Ways to Think Like a 21st-Century Economist.* White River Junction, VT: Chelsea Green, 2017.

Sahlins, Marshall. *Stone Age Economics.* London: Routledge Classics, 2017. Originally published 1974.

Sapolsky, Robert. *A Primate's Memoir: A Neuroscientist's Unconventional Life among the Baboons.* New York: Touchstone, 2001.

Schumacher, E. F. *Small Is Beautiful: Economics as if People Mattered.* London: Blond & Briggs, 1973.

Conclusion: Serving in Civic Space

Etmanski, Al. "Slow Change." June 23, 2015. http://aletmanski.com/impact/slow-change/.

Hirschman, Albert O. *Exit, Voice and Loyalty: Responses to Decline in Firms, Organizations, and States.* Cambridge: Harvard University Press, 1970.

Keane, John B. "The Ballad of Con Carey." June 2, 1978, https://static.rasset.ie/documents/doc-on-one/the-ballad-of-con-carey.pdf

Index

Figures are indicated by "f"
after the page number.

ABCD. *See* asset-based community
    development
abundance
    community abundance, 84, 101
    scarcity versus, 45–47, 63, 65, 79, 81,
        227f, 228
Abundant Community (McKnight and
    Block), 60
affluenza, 45–46
aggression, nature of, 215
aging, in the West. *See* growing old, in
    the West
Alinsky, Saul, 62, 172
Althusser, Louis, 188
Amqui, Quebec, community problem-
    solving in, 21–22, 24
Angelou, Maya, 155
Anthropocene, 215
anticolonialism, 183
Apffel-Marglin, Frédérique, 70–71
appropriate technology, 57, 58, 59, 75
Arendt, Hannah, 190–91
"The Art of Well-Being" (Gawande),
    111
asset-based community development
    (ABCD), 13–23
    in Ayrshire, Scotland, 106–9
    citizen participation in, 21–23
    conclusions on, 23
    deficit model versus, 227–29, 227f
    description of, 180–81
    essential pieces of, 171–72

focus of, 29
    introduction to, 9, 13–15
    neighborhoods as units of
        democracy, 18–20
    prevalence of, 180
    principles and practices of, 15–18
Asset-Based Community Development
    (ABCD) Institute, 28–29
Asset-Based Community Development
    (Russell), 9
assets
    asset-based economies, 58
    asset-based practices, 16
    asset maps, 20, 230
    community building blocks, 28
    consequential to health, 111–12
    importance of knowledge of, 213–14
    nature of, 58
    primary assets, mobilization of,
        73–76
associational life (relational power), 7,
    15, 93, 95, 117, 199–200, 200f
associational world, 60
associations
    associations of, 172, 193–201
    under austerity measures, 48
    of connectors, 175
    functions of, 41
    Hallett on, 60
    smaller mediating hybrid
        associations, 158–59

attachment, as metric for communities, 132

austerity, cargo cults and, 43–53

Austin, Chicago, Westside Health Authority, 181–82

Australia, cultural history of Indigenous Australians, 5–6

authentic voices, 225

authority, locus of, 227f, 228

autos, bikes versus, 63

BACA (Bikers Against Child Abuse), 144–45

balanced living, 54–62

"The Ballad of Con Carey" (Keane), 223

Bar-On, Yinon M., 215

Barber, Benjamin, 133

Barrett, Al, 173–74

Baylis, Trevor, 126–27

Bentham, Jeremy, 71

Bernays, Edward, 33–35, 40, 212, 221

Bernays curse. See hidden persuaders, countering tactics of

Berry, Wendell, 52, 83, 99, 177, 179

Betty Crocker cake mixes, 36

Bikers Against Child Abuse (BACA), 144–45

bikes, cars versus, 63

Birmingham, England, Industrial Revolution in, 95

Black Swan theory, 24

Block, Peter
  Abundant Community, 60
  on children, caring for, 142
  on dissent, 110
  mentioned, 20
  on neighborly economy, 77–78, 214
  on questions and answers, 138

book exchanges, 144

Borlaug, Norman, 66–67

bottom-up community building, xiv

boundaries, of communities, 17

Bowie, David, 210

Boyte, Harry, 203

breastfeeding, 61–62

Brexit, 94

Brigham Young University, study of loneliness, 4–5

Bristol, UK, citizen action in, 189

Brooks, David, 18–19

Brueggemann, Walter, 203

Building Communities from the Inside Out (McKnight and Kretzmann), 28

bullshit jobs, 80–81

BY space, 155–56, 156f, 210, 214f, 222

Camp Kulin, 75–76

Canada
  loneliness in, 4–5
  Mincome experiment, 83
  veterans, support for, 82

Canadian Conference of Community Development Organizations, 22

care and caring, 39–40, 118

Carey, Con, 222–25

cargo cults, austerity and, 43–53
  cargo cults narrative, 44–45
  conclusions on, 53
  disabling professionals, 47–49
  introduction to, 43–44
  scarcity versus abundance and, 45–47
  welfare systems, sympathy versus empathy in, 49–53

Carin (community center creator), 1–2, 229–30

cars, bikes versus, 63

Carter, Damian, 189

celebrating, 230

Center for Urban Affairs (Northwestern University), 194–95

certainties, questionable, xvi, 210–17

change
  change spectrum model, 227–29, 227f
  enduring change, sequence of, 168–69
  social change, leadership and, 123–24
  social change, tools for, 193–201
  social change movements, nature of, 130
  sources of, 123–28
  speed of, 229
  units of, 172, 179

Chicago
  heatwave deaths in, 26

Westside Health Authority, 181–82
children
    child care, traditional nature of, 2
    ensuring safety of, 146–52
    raising powerful, 92–93
    in shame-based cultures, 181–82
    supporting through community
        building, 139–45
Chipko movement, 65–66
Chiquita Brands International, 35
chronos (time), 227f, 229
cigarettes, women and, 36
Citizen Credo, 135–36
The Citizen Solution (Boyte), 203
citizens and citizenship
    building pathways to, 139–45
    citizen-led practices, 15
    citizen participation, support for
        creation of, 21–23
    citizen space, reduction in, 57
    citizen-to-citizen participation, 8,
        221, 226
    citizens as co-creators, 155–56, 156f
    clientship versus, 4
    consumers versus, 196, 204
    critical functions of, 19–20
    institutions versus, 7–8, 227f, 228
    professionalism versus, 161, 170
    role of, 210, 231
    subjects versus, 136–37
    See also communities
civic life
    children's relationship to, 148
    civic action, as senior citizen
        competence area, 94–95
    civic inventiveness, 196–97
    civic libraries, 144
    civic professionals, 103, 201
    critical functions of, 19–20
clientship, 4, 48, 136–37, 188
co-operatives, 76
Cohen, Leonard, 166
Collier, Paul, 64
colonialism, 183, 188
the commons, 69, 79
communities (neighborhoods)
    assets of, 13
    boundaries of, 17
    building resilient, 93

children's safety and, 147–51
    citizen-professional relations in,
        101–2, 104
    "community" as term, meaning of,
        177–78
    community care, 61
    community kitchens, 51–52
    community safety, 90
    consumerism versus, 29–30, 60–61,
        210
    critical functions of, 19–20
    health, role in, 100, 104–9 (See also
        medical heretics, search for)
    identifying existing capacities of,
        159–62
    impact of austerity measures on,
        47–48
    importance of, 7–8, 60–61, 217
    institutions versus, 52, 54–57, 61,
        65, 116–17, 135
    neighborliness, 16–17, 76–80
    optimum population size of, 178–79
    as prisons, 146
    as sites of power, 131
    souls of, 131–34
    as units for change, 14, 16, 18–20,
        123, 211, 228–29
    village economies, as homes for
        consumers, 38–39
    villages, functions of, 39
    well-being of, 138
    See also asset-based community
        development; citizens;
        community building;
        deschooling society
community, connection with state,
        187–218
    associations, association of, 193–201
    questionable certainties, 210–17
    sphere of influence, widening of,
        187–92
    technocracy, consumerism, and
        globalization, 202–9
community, deepening of, 123–53
    collective power, 129–38
    deschooling society, 139–45
    leadership, question of, 123–28
    youth and, 146–52

community, rekindling of, 33–85
  balanced living, 54–62
  cargo cults and austerity, 43–53
  development, critique of, 63–71
  hidden persuaders, countering
      tactics of, 33–42
  local economies, rekindling of,
      72–84
  See also *detailed entries for these
      concepts*
community building
  characteristics of, 208–9
  community building blocks, 28
  healthcare and, 109–11
  human scale of, 168–76
  measurements of, 167
  methods for, 229–31
  principles of, 155–62, 166–67,
      169–76
  relief versus, 227, 227f
  supporting children through,
      139–45
  See also asset-based community
      development
community-building principles,
      application of, 155–85
  community building, principles of,
      155–62
  human scale of community
      building, 168–76
  trust, 163–67
competition, 39, 215
Competition Is Ruining Us! (Kohn), 215
conductors, social inventors as, 126–28
connectors and connectorship, 124–26,
      128, 168–76
consent, engineering of, 34
consumerism
  addictive consumption, 35–37, 165
  assumptions of, 76
  Bernays and, 34–35
  as cargo cult, 45
  characteristics of, 30
  consumer economy, 78
  consumer rights, 130
  consumers, citizens versus, 196, 204
  culture of, xi
  delivery in, 213–14

  effects of, 37–38, 39, 165, 221
  need for shift from, 138
  neighborhoods versus, 29–30,
      60–61, 210
  question of benefits of, 212
  technocracy and globalization and,
      202–9
  on working, 81
  youth, impact on, 150
"Contempt for Small Places" (Berry),
      177
corporate greed, 35
Cousins, Norman, 219
COVID-19, 219
creative outlets, as compelling need, 36
crime, fear of, 143
cruise industry, 49
Crystallizing Public Opinion (Bernays),
      33
cults, 44–45
  See also cargo cults, austerity and
culture
  community, cultural functions of,
      19–20, 180–82
  cultural heritage, under austerity
      measures, 48
  shame-based cultures, 181–82
curiosity, helpfulness versus, 155, 160,
      162
currencies, 78, 79
customers, nature of, 137

data, question of role of, 213
deafness, in Martha's Vineyard, 197–98
death and dying, 222–25
Declaration of Independence, "subjects"
      versus "citizen" in, 136
decolonization, 52
deficiencies
  cargo cults and, 46
  deficiency mindset, in modern
      economies, 78
  deficit model versus ABCD, 227–29,
      227f
  deficit-oriented processes, 169–70
  humans as defined by, 211
  inappropriate focus on, 28, 87, 170
  public health focus on, 100

as supposed cause of societal
breakdowns, 190
deforestation, 65–66
deinstitutionalization, 118
deliverables, 13–14
delivery, question of benefits of, 213–14,
214f
democracy
central task of, 18
characteristics of flourishing
democracy, 156
chemistry of, 206–8
child safety as measure of, 148
citizen-centered, 191–92, 196–97,
207–9
functions of citizens in, 19
local, as way of living, 135
locus of, 138
redefinition of, 3–5
as term, origins of, 136, 221
democracy, rekindling of
asset-based community
development, 13–23
associations, association of, 193–201
balanced living, 54–62
cargo cults and austerity, 43–53
children, ensuring safety of, 146–52
collective power, 129–38
community building, principles of,
155–62
community building, supporting
children through, 139–45
conclusions on, 219–31
connectorship, art of, 168–76
development, critique of, 63–71
growing old, in the West, 87–98
hidden persuaders, countering
tactics of, 33–42
human scale of community
building, 168–76
institutional radicals, learning from,
113–20
introduction to, 1–9
leadership, question of, 123–28
local economies, rekindling of,
72–84
medical heretics, search for, 99–112
policymakers, questionable
certainties of, 210–17

sphere of influence, widening of,
187–92
technocracy, consumerism, and
globalization, 202–9
top-down approaches, failures of,
24–29
trust, 163–67
See also detailed entries for these
topics
DEMOS, report on local power, 132–33
Denning, Stephen, 96
Department of Youth Services
(Massachusetts), 115
DePaul University, Asset-Based
Community Development
Institute, 28–29
dependence, 40, 51, 117, 221
deschooling society, 139–45
development, critique of, 63–71
Deventer, Netherlands, community
center development in, 1–3
Diagnostic and Statistical Manual of
Mental Disorders, Fifth Edition
(DSM-5), 105
Diers, Jim, 133, 134
disabilities, locus of definition of,
197–98
disabling professionals, 47–49
discoverables and discovering, 13–14,
229
Dissent in Medicine (Mendelsohn),
102–3
distancing, dangers of, xv–xvi
divorce, reasons for, 142
D'Onofrio, Leonardo, 146
Doughnut Economics (Raworth), 77
dreams, 192
drugs, overmedicalization, 111
DSM-5 (Diagnostic and Statistical
Manual of Mental Disorders,
Fifth Edition), 105
Dublin Docklands area, senior health
and safety in, 89
Dumbing Us Down (Gatto), 149
Dunkelman, Marc, 204
dynamos, as metaphor for social change,
124–25

Easterly, William, 64
ecocide, 62, 179, 205–6
ecofeminism, 65
ecologies, under austerity measures, 48
economics and economies
    asset-based economies, 58
    under austerity measures, 48
    economic development, inside-out
        orientation to, 73
    economic floors and safety nets, 82
    economic sovereignty, 205
    economically marginalized
        communities, 27, 44, 46–47, 52,
        159, 190
    economically marginalized people,
        4, 19, 44–45, 72, 83, 169, 182,
        194, 211
    grants economy, 58
    industrial economy, 78
    local economies, nurturing of,
        90–92
    modern economies, critiques of, 76
    modern economies, gift economies
        versus, 71
    neoliberal economies, question of
        extent of, 214–15
    of scarcity, health and, 100–101
    society, relationship to, 72–73
    Stone Age economics, 76–77
    trickle-down theory of, 77
    See also marketplace and market
        economies
educational techniques, at Strange
    School, 3
ego gratification, as compelling need, 36
electric toothbrushes, 59–60
Eliot, George, 163
Elis, Rudy, 74
emergency response, as senior citizen
    competence area, 95
emergent invention, 208
Emilia-Romagna, Italy, co-ops in, 76
emotional security, as compelling need,
    35
empathy, sympathy versus, 49–53
employment, nature of, 83
energy providers, 124–25

entrenchment. See austerity, cargo cults
    and
environment
    ecofeminism, 65
    ecologies, under austerity measures,
        48
    environmental/social change, 14
    as senior citizen competence area,
        90–91
equality feminism, 70
Etmanski, Al, 229
Europe
    European Troika, 205
    heat waves in, 25–27
Everybody's Autobiography (Stein), 61
Everyone Here Spoke Sign Language
    (Groce), 197–98
exchange, 63, 68–69, 71, 78–80

fake news, 38
fear, of crime, 143
Featherstone, Brid, 145
feminism. See women and feminism
Fire Souls, xi
Food, Energy, Soil, Water, Air and Waste
    (FESWAW), 58, 59–60, 63
food, safe production of, 92
food banks, 49–50
FOR space, 155–56, 156f, 210, 214f,
    220, 222
Foucault, Michel, 71
France
    British second homes in, 91
    heat wave deaths, 25
Fredrickson, Barbara, 7
free market, question of benefits of, 212
Freire, Paulo, 41, 207
Freud, Sigmund, 33
Freudian slips, 33
Friedman, Thomas, 205

GAH (gift exchange, associations, and
    hospitality), 79
Gallup organization, survey on
    community power, 131–32,
    215–16

gaman (fortitude in times of unbearable challenge), 95
Ganz, Marshall, 19
garaiocht (proximity), 137
gardens, community gardens, 92
Gatto, John Taylor, 149
Gawande, Atul, 111
gender divisions, green revolution and, 67–68
generational divides, 94
George, Robert M., 145
G.I. Bill (Servicemen's Readjustment Act, 1944), 82–83
gift economies
    associations and, 41
    exchange versus gift giving, 63, 71
    gifts, labels and, xvi
    in Papua New Guinea, 49
    Tanna as, 45
    village economies as, 38
    Voorstad-Oost community center and, 2
    women and, 68–69
gift exchange, associations, and hospitality (GAH), 79
Global South
    changing attitudes toward, 64–65
    electrification of, 126
    green revolution and, 66–68
    impact of globalization on, 69
globalism (globalization), 69, 205–6, 212, 221
Godrej, Dinyar, 104–5
Goebbels, Joseph, 33
Goldfarb, Jeffrey C., 189
Goldman, Emma, 129
good life
    changing citizen beliefs about, 4
    consumerism and, 30, 38, 81
    impact of, 7
    political parties' beliefs on, 193–94
    question of sources of, 212
    social prescribing and, 110
Gotong ryong (neighborly giving), 137
government, role of, 8
GR (green revolution), 66–68
Graeber, David, 80

Grand Ledge, Michigan, Strange School, 3
grants economies, 58
The Great Transformation (Polanyi), 38, 72, 84
"A Great Transition" (Wallis), 205
Greece, citizen action in, 189
greed, sufficiency versus, 63–71
Green, Mike, 116
green revolution (GR), 66–68
greenhouses, 59
Groce, Nora, 197–98
gross domestic product (GDP), as benchmark, critiques of, 77
growing old, in the West, 87–98
    conclusions on, 97–98
    introduction to, 87–88
    loneliness and, 96–97
    senior citizens, competences of, 88–96
Guatemala, U.S. interference in, 35
Gupta, Anna, 145
Guzmán, Jacobo Árbenz, 35

Hackney, London, citizen action in, 189
Hallett, Stan, 57–60, 62, 67, 79
health
    assets consequential to, 111–12
    cocreation of, 104–6
    in communities, 14, 109–11
    determinants of, 194–95
    nature of, 7–8
    as senior citizen competence area, 88–89
    See also medical heretics, search for
heat waves, 25–27
helping and helpfulness, 155, 160, 162, 210
Hennezel, Marie de, 40
hidden persuaders, countering tactics of, 33–42
    care services, rise of, 34–35
    compelling needs fulfilled by, 35–37
    conclusions on, 41–42
    institutional elevation and, 56–57
    introduction to, 33–34
    online safety and, 149
    tactics of hidden persuaders, 37–41

The Hidden Persuaders (Parkard), 35–36
hierarchies
    in food banks, 49
    harms from, 199
    networks versus, 191, 193
    scarcity model and, 228
Hirschman, Albert, 225
history, question of nature of, 212
HIV/AIDS, in Africa, 126–27
Hobbes, Thomas, 212
Hodge Hill, Birmingham, UK, unsung
    heroes in, 173–74
Hoffer, Eric, 37, 212
Horton, Myles, 207
hospitals, overreach by, 100
Huber, Machteld, 7
Humpty Dumpty, xiii, xiv, 231
hunter-gatherer societies, 46
Hydon, Brenda, 3
hydraulic effect
    community building and, 161
    conclusions on, 220
    of deinstitutionalization and
        interdependence, 61
    institutional radicals and, 117
    of institutions and communities, 52,
        53, 54–56, 55f, 56f, 104
    relevance of, 118

ideology, nature of, 188
Illich, Ivan
    Deschooling Society, 139–40
    influences on, 60
    on institutional overreach, 65
    Limits in Medicine, 99–102
    mentioned, xvi
    Miller on, 116
    on progress, 193
    on useful unemployment, 81
    on war on global poverty, 64
immortality, as compelling need, 36
incarceration, community alternatives
    to, 55
inclusion-focused practices, 17–18
India, impact of green revolution on
    Punjab, 66
indigenous communities and societies,
    5–6, 68–69, 191

individualism, 204
individuals, organization of life by, 16
Industrial Revolution, 95
innovation, 110, 123–28
Institute for Local Self-Reliance, 125
institutional radicals, learning from,
    113–20
institutions
    under austerity measures, 48
    citizens versus, 7–8, 227f, 228
    communities versus, 52, 54–57, 61,
        65, 116–17, 135
    counterproductivity of, 101
    in democracies, 3–4
    dependence on, xi, 40
    desired actions of, 209
    hidden persuaders in, 71
    human service institutions, 34
    institutional assumption, 18, 194–
        97, 209, 220
    institutional capacity, civic
        inventiveness and, 196–97
    institutional reformers, 116
    medical institutions, Illich on, 100
    operational modes of, 191
    place-based actions versus, 16
    primary functions of, 6
    reasons for impact of, xv
intangibles, exchange of, 78, 79
integrative feminism, 70
interdependence, xv, 118
Intergenerational Foundation, 92
invisibles, visibility of, 159–62
Ireland
    Con Carey incident, 222–25
issues, values versus, 227–28, 227f

Jacobs, Jane, 133
James, Oliver, 45–46
John S. and James L. Knight
    Foundation, 131–32, 215–16
Johnson, Lyndon, 64
Jubilee years, 84
Judaism, Sabbath proscriptions, 225
Jung, Carl, 192

Kafka, Franz, 190

kairos (time), 227f, 229
Keane, John B., 223
Keller, Helen, 123
Keller, Richard C., 26
Kennedy, Robert, 77
Kenyon, Peter, 75
Keynes, John Maynard, 80
Klein, Naomi, 206
Klinenburg, Eric, 26
Knight Foundation, 131–32, 215–16
knowledge
    knowledge economy, 78
    as senior citizen competence area,
        95–96
Kohn, Alfie, 39, 215
Kohr, Leopold, 60
Kretzmann, Jody, 20, 27–28, 58, 180
Kula exchange system, 49
Kulin, Australia, community action in,
    75–76

La Leche League International (LLLI),
    61–62, 117
labeling, xv–xvi, 27, 150, 182
Last One Over the Wall (Miller), 113
Le Bon, Gustave, 33
leaders, connectors versus, 173
leadership, question of, 123–28
learning conversations, 229–30
Lego blocks, 207–8
Leviathan (Hobbes), 212
Lewis, John, 124
libraries, 144
life, purpose in, 107
    See also civic life; good life;
        relational power (associational
        life)
Limerick, Ireland, senior safety in, 89
Limits in Medicine: Medical Nemesis
    (Illich), 99–102
Linhart, Mary and Margaret, 74
listening campaigns, 229–30
LLLI (La Leche League International),
    61–62, 117
lo hei (yu sheng, Chinese New Year
    tradition), 50–51
local economies, rekindling of, 72–84

bullshit jobs, 80–81
conclusions on, 84
introduction to, 72–73
neighborly economy, movement
    toward, 76–80
policy revisions, need for, 81–84
primary assets, mobilization of,
    73–76
local hosts, in community building,
    157–59
local invention, 160, 161
London, England, heat wave deaths, 25
loneliness, 4–5, 96–97, 149
longevity, 7
Lord of the Rings (Tolkien), 165
Lorde, Audre, 33, 187
L'Oreal, 35–36
Lotte (community center creator), 1–2,
    229–30
love, mask of, 41
love objects, as compelling need, 36
Lunar Society of Birmingham, 95

malaria, 127
Malinowski, Bronisław, 49
managerialism, 203
Manitoba, Canada, Mincome
    experiment, 83
March on Washington for Jobs and
    Freedom (1963), 123
marketplace and market economies
    free market, question of benefits
        of, 212
    gift economies versus, 68–69
    neighborly economy versus, 78–79
    paradox of, 72
    See also economics and economies;
        local economies, rekindling of
Marmot, Michael, 105–6
Martens, Helen, 74
Martha's Vineyard, deafness in, 197–98
mask of love, 41
mass manipulations, 34–35
Massachusetts, reformatories in, 114–15
Mayo, Elton, 203
mayors, as locus of power, 133
McDonald's, 36

McGarvey, Darren, 109
McKnight, John
  Abundant Community, 60
  at Canadian Conference of
    Community Development
    Organizations, 21–22
  on children, caring for, 142
  community research, 27–28
  foreword by, xi
  on Hallett, 58
  on health, determinants of, 194–95
  on mapping people, 27
  on Mendelsohn, 103
  on Miller, 116
  poker group experiences, 99
  on poor, needs of, 58
  on power from and to the people,
    131
  primary focus of, 180
  Schumacher and, 57–58
McNamara, Robert S., 64
medical heretics, search for, 99–112
  conclusions on, 111–12
  introduction to, 99
  lessons learned, 109–11
  Medical Nemesis, 99–102
  Mendelsohn, Robert S., 102–4, 110,
    111, 117, 194–95
  mental health, cocreation of, 104–6
  mental health project, Ayrshire,
    Scotland, 106–9
Mendelsohn, Robert S., 102–4, 110, 111,
  117, 194–95
mental health, 104–6
methicillin-resistant *Staphylococcus
  aureus* (MRSA), 100
microscopes, 127
Miles, Angela, 69, 70
Miller, Jerome (Jerry), 113–16, 195–96,
  216
Miłosz, Czesław, 193
Milton, John, 43
Mincome, 83
Mollison, Bill, 129–30
Molnar, Beth E., 145
money, 78, 80
Monsanto, 48
Moyo, Dambisa, 64–65

MRSA (methicillin-resistant
  Staphylococcus aureus), 100
mu (re-ask the question), 138
multilities, 59–60, 67
Municipal League of King County, 134
Murray, Ed, 134

Nation Health Service (NHS)
  Endowment Fund for the
  Ayrshire and Arran NHS Trust,
  106–7
Nazi propaganda, 41
Nebraska Community Foundation
  (NCF), 73–75
needs
  compelling needs, 35–37
  institutional, 188, 211, 221
  needs analysis, problematic nature
    of, 117
"Neighborhood-Level Social Processes
  and Substantiated Cases of
  Child Maltreatment" (Molnar et
  al.), 145
Neighborhood Matching Fund (Seattle),
  133–34
neighborhoods. *See* communities
neoliberalism, 66–68, 170, 214–15
NESTA, Mass Localism discussion
  paper, 132
networks, hierarchies versus, 191, 193
New Deal, 34, 47
NHS (Nation Health Service)
  Endowment Fund for the
  Ayrshire and Arran NHS Trust,
  106–7
Northwestern University, Center for
  Urban Affairs, 194–95
not-for-profit organizations, 209

Obama, Michelle, 1
older people, 26, 87–98, 151
O'Neill, Nebraska, revitalization effort,
  74–75
online world, supposed safety of,
  148–49
outliers, 24

outsiders, community and, 17
Oxford English Dictionary, on cults,
    44–45

P-Patch Program (historic preservation
    program, Seattle), 134
Packard, Vance, 35–37
Pahl, Greg, 125
Pan American World Airways, 115
pandemics, impact of, 219
Papua New Guinea, Kula exchange
    system, 49
Pascal, Blaise, 54
People of Paradise, 53
perfection, pursuit of, 39
philanthropic economy, 78
pinch points, 20
Pirsig, Robert, 138, 139–40, 141–44
place
    place-based practices, 16–17
    power of, 197–200
    silos versus, 227*f*, 228–29
    small places, 177
    See also communities
        (neighborhoods)
Plato, 216
Polanyi, Karl, 38, 72, 84
police, safety and security and, 146–47
policy revisions, need for, 81–84
policymakers, questionable certainties
    of, 210–17
poor people, as label, xvi
portrait making, 230
positive life. *See* good life
post offices, importance to community
    life, 96
poverty, 64–65, 109
power (electricity) generation, 124–26
power (might)
    Arendt on, 190–91
    of citizens, 161
    collective power, 129–38
    community power, 131–32
    competitive versus cooperative
        power, 129–30
    internal resources and, 172
    nature of, 120

    from and to the people, 130–31
    of place, 197–200
    power struggles, sources of, 220–21
    relational power, 15
    of schools, 140
    sense of, as compelling need, 36
practices and prohibitions, list of, 226*f*
Prakash, Manu, 126–27
prescribing, proscribing versus, 111
preventive maintenance, 143
primitive societies, 211–12
production, mythologization of
    collective, 40
professionals and professionalism
    citizen-professional relations, 101–2,
        104
    citizens versus, 161, 170, 220
    dangers of outsourcing to
        professionals, 141–42
    disabling professionals, 47–49
    neighborhoods, lack of connection
        to, 203
    threat of, xi
progress, question of definition of,
    211–12
prohibitions and practices, list of, 226*f*
propaganda, 33–35, 41
proportionality, 60
proscribing, prescribing versus, 111
Protecting Children: A Social Model
    (Featherstone and Gupta), 145

Quakers, meal traditions, 182

radicals, learning from, 113–20
radios, 127
Rankine, Claudia, 168
rationalism, 71
Raworth, Kate, 72, 77, 214
Real Junk Food Project, 50
reform and reformers, 116, 119
"Regenerating Community"
    (McKnight), 194
rekindling democracy. *See* democracy,
    rekindling of
relational power (associational life), 7,
    15, 93, 95, 117, 199–200, 200*f*

relationship-oriented practices, 15
relief, community building versus, 227, 227f
resilience, as senior citizen competence area, 93
resources, question of keepers of, 227f, 228
Rice, Norm, 133
The Right to Useful Unemployment (Illich), 81
rituals, sympathy versus empathy and, 50–51
Rogers, Carl, 175
rooftops, greenhouses on, 59
Roosevelt, Franklin D., 34, 47, 136
roots, as compelling need, 36
Rousseau, Jean-Jacques, 149
Royer, Charles, 133
Ruest, Gaëtan, 21
Russell, Cormac, 75, 99, 113, 140
Rwanda, schools in, 140

Sachs, Jeffery, 64
safety and security, 89–90, 149–51
Sahlins, Marshall, 76–77, 101, 212
Sampson, Robert J., 90, 147
Sapolsky, Robert, 215
Sargent, Francis, 114
scale (size), 38–39, 168–76, 215
scarcity
    abundance versus, 45–47, 63, 227f, 228
    consumerism and, 76, 203–4
    in economic global system, 188
    growth-created, 66–68
Schell, Paul, 133
schools, power of local, 140
Schumacher, E. F. ("Fritz"), 57–58, 60, 62, 75, 157, 215
Scott, Evelyn, 24
Seattle, Office of Neighborhoods, 133–34
segregation, 92, 151
self
    culture of, 37–38
    hidden selves, 41
    as tripartite construct, 70–71
senior citizens, 26, 87–98, 151

Servicemen's Readjustment Act (G.I. Bill, 1944), 82–83
services
    belief in, 4, 6, 27, 53
    care services, 34–35
    clientelism versus, 48
    confusion of needs with, 221
    consumerism and, 30
    hierarchies and, 155–56
    impact of, 221
    modern austerity and, 48
    neighborliness versus, 16
    political beliefs in, 193–94
    question of use of, 216
    recipients of, as deficient, 170
    reliance on, 40, 117, 135
    Seattle's provision of, 133
    senior citizens and, 88, 97
    service economies, 188
    serviceland, 4, 190
    serving while walking backward, 52, 55, 102, 117, 225, 226
    social services, provision of, 76
    ubiquity of, 210–11
    See also trust
sharing, 230
Shaun (Harbourside community builder), 108
Sher, Jonathan, 140
Shiva, Vandana, 65, 66, 67–68, 69
Silas Marner (Eliot), 163–67
silos, 15, 17, 179, 227f, 228–29
Singapore, We Wish You Enough program, 50
size
    bigness, question of benefits of, 215–16
    small places, Berry on, 177
    too small to fail, 57–58
Small Is Beautiful (Schumacher), 57, 58, 215
small places, 177
    See also scale; size
society
    deschooling of, 139–45
    indigenous societies, gift giving by, 68–69
    marginalization of, 72–73
    proper functions of, 80

social capital, 46, 78
social challenges, deficit-based
    views of, 27
social change, 123–24, 130, 193–201
social connections, importance of, 5
social/environmental change, 14
social inventors, as conductors,
    126–28
social isolation, 147
social movements, 17, 192
social prescribing, 110
societal breakdowns, causes of,
    187–88, 190
technology versus, 67
society, rekindling of, 13–31
    asset-based community
        development, 13–23
    top-down approaches, failures of,
        24–31
    See also *detailed entries for these
        concepts*
Socrates, xiv
songlines, 5–6, 68, 91, 200, 211, 213,
    222
Soul of Community study, 215–16
South Africa, Jung in, 192
spaces (BY, FOR, TO, WITH), 155–56,
    156f, 210, 214f, 220, 222
Spain, British pensioners in, 91
speed of trust. *See* trust
sphere of influence, widening of, 187–92
springboard stories, 96
state, connection with community,
    187–218
    associations, association of, 193–201
    questionable certainties, 210–17
    sphere of influence, widening of,
        187–92
    technocracy, consumerism, and
        globalization, 202–9
*Staying Alive: Women, Ecology and
    Development* (Shiva), 65
Stein, Gertrude, 61
stewardship, limitations of, 224–29
Stockholm Resilience Centre, 206
Stone Age Economics (Sahlins), 76–77,
    101
stories, nature of, 164–65

Strange School (Grand Ledge,
    Michigan), 3
Subaru Love Promise advertising
    campaign, 36
subjects, citizens versus, 136–37
sufficiency, greed versus, 63–71
surveillance society, 71
Swedish National Social Care
    Convention, 118
swing (in jazz), 192
sympathy, empathy versus, 49–53
system reform, question of benefits of,
    216

Taleb, Nassim Nicholas, 24
tangibles, exchange of, 78, 79
Tanna island, 43–47, 52–53
technocracy, 3–4, 202–9, 216–17
technology
    appropriate technology, 57, 58, 59,
        75
    question of benefits of, 216
    society versus, 67
Thompson, Marian, 53
time, chronos versus kairos, 229
Timebanking, 79
Tin Horse Highway, 75
TO space, 155–56, 156f, 210, 214f, 220,
    222
Tompson, Marian, 61–62, 102, 110
tools
    for social change, 193–201
    unitilities and multilities, 59–60
Tools for Conviviality (Illich), 60, 100
top-down approaches, failures of, 24–29
Trotter, Wilfred, 33
Trudeau, Pierre, 83
Truman, Harry S., 64
trust, 163–67, 175
Tsai, Ing-wen, 203
Tsakos, Matasha, 113
Twain, Mark, 147
Twelve Apostles (in Carey reburial
    incident), 223–24

unconditional positive regard, 175
United Fruit Company, 35

United Kingdom
  austerity in, 52
  Bristol, citizen action in, 189
  Hodge Hill, Birmingham, unsung
    heroes in, 173–74
  loneliness in, 5
  universal health service, 46
unitilities, 59–60, 67
Universal Unconditional Basic Income,
  80–81
The Unnamable (Beckett), 95
urbanization, 26
useful unemployment, 81

values, issues versus, 227–28, 227*f*
The Vanishing Neighbor (Dunkelman),
  204
Vassey, Liz, 177
Vaughan, Genevieve, 63
Vernooij-Dassen, Myrra, 5
veterans, support for, 82–83
villages. *See* communities
  (neighborhoods)
violence, power and, 191
The Violence of the Green Revolution
  (Shiva), 66
visioning, 230
volunteering, limitations of, 132
Voorstad-Ost community center
  (Deventer, Netherlands), 1–3
voting, senior citizen participation in,
  94

Walburg, Jan, 7
Waldinger, Robert, 7
Wallis, Stewart, 205–6
We Wish You Enough program, 50
wealth distribution, 48, 82, 206
welcoming, 229–30
welfare states, central crisis of, 87–88
welfare systems, sympathy versus
  empathy in, 50–53
well-being, 87–121
  determinants of, 6–7, 195
  growing old, in the West, 87–98

institutional radicals, learning from,
  113–20
medical heretics, search for, 99–112
as senior citizen competence area,
  88–89
the West. *See* growing old, in the West
Westside Health Authority (Austin,
  Chicago), 181–82
"When Disaster Strikes, It's Survival of
  the Sociable" (Sampson), 147
"Why Mayors Should Rule the World"
  (Barber), 133
Willard, Nancy, 139
Williams, M. J., 24
Window Wanderland (Bristol, UK), 189
wisdom, as senior citizen competence
  area, 95–96
WITH space, 155–56, 156*f*, 210, 214*f*,
  222
women and feminism
  characteristics of feminism, 69
  ecofeminism, 65
  gift economy and, 68–69
  green revolution and, 67–68
  integrative feminism, 70
Women and the Gift Economy
  (Vaughan), 68–69
Wong, Penny, 87
workforce, commodification of, 70–71
World Bank, electrification of Global
  South, 126
World Health Organization, 7
World War II, Tanna island during,
  43–47, 52–53
worth, reassurance of, as compelling
  need, 35–36

Yeats, W. B., 13
Young, Andy, 105
youth. *See* children
yu sheng (*lo hei*, Chinese New Year
  tradition), 50–51

*Zen and the Art of the Motorcycle
  Maintenance* (Pirsig), 138,
  139–40, 141–44